DISASTER RESILIENCE

DISASTER RESILIENCE

An Integrated Approach

By

DOUGLAS PATON, Ph.D., C. Psychol.

School of Psychology
University of Tasmania,
Launceston, Tasmania, Australia

and

DAVID JOHNSTON, Ph.D.

Institute of Geological and Nuclear Sciences
Lower Hutt, New Zealand

CHARLES C THOMAS • PUBLISHER, LTD.
Springfield • Illinois • U.S.A.

Published and Distributed Throughout the World by

CHARLES C THOMAS • PUBLISHER, LTD.
2600 South First Street
Springfield, Illinois 62704

© 2006 by CHARLES C THOMAS • PUBLISHER, LTD.

ISBN 0-398-07663-4 (hard)
ISBN 0-398-07664-2 (paper)

Library of Congress Catalog Card Number: 200644509

With THOMAS BOOKS *careful attention is given to all details of manufacturing
and design. It is the Publisher's desire to present books that are satisfactory as to their
physical qualities and artistic possibilities and appropriate for their particular use.*
THOMAS BOOKS *will be true to those laws of quality that assure a good name
and good will.*

Printed in the United States of America
MM-R-3

Library of Congress Cataloging-in-Publication Data

Paton, Douglas
Disaster resilience : an integrated approach / by Douglas Paton and
David Johnston.
p. cm.
Includes bibliographical references and index.
ISBN 0-398-07663-4 – ISBN 0-398-07664-2 (pbk.)
1. Disasters–Social aspects. 2. Natural disasters–Social aspects.
3. Hazardous geographic environments. 4. Risk management. 5. Emergency management. 6. Preparedness. 7. Community organization. 8. Resilience (Personality trait). I. Johnston, David Moore, 1966-II. Title.

HV553.P37 2006
363.34'7–dc22

2006044509

PREFACE

The Boxing Day 2004 Indian Ocean tsunami and the impact of Hurricane Katrina on New Orleans in 2005 provided unfortunate reminders of the susceptibility of many communities to devastating losses from natural hazards. These events provided graphic illustrations of how extreme hazard events adversely impact on people, affect communities, and disrupt the community and societal mechanisms that serve to organize and sustain community capacities and functions. It would, however, be incorrect to automatically assume that the deficit and loss outcomes that are often the most visible and publicized aspects of these events should be regarded as a fait accompli of exposure to disaster. Rather, deficit and loss outcomes co-exist with a capacity to confront challenging circumstances in ways characterized by adaptation and growth. Recognition of the co-existence of these outcomes opens up new opportunities for managing natural hazard risk. This book discusses how risk can be managed by identifying factors that influence a capacity for co-existence with periodically hazardous, but often beneficial, environmental elements. It identifies values, beliefs, competencies, resources and procedures that societies and their members can utilize to proactively develop a capacity to adapt to adverse natural hazard consequences and sustain societal functions in the face of significant perturbations to the fabric of everyday community life. That is, to make societies and their members resilient.

DOUGLAS PATON
DAVID JOHNSTON

CONTRIBUTORS

TREVOR AULD, DIP. EM. MGNT.

Trevor Auld is the Emergency Management Officer with the Manawatu District Council in New Zealand. He has extensive experience in developing emergency response policies and plans and in applying them to manage natural hazard processes. The content of the chapter he contributed to draws upon his experience in managing a large flood disaster in 2004.

JULIA BECKER, B.SC.

Julia studied both resource management and natural hazards at Waikato University in New Zealand before joining the Institute of Geological and Nuclear Sciences (GNS) in 2000. She has completed studies in social science research, and has undertaken social surveys looking at people's perceptions and awareness of social, environmental and hazard issues. In addition to her work at GNS, Julia spent two years in the U.K. from 2002–2004 working on environmental impact assessment, energy issues and urban development. Currently, she is involved with research into effective planning and policy for natural and environmental hazards in New Zealand.

PHILIP BUCKLE, B.SC.

Philip Buckle has extensive experience in planning and managing recovery programs for natural and anthropogenic disasters. He has contributed top policy debates in Australia and the U.K. and has researched and taught in a number of Universities in Australia and the U.K., currently at the Coventry Centre for Disaster Management at Coventry University. He has published numerous papers, guidelines, program documents and books, focusing mainly on recovery, vulnerability assessment and capacity development.

PETRA T. BÜRGELT, M.A.

Petra T. Bürgelt is currently conducting her Ph.D. project in which she qualitatively explores the experiences of German migrants to New Zealand and Australia by accompanying them throughout their migration process. She has also been involved with the design and analysis of several qualitative research projects on modeling preparedness for bushfires (Australia) and identifying indicators of warning effectiveness for tsunami hazards (Washington State Government, U.S.A.). In addition to her publications in this area, Petra is currently completing a book on adaptation and migration. This work is based on her Masters research with German migrants to New Zealand that examined migration within a salutogenic paradigm.

LYNNE COHEN, PH.D.

Lynne Cohen is a Senior Lecturer and is Undergraduate Coordinator in the School of Psychology at Edith Cowan University (ECU). She teaches in both the undergraduate and postgraduate psychology programs and has recently been awarded a National Teaching Award by the Australian University Teaching Committee. Her research focuses on issues in higher education and has many publications and presentations on learning and teaching in higher education. She is the current editor of the community psychology journal *Network*. Dr. Cohen is also a community psychologist and researches and teaches in the area of sense of belonging and its relationship to successful outcomes for students.

ALISON COTTRELL, PH.D.

Alison Cottrell is with the Centre for Disaster Studies in the School of Tropical Environment Studies and Geography at James Cook University in Townsville, Queensland, Australia. The focus of her research is communities and their relationships with hazards. Perceptions of risk, vulnerability and resilience at the individual, household and community levels are of prime concern. Previous research in hazards has covered issues of women's experiences preparing for flooding and community participation in flood mitigation activities. Current research includes a project with the Bushfire Cooperative Research Centre on understanding the relationships between government policy, planning, service delivery and community responses to bushfires. This research is linked to an assessment of appropriate community-based strategies for enhancing community resilience to hazards in general. Her teaching activities include cultural aspects of environmental issues, disaster studies, community studies and qualitative social research methods.

JIM COUSINS, B.SC.

Jim Cousins has been employed with GNS Science and the Physics and Engineering Laboratory (DSIR), New Zealand, since 1973. His research is focused on reducing the vulnerability of people, buildings and infrastructure to natural hazards. He has been involved in the modeling of damage and casualties caused by earthquakes, volcanoes, tsunami and post-earthquake fire. For nearly two decades, he has been helping clients from commerce, industry and government bodies understand their risks from earthquakes.

MICHAEL DOHERTY, B.SC.

Michael graduated with an Honors Degree in Science from the University of Sydney in 1986, majoring in plant ecology. Working on a wide range of vegetation management projects for Australian State and Federal Agencies he has developed expertise in the ecology of southeastern Australian vegetation communities as well as detailed knowledge of environmental legislation. In addition, he has worked on a variety of consulting projects both locally and overseas. In his current role with CSIRO Sustainable Ecosystems, Michael's research focus is in the dynamics and management of temperate ecosystems, particularly in relation to fire, forestry, and peri-urban expansion.

CHRIS GREGG, PH.D.

Chris Gregg is an Assistant Professor of Geology at East Tennessee State University in Johnson City, Tennessee. He received his Ph.D. in Geology and Geophysics from the University of Hawaii and his post-graduate Diploma from the University of Canterbury, New Zealand. He specializes in exploring social cognitive factors that influence community preparedness for geologic hazards (volcanic and tsunami). He is actively working on public understanding of warning signals for tsunami in Hawaii, Thailand, and the coastal US and Puerto Rico. Chris has an extensive background in the U.S.-based environmental industry, which compliments his natural hazards research.

KATE HILL, M.A.

Kate Hill is drawing upon her business expertise to conduct doctoral research into business continuity planning. While her contribution to this chapter focuses on large-scale events, the focus of my doctoral work is on the procedures and processes required to ensure continuity during local disruptions.

BRUCE HOUGHTON, PH.D.

Bruce Houghton is the Gordon MacDonald Professor in Volcanology at University of Hawaii at Manoa and Hawaiian State Volcanologist and a Fellow of the Royal Society of New Zealand. Previously, he had a career of 25 years as a volcanologist in New Zealand, culminating in the leadership of the scientific response to the 1995–1996 eruption of Ruapehu volcano. Bruce has published over 150 research papers in international journals and was an editor of the *Encyclopaedia of Volcanoes* in 2000. In his career he has studied active volcanoes in Alaska, Chile, El Salvador, Greece, Hawaii, Iceland, Italy, Germany, Nicaragua, and New Zealand.

PETER HUGHES, M.A.

Peter Hughes teaches Media Studies at La Trobe University, Melbourne, Australia. His main areas of research and publication are in the fields of documentary film and television, and new cultural technologies. He is author, with Ina Bertrand, of Media research methods: Institutions, texts, audiences (published by Palgrave, Basingstoke, New York, 2005) and is currently engaged (with Peter White and Erez Cohen) on research into Media and Bushfires through the Bushfire CRC.

LI-JU JANG, PH.D.

Li-ju is an assistant professor in the School of Medical Sociology and Social Work at Chung Shan Medical University, Taiwan. She holds a doctorate from the University of Denver in Social Work. Her interest areas are human response to natural disaster, disaster resilience, and posttraumatic growth. Her focus has been on the effects of cultural factors on resilience and posttraumatic growth. Li-ju also supervises a group of voluntary outreach workers whom themselves were the survivors of the 921 Earthquake. Those survivors now reach out to people in need. Their roles have changed from service receivers to helpers.

DAVID JOHNSTON, PH.D.

David Johnston has been employed with the Institute of Geological and Nuclear Sciences, New Zealand since 1993, and his research is focused on reducing the vulnerability of society, economy, and infrastructure to hazards. He has been involved in developing integrated risk management strategies for many different hazard events, using techniques such as scenario development, mitigation planning and community education programs. He is also interested in assessing social and economic impacts of natural and environmental hazard events. David has had long-term relationship with a wide number of end-users through his research, consulting, and outreach activities.

GAIL KELLY, PH.D.

Gail's research focuses on understanding community change processes and strategies (initially in the context of forest industry restructuring). She has published a Social Impact Assessment on the plantation industry, and led a conflict resolution process investigating aerial spraying of commercial eucalypt plantations. Gail currently leads the Sustainable Urbanization research stream within the Resource Futures Program at CSIRO Sustainable Ecosystems. Her current areas of focus include understanding the social dimensions of community resilience and developing linkages between quality of life and biophysical measures of sustainability in coastal regions.

DAVID KING, PH.D.

David King is an Associate Professor of Geography in the School of Tropical Environment Studies and Geography at James Cook University, and is both Director of the Centre for Disaster Studies, and the Centre for Tropical Urban and Regional Planning. He has worked in North Queensland for 15 years and was formerly at the University of Papua, New Guinea. His research specializes in social impact and evaluation in such areas as planning, natural hazard vulnerability and resilience, disaster mitigation and recovery, as well as the social impact of mining projects, third-world development, and census analysis.

PROF. WALTER LAMENDOLA, PH.D.

Walter LaMendola is Professor at the Graduate School of Social Work, University of Denver, Denver, Colorado, U.S.A. He teaches social theory as well as research courses in the PhD and Master of Social Work program. His scholarly interests have ranged across issues that involve the use and application of information and communication technologies in human services, particularly when they are directed toward, or otherwise involve themselves in the everyday life of people experiencing social problems, such as mental illness. He has recently completed a multi-year study of the effects of technology mediation on learning outcomes and resilience among children living in public housing.

JOHN MCCLURE, PH.D.

John McClure is Associate Professor of Psychology at Victoria University of Wellington. His research relating to disasters focuses on reducing people's fatalism about hazards such as earthquakes and on clarifying people's biases in the risk judgments about these hazards. He has examined the way that people's attributions for damage following earthquakes mediates their fatalism. People who attribute the damage solely to the force of the earthquake are more fatalistic than people who attribute the damage in part to the design of the damaged buildings. He has also clarified why people have a tendency to underestimate the risk from harmful low-frequency events.

MOIRA O'CONNOR, PH.D.

Moira O'Connor is a senior lecturer in the School of Psychology at Edith Cowan University, Western Australia. Moira teaches community psychology, environmental psychology and applied social psychology, as well as qualitative research methods. Her research interests include sense of place and the importance of place to people's psychological well-being; psychosocial aspects of living with cancer; psychological aspects of palliative care; women's health, particularly during life transitions; parenting and domestic violence and women's safety. What ties these research interests together is an interest in people's stories and experiences and a focus on health and well-being. Moira's involvement in community responses to natural disasters comes from an interest in sense of community and sense of place in rural Australia.

DOUGLAS PATON, PH.D.

Douglas Paton is a Professor at the University of Tasmania. He researches community resilience to natural hazards. This work involves working with communities susceptible to seismic, volcanic, bushfire, tsunami and flooding hazards. He recently served on a NATO working party on resilience to terrorism and was the Australian delegate to the UNESCO Education for Natural Disaster Preparedness in the Asia-Pacific program. He has published some 170 papers and chapters and 12 books on resilience and vulnerability to disaster and traumatic events. He is chief psychological advisor to the Cities on Volcanoes Commission (IAVCEI), editor of the *Australasian Journal of Disaster and Trauma Studies,* and is on the Editorial Board of *Disaster Prevention and Management.*

JULIE ANN POOLEY, PH.D.

Dr. Julie Ann Pooley is a Senior Lecturer in the School of Psychology at Edith Cowan University since 1991. She is involved in teaching in both the undergraduate and postgraduate psychology programs and has recently been awarded a National Teaching Award by the Australian University Teaching Committee. Her current research is focusing on communities facing natural disasters, through which she is trying to determine what enables communities to become resilient to impending threats. She is also interested in the area of environmental education and attitudes towards the environment.

ADAM ROSE, PH.D.

Adam Rose is Professor of Energy, Environmental, and Regional Economics in the Department of Geography at The Pennsylvania State University where he researches the economics of natural and man-made hazards, and the economics of climate change. He recently served as a lead researcher on a report to the U.S. Congress evaluating the net benefits of FEMA hazard mitigation grants and on a National Research Council study on the benefits of advanced seismic monitoring. He is a faculty affiliate of the DHS Center for Risk and Economic Analysis of Terrorism Events and of the NSF Multidisciplinary Center for Earthquake Engineering Research, where his work emphasizes resilience to natural disasters and terrorism at the levels of the individual business, market, and regional economy. Professor Rose is the co-author or co-editor of ten books, published by Oxford and Johns Hopkins University Press among others, and has published 70 refereed articles. He serves on the editorial boards of several journals, as well as on the advisory boards of several research units at Penn State. He has served as the American Economic Association Representative to the American Association for the Advancement of Science and currently serves on the Board of Directors of the American Association of Geographers Energy and Environment Specialty Group. He is also the recipient of a Woodrow Wilson Fellowship, an East-West Center Fellowship, an Earthquake Engineering Research Institute Special Recognition Award, and the American Planning Association Outstanding Program Planning Honor Award.

ROBERT O. SCHNEIDER, PH.D.

Professor Robert O. Schneider is currently serving as Acting Associate Vice Chancellor for International Programs at the University of North Carolina at Pembroke (UNCP). He has previously served as Department Chair and Professor in the Department of Political Science and Public Administration at UNCP. Dr. Schneider's research includes published work in hazard mitigation, the ethical dimensions of emergency management, and emergency management policy. He has also worked on several (local and national) curriculum development projects in emergency management.

LEIGH SMITH, M.A.

Leigh Smith is an Associate Professor in the School of Psychology at Curtin University of Technology, Perth, Western Australia. His fields of expertise include research design and analysis, measurement, and disaster research. He also has research interests in cognitive development and psych-motor development. He is currently the program leader for the Organizational Psychology stream within the School of Psychology.

PETER B. WHITE, M.A.

Peter B. White teaches Media Studies at La Trobe University in Melbourne, Australia. His main area of teaching and research deals with the social and regulatory implications of new media. Recent work with Naomi Rosh White examines the role of new media such as mobile phones, SMS, and internet-based communications in the lives of tourists. He is currently engaged (with Peter Hughes and Erez Cohen) on research into media and bushfires through the Bushfire CRC.

CONTENTS

DISASTER RESILIENCE

Chapter 1

DISASTER RESILIENCE: BUILDING CAPACITY TO CO-EXIST WITH NATURAL HAZARDS AND THEIR CONSEQUENCES

Douglas Paton

Keep my words positive, because my words become behaviors.
Keep my behaviors positive, because my behaviors become habits.
Keep my habits positive, because my habits become my values.
Keep my values positive, because they become my destiny.

Mahatma Gandhi

INTRODUCTION

A long history of development in locations which has resulted in increased societal susceptibility to experiencing adverse impacts from interaction with natural processes, such as volcanic, wildfire, storm, flooding, tsunami and seismic events, has stimulated interest in understanding how to manage the associated risk. This is no easy task. Objectively, societal risk from natural hazards is constantly increasing. Even if the probability and intensity of hazard activity remain constant, continuing population growth and economic and infrastructure development results in a concomitant increase in the potential magnitude and significance of loss and disruption associated with hazard activity, and consequently, risk. In this book, the focus is on managing risk through influencing the consequences of hazard exposure. It does

3

so by identifying factors that influence a capacity for co-existence with periodically hazardous, but often beneficial, environmental elements. This involves developing a capability to sustain societal processes should disaster occur through the proactive development of a capacity to adapt or adjust to the consequences of hazard activity.

The most effective strategy for achieving this outcome is planning to avoid development in areas susceptible to hazard impacts (Burby, Deyle, Godschalk, & Olshansky, 2000). While this approach must retain a prominent position in the battery of hazard mitigation strategies, particularly with regard to decisions about future development in areas susceptible to hazard activity and post-disaster rebuilding, it does not cater for all circumstances.

Much economic, infrastructure and social development has already occurred in areas susceptible to disruption and loss from hazard activity. For example, in her review of research from United States Geological Survey and Smithsonian Institute sources, Mayell (2002) describes how there are some 457 volcanoes with cities that house one million or more people within 100km of them. Depending on prevailing meteorological conditions, whose distribution cannot be planned for, hazards such as volcanic ash may find them. The city of Auckland, New Zealand is built on a volcanic field, the location of whose future eruptions cannot be predicted. It is difficult to plan where future development should occur if the location and distribution of future hazard activity cannot be specified in advance. While many of these cities have, so far, been spared a need to confront significant hazard events, others have. Experience of hazard activity is not, however, necessarily a disincentive for societal development.

For example, some 3.75 million people live in Naples, which has a history of experiencing adverse consequences over several millennia as a result of its proximity (within 30km) to Vesuvious. Popcate´petal, which has erupted 15 times in the past 400 years, is located 60km from Mexico City and its 20 million inhabitants (Mayell, 2002). The cities of San Francisco (U.S.) and Wellington (New Zealand), to name but a few, are built on active fault lines that have been active in historical times. These cities thus remain susceptible to experiencing considerable devastation from future seismic activity. Even if a decision to halt future development was made, a need to develop a capability to confront the consequences of hazard activity is an important component in any plan designed to facilitate a societal capacity to co-exist with the potentially hazardous elements of its environment.

Co-existing With a Hazardous Environment

As the opening quote alludes, this starts from hazard issues being the subject of community discourse that supports choosing to develop adaptive capacity. It also involves ensuring that the choices that reflect the substance of this discourse are translated into beliefs and behaviors that, over time, become established within the fabric of society. When such values are established, societies and their members lay the foundation for a destiny that includes a capacity for their sustained co-existence with a hazardous environment.

That developing a capacity for co-existence with natural hazards is feasible, is evident from observation of communities that face regular exposure to hazard activity. For example, because it receives ashfall and ballistic debris on some 113 days/year from its proximity to Sakurajima volcano, the town of Kagoshima in Japan has developed building codes, ash removal practices and community attitudes and preparedness to facilitate continuity of societal functions during periodic volcanic episodes (Johnston, 2004). That is, when a need to confront hazard consequences prevails, adaptive mechanisms can be established within the fabric of a society.

In locations characterized by less frequent hazard activity, however, a more challenging risk management environment faces the emergency planner. If they are to rise to this challenge, emergency management planners need knowledge of the characteristics and processes that underpin a capacity to adapt to hazard consequences and they need to develop strategies to instill these into the fabric of communities at risk. Furthermore, they have to do so in the context of evolving hazard-scapes.

The hazards that communities will face will change over time. For example, growth of residential development in the peri-urban environment has increased risk from wildfire hazards. Changes in land use patterns (e.g., farming, land clearance, industrial development) have increased environmental degradation. Change is also emanating from factors such as global warming. This may result in areas which have previously enjoyed relatively benign relationships with their environment experiencing risk from new sources. Clearly, understanding the hazards that represent the source of adaptive pressures is an important activity.

The systematic scientific analysis of hazards and their distribution is still a relatively youthful endeavor. Until relatively recent times, knowledge of hazards in an area would have relied on firsthand experience or historical accounts. For hazards with long return periods, and thus extended periods of hazard quiescence, humankind has been denied the opportunity to gain comprehensive experience or knowledge of the hazard phenomena it may have to contend with. As a result, development has often taken place in ignorance of potentially hazardous circumstances. Articulating the nature of the hazard-scape (present and future) describes the context in which societal response and adaptation will occur.

Irrespective of whether they were made in light of knowledge of hazards or not, decisions regarding the location of societal development often reflect the association between geological and other natural processes and the resources and amenities (e.g., fertile soils, natural harbors, navigable rivers that serve as commercial highways, coastal scenery) they create for human populations. To fully realize the potential individual, community and societal benefits that can accrue from development in these locations, planning must address how to minimize the costs that arise when natural processes interact with human settlement in ways that create loss and disruption. That is, when they become hazards.

Hazards impact on people, they affect communities, and they disrupt the community and societal mechanism that serve to organize and sustain community capacities and functions. When hazard activity results in significant loss or disruption to established social processes, functions, activities and interactions, it can be defined as a disaster. Disasters expose populations and social systems to demands and consequences that fall outside the usual realm of human experience. This can occur suddenly, as is the case with earthquakes, or, as with environmental hazards such as salinity, more insidiously over periods of time that can be measured in decades. With rapid onset hazards in particular, the extent, distribution and complexity of their consequences generally exceed routine capacities and present significant nonroutine demands that call for novel, creative solutions to emergency problems. Extensive loss of or disruption to the physical, social and administrative infrastructure means that, in the absence of activities implemented specifically to develop a capability for continued functioning, normal routines will no longer be supported or maintained within an affected area. It follows from this that adaptive pressures on communities will depend on the hazards they will have to contend with.

The information required to define this context extends beyond knowledge of hazards (e.g., volcanic, seismic) per se to include understanding of hazard characteristics and behavior. For example, for volcanic events, hazard characteristics include tephra, lava, ballistic material and gas. Seismic hazard characteristics include, for example, ground acceleration and liquefaction. Hazard behavior includes, for example, return and precursory periods, speed of onset, intensity, and duration. It is how hazard characteristics and behavior interact with the physical and social environment that defines the adaptive pressures on communities should hazard activity occur. The particular mix of hazard characteristics and behaviour will differ from place to place, as will the communities with which they will interact. Given the permutations that can arise from the interactions between community and hazard characteristics, planning for adaptive capacity is no easy task. If it is to occur, an important issue is identifying how adaptation can be facilitated.

RESILIENCE AND ADAPTIVE CAPACITY

This book is concerned with identifying the values, beliefs, competencies, resources and procedures that societies and their members can call upon to facilitate their capacity to adapt to these circumstances and sustain societal functions in the face of significant perturbations to the fabric of everyday community life. That is, to identify the factors that makes societies and their members resilient. First, it is pertinent to consider what is meant by "resilient"?

The term resilience is often used in a manner synonymous with the notion of "bouncing back." This reflects its derivation from its Latin root, *resiliere,* meaning "to jump back." It implies a capability to return to a previous state. This usage, however, captures neither the reality of disaster experience nor its full implications. Even if people wanted to return to a previous state, changes to the physical, social and psychological reality of societal life emanating from the disaster can make this untenable. That is, the post-disaster reality, irrespective of whether it reflects the direct consequences of disaster or the recovery and re-building activities undertaken, will present community members with a new reality that may differ in several fundamental ways from that prevailing pre-disaster. It is the changed reality (whether from the dis-aster itself or the societal response to it) that people must adapt to.

A definition based on the notion of "bouncing back" fails to capture this reality. Nor does it encapsulate the new possibilities opened up by the changes wrought by a disaster. In this context, disaster can be con-ceptualized as a catalyst for change; if mother nature does the demoli-tion work, society can make choices about how to rebuild itself. Opportunities for development also extend to the social context. For example, disasters can generate a stronger sense of community amongst those affected than had prevailed prior to the disaster. Decisions can be made to reorganise social and institutional relation-ships in ways that sustain this new quality of life and so contribute to the social capital of the affected area in ways that will endure long after the disaster has passed into history. None of these outcomes will hap-pen by chance. People, communities and societal institutions must choose to make it happen. If such choices are to be made, it is first nec-essary to define what it is that is intended to be achieved. Once this has been done, the next step is to consider how it can be achieved.

In this book, resilience is a measure of how well people and societies can adapt to a changed reality and capitalize on the new possibilities offered. To accommodate the former, the definition of resilience used here embodies the notion of adaptive capacity (Klein, Nicholls & Thomalla, 2003). To encapsulate the potential for new possibilities, an element of learning and growth should also be implicit in its concep-tualization, as should the notion of disaster as a catalyst for develop-ment. Neither a capacity to adapt nor a capacity for post-disaster growth and development will happen by chance. Achieving these out-comes requires a conscious effort on the part of people, communities and societal institutions to develop and maintain the resources and processes required to ensure this can happen and that it can be main-tained over time. In particular, it is important to ensure that civic agen-cies and institutions with a role in emergency planning and communi-ty development nourish this capacity in community members. This can facilitate the development and maintenance of a societal capabili-ty to draw upon its own individual, collective and institutional resources and competencies to cope with, adapt to, and develop from the demands, challenges and changes encountered during and after disaster.

THE NATURE OF ADAPTIVE CAPACITY

In this context, resilience can be defined as comprising four general components (Paton, 2000; Paton & Bishop, 1996). Firstly, communities, their members, businesses and societal institutions must possess the resources (e.g., household emergency plans, business continuity plans) required to ensure, as far as possible, their safety and the continuity of core functions in a context defined by hazard consequences (e.g., ground shaking, volcanic ash fall, flood inundation) that can disrupt societal functions. Secondly, they must possess the competencies (e.g., self-efficacy, community competence, trained staff, disaster management procedures) required to mobilize, organize and use these resources to confront the problems encountered and adapt to the reality created by hazard activity. Thirdly, the planning and development strategies used to facilitate resilience must include mechanisms designed to integrate the resources available at each level to ensure the existence of a coherent societal capacity, and one capable of realizing the potential to capitalize on opportunities for change, growth and the enhancement of quality of life. Finally, strategies adopted must be designed to ensure the sustained availability of these resources and the competencies required to use them over time and against a background of hazard quiescence and changing community membership, needs, goals and functions.

Understanding how interdependencies between people, their communities, and societal institutions and organizations influence adaptive capacity thus becomes important. That is, it is necessary to describe resilience, or adaptive capacity, at several interdependent levels (Buckle, Marsh, & Smale, 2000; Paton 2000; Paton & Bishop, 1996; Tobin, 1999). For example, the ability of a community to adapt to adverse or challenging circumstances and recover using its own resources requires that attention be directed to safeguarding the physical integrity of the built environment (e.g., land use planning, design standards, building codes, lifeline engineering, retrofitting buildings).

At another level, resilience can be conceptualized as a social resource (e.g., facilitating community members' commitment to reduction and readiness activities) whose existence is sustained by ensuring an equitable distribution of the costs and benefits associated with hazard reduction and readiness activities. Resilience also comprises a behavioral level concerned with encouraging the sustained adoption of preparatory adjustments and the ability to respond to and adapt to adverse hazard effects. It must also encompass the social, cultural and environmental contexts within which societal activities occur. The latter includes ensuring economic, business and administrative continuity (including emergency management and social institutions), and promoting heritage and environmental sustainability (Buckle et al., 2000; Mileti, 1999; Paton, 2000; Spenneman & Look, 1998).

If emergency planners are to act on this, they need knowledge of the hazard-scape prevailing within their jurisdiction and the elements that can be mobilized to develop a capacity to adapt to hazard activity. These issues are addressed in the next chapter.

REFERENCES

Buckle, P., Marsh, G., & Smale, S. (2000). New approaches to assessing vulnerability and resilience. *Australian Journal of Emergency Management, 15,* 8–14.

Burby, R. J., Deyle, R. E., Godschalk, D. R., & Olshansky, R. B. (2000). Creating hazard resilient communities through land-use planning. *Natural Hazards Review, 1,* 99–106.

Johnston, D. (2004, October). Cities Coping with Volcanic Ash. Volcanoes and Society Workshop, Wairakei Research Centre, Taupo, New Zealand.

Klein, R., Nicholls, R., & Thomalla, F. (2003). Resilience to natural hazards: How useful is this concept? *Environmental Hazards, 5,* 35–45.

Mayell, H. (2002). Volcanoes loom as sleeping threat for millions. *National Geographic News.* Retrieved on 24th October 2005 from http://www.rense.com

Mileti, D. (1999). *Disasters by design.* Washington, DC.: Joseph Henry Press.

Paton, D. (2000). Emergency Planning: Integrating community development, community resilience and hazard mitigation. *Journal of the American Society of Professional Emergency Managers, 7,* 109–118.

Paton, D. & Bishop B. (1996). Disasters and communities: Promoting psychosocial well-being. In D. Paton and N. Long (Eds.) *Psychological aspects of disaster: Impact, coping, and intervention.* Palmerston North, Dunmore Press.

Spenneman, D.H.R. & Look, D.W. (1998). *Disaster management programs for historic sites.* San Francisco and Albury: Association for Preservation Technology and the Johnstone Centre.

Tobin, G.A. (1999). Sustainability and community resilience: The holy grail of hazards planning. *Environmental Hazards 1,* 13–26.

Chapter 2

IDENTIFYING THE CHARACTERISTICS OF A DISASTER RESILIENT SOCIETY

DOUGLAS PATON AND DAVID JOHNSTON

INTRODUCTION

To develop resilience, it is necessary to identify its constituent components. This chapter introduces the resources and processes that people, communities, and social systems can utilize to facilitate their capacity to adapt to the challenges posed by disaster, recover as quickly as possible, and use the disaster experience as a catalyst for future growth and development. It commences with an introduction to the circumstances that will challenge adaptive competencies.

Gregg and Houghton (Chapter 3) introduce hazards in terms of characteristics such as their frequency, magnitude, precursory and reaction times, and their spatial and temporal distribution. In conjunction with the assessment of how these characteristics interact with the built and social environment over time, hazard analysis thus plays an important role in risk assessment and in the development of effective mitigation plans and strategies by identifying the causes and consequences of hazard activity that societies will have to adapt to. An important target of this planning derives from understanding how hazard activity impacts on those elements of the built environment that facilitate the performance of societal functions.

Johnston, Becker and Cousins (Chapter 4) discuss how hazards can impact on the infrastructure, services, utilities and linkages that sustain societal functions (see also Chapter 14). They present several case studies that illustrate the diverse consequences that hazard activity can have for these lifelines. They go on to discuss how lifeline technology and processes can be integrated to formulate strategies designed to facilitate their sustained operation in the event of a disaster.

The development of this capacity is a costly endeavor. Building resilience and redundancy into these systems is expensive. Because decisions made regarding the level of capacity in these systems are derived from estimates of risk and from cost-benefit analysis, it is possible that certain hazard parameters (e.g., magnitude, intensity, duration) could exceed planning estimates of infrastructure resilience. Consequently, the pragmatics of structural mitigation can never guarantee continuity of functioning under all possible conditions. Thus, under certain circumstances and in certain locations, loss of lifelines can constitute a significant secondary hazard. Lifeline failure must be factored into the process of estimating the parameters of societal adaptive capacity (see also Chapter 14).

While ensuring that the physical environment and lifelines are as robust as possible, resilience, at this level, describes only the degree to which the infrastructure required to support societal activity will continue to be available. It only contributes to societal resilience if it can be used by people and organizations to adapt to hazard consequences in ways that ensure their continued functioning. People and organizations must have taken steps to ensure their ability to utilize this infrastructure. If the latter capabilities are absent, there will be no return on the investment in infrastructure resilience.

What happens when a disaster strikes is very much a function of the quality of the mechanisms developed to facilitate the adaptive capacity of a society, its citizens and its core social functions (Paton, 2000). The remaining chapters explore the social elements exposed to hazard consequences and discuss what can be done to develop their adaptive capacity. It commences with consideration of societal mechanisms specifically developed to manage risk.

Emergency management planning takes place not during periods of hazard activity, but rather during periods of hazard quiescence when hazards may well be the furthest thing from peoples' minds. To maximize the likelihood that communities can realize their resilient potential under these circumstances, Schneider (Chapter 5) argues that emergency management agencies play a pivotal role in the community planning and development required to facilitate disaster resilience.

Schneider outlines how, since it takes place against a backdrop of increasing community diversity, motivating and sustaining activities designed to anticipate, prevent and mitigate hazard consequences is becoming progressively more complex. He continues by discussing the need for emergency management agencies to engage people and political and social institutions in ways that link public policies with community sustainability (see also Chapter 7). To do this it is necessary to understand the constituent components of adaptive capacity that can inform the substance of these policies.

Following a brief overview of current definitions of resilience, Buckle (Chapter 6) discusses these constituents and the assessment processes by which their availability can be estimated. He reiterates a point made by Schneider regarding the need to stop viewing communities as homogenous entities. In addition to accommodating the intrinsic diversity (e.g., demographic) of communities, Buckle argues that conceptualizing resilience requires that interaction within and between levels (e.g., individual, community, institutional, environmental) is fundamental to comprehensive resilience assessment. His review of the elements that comprise a resilient community (e.g., knowledge, shared values, social infrastructure) introduces several issues that are explored in more detail in subsequent chapters. Two of these issues, regarding community members' hazard knowledge and their disaster preparedness, are discussed next.

Paton, McClure and Bürgelt (Chapter 7) discuss how, even when it is intended to inform them about significant issues in their environment, people are not passive recipients of hazard information. People make judgments about the information presented to them and actively interpret it within socially constructed frames of reference defined by their expectations, experience, beliefs and misconceptions about hazards. Facilitating preparedness, according to this view, requires more than just making information available to people; it must meet the needs of diverse groups, make sense to them, and assist their making decisions regarding the adoption of protective measures. Furthermore, they argue, strategies must extend beyond information provision to engage community members in ways that facilitate their adoption of protective actions.

Cottrell, in Chapter 8, expands on the decision-making theme in her discussion of the relationship between socially constructed models of hazards, their mitigation and their management. She focuses on one

specific group, women, and how culture, social networks and personal characteristics influence choices made regarding adaptive strategies
for dealing with wet season hazards in northern Australia. Cottrell reiterates issues discussed in Chapter 6 regarding how structural mitigation and infrastructure development can actually reduce the likelihood
that people will take responsibility for preparing and how beliefs
regarding when to prepare make independent contributions to the
diversity that must be accommodated within the planning process.

Both the previous chapters discussed how individual choices and
actions are embedded in the social contexts in which decisions are
made. Smith (Chapter 9) develops a framework within which this
interaction can be conceptualized and systematically studied. He
focuses specifically on how social context influences hazard and risk
perception. Smith then proceeds to discuss the value of multilevel
models for articulating these relationships.

While, on the one hand, such models constitute a more representative model of adaptive capacity, integrating these levels of analysis also
raises new challenges for risk management. Smith discusses how reconciling individual and community costs and benefits can introduce
another source of conflict into community life that has implications for
readiness planning, even when dealing with hazards with the potential
to impact all citizens.

Planning occurs during periods when issues regarding the costs and
benefits of mitigation stand out against a background of hazard quiescence. Under these circumstances, community members will be well
aware of the costs associated with risk management, but less likely to
appreciate the benefits that could arise from their adoption (particularly if dealing with infrequently occurring events). This problem is
compounded by the limited period within which systematic hazard
analysis has taken place (see Chapter 3) and during which only a limited range of the possible permutations of hazard consequences will
have made their presence felt. Consequently, equity and fairness
regarding the distribution of risk throughout different sectors of the
community and community engagement in decision making about
acceptable levels of risk and the strategies used to mitigate this risk
become increasingly important components of strategies designed to
facilitate resilience (Paton, 2005; Paton & Bishop, 1996). Strategies
based on social justice principles can inform the understanding of
processes that influence risk acceptance and responsibility for safety.

Ensuring that this can be built into hazard reduction and readiness planning requires that mechanisms capable of providing insight into perceived fairness are available.

Candidates for mechanisms capable of evaluating perceived fairness are presented by Poolley, Cohen and O'Conner (Chapter 10) in their discussion of the role of social networks and community competence as resilience resources. In the context of a case study of Australian communities impacted by cyclones, they discuss not only how community and personal attributes affect adaptive capacity, but also how disaster can constitute a catalyst for individual and community growth.

To this point, discussion has concentrated on Western populations. Jang and LaMendola (Chapter 11) discuss how indigenous cultural characteristics can inform understanding of adaptive capacity. In a study of Taiwanese populations affected by an earthquake, they illustrate how elements of the Hakka Spirit predict resilience and post-traumatic growth. Jang and LaMendola discuss how this cultural predisposition contributes to resilience in two ways. Firstly, it does so through its influence on the way in which the relationship between people and environment is perceived. Secondly, it provides affected populations with an intrinsic set of social and psychological resources that facilitate their capacity to adapt to disaster.

The likelihood of a similar cultural predisposition toward positive social-ecological relationships developing in Western populations is low. Consequently, it becomes necessary to specifically consider the management of social-ecological interaction when developing comprehensive conceptualizations of resilience (Mileti, 1999).

In Chapter 12, Paton, Kelly and Doherty discuss social-ecological interaction from three perspectives: the capacity of an ecological system to adapt to the demands made upon it that are independent of human involvement; human action as a demand on the adaptive capacity of ecological systems; and social-ecological interaction as a source of adaptive capacity for people and communities. Their discussion focuses on identifying factors that can inform the development of sustainable environmental practices that both reduce natural hazard risk and enhance peoples' adaptive capacity.

A common thread running through the preceding chapters is the emphasis on resilience reflecting a capacity to make choices within social contexts. To make these choices, people need information. While having a prominent role to play in this regard, emergency management and civic agencies responsible for risk management are not the only sources of information. Information is also available, to civic agencies and citizens alike, from the media. In many cases, the media are the more active source, particularly when it comes to reporting response and recovery efforts. How issues are reported can exercise a significant influence on peoples' perceptions of hazard characteristics, their consequences and how they should be managed. This confers upon the media a substantial capability to influence peoples' future adaptive capacity (see also Chapter 7). The importance of the media can also be attributed to the fact that it often delivers information that is filtered, processed and interpreted to varying extents and with varying degrees of accuracy.

Given the implicit uncertainty associated with hazard activity and the fact that, by definition, a disaster is an event that exceeds the capacity of societal resources to meet all needs generated (i.e., no response can be 100% effective), this is a fertile area for misinterpretation. Not all those who receive media coverage will be able to weave their way through the maze of issues required to construct an objective view of these matters. Thus, how the media treat the complexity and uncertainty that is an implicit characteristic of the hazard context can influence both adaptive capacity and trust in formal sources of information, advice and recommendations (e.g., civic and scientific agencies). As a result, the media can exercise a powerful influence on the debate that occurs regarding the causes and mitigation of hazard consequences. Media coverage can also influence public perceptions of agencies with a civic responsibility for managing hazards.

Hughes and White (Chapter 13) discuss the relationship between the media and societal resilience in the context of wildfire hazards. They discuss media influence from several perspectives; reporting events, the relationship between different media and public beliefs regarding mitigation and response, and building relationships between civic and media agencies. The effective management of this relationship will also influence whether media coverage enhances or hinders adaptive capacity (e.g., through its influence on the sustained adoption of protective measures (see Chapter 7).

Fundamental to societal resilience is the degree to which its economic systems can respond to and adapt to the consequences of hazard activity. Drawing upon ecological, engineering and organizational theory definitions of resilience, Rose (chapter 14) fills a gap in the existing literature by offering an operational definition of economic resilience that demonstrates its utility as a device for managing catastrophic risk through actively incorporating economic issues into holistic natural hazard planning models. In pursuing this objective, Rose discusses how to quantify and measure economic resilience. He emphasizes the need to consider this issue in the context of the specific hazard characteristics (e.g., their duration and severity, see Chapter 3) that a society may have to contend with. By emphasizing the contribution of microeconomic levels to economic resilience, Rose also introduces the need to consider how commercial and business continuity contributes to economic resilience and the continuity of employment.

Paton and Hill (Chapter 15) discuss the procedures and competencies that contribute to business resilience through disaster continuity planning. The processes they discuss also have implications for ensuring functional continuity in agencies with response, recovery and rebuilding roles and responsibilities. One group for whom a capacity for sustained operations is essential are those agencies with responsibility for managing the consequences of disaster.

Paton and Auld (Chapter 16) discuss the relationship between resilience in emergency managers and effective response management. They discuss adaptive capacity in this population as a process that involves matching the consequences and demands to be managed with the individual, team and organizational resources that can be mobilized to confront hazard consequences. While emergency management agencies play pivotal roles in all phase of disaster planning, reduction (mitigation), readiness, response, recovery and rebuilding, the effectiveness of the societal response, as a whole, is a function of the degree to which emergency planning and management roles are complemented by the activities of many other groups and agencies.

King (Chapter 17) emphasizes that planning for resilient communities is the responsibility of all community members, agencies and organizations. He does so by arguing that closer integration of planning with the concepts of sense of place and sense of community (see also Chapters 7, 10, 12) will help embed planning processes within the culture of a community (see also Chapter 11). That is, to develop resilience as a capacity that grows out of people and their communities rather than as something that is imposed upon them. He discusses how this can be done within mitigation and response planning initiatives.

The content areas introduced here describe core issues to be included in planning agenda designed to develop disaster resilient communities. The quality and effectiveness of planning initiatives are put to the test when natural processes interact with societal elements in ways that result in their becoming hazards. Consequently, an appropriate starting point for a book on disaster resilience is a discussion of the characteristics of the natural processes that define the context in which societal adaptation will take place should disaster occur.

REFERENCES

Mileti, D. (1999). *Disasters by design.* Washington, DC.: Joseph Henry Press.

Paton, D. (2000). Emergency Planning: Integrating community development, community resilience and hazard mitigation. *Journal of the American Society of Professional Emergency Managers, 7,* 109–118.

Paton, D. (2005). Community Resilience: Integrating Hazard Management and Community Engagement. *Proceedings of the International Conference on Engaging Communities.* Brisbane. Queensland Government/UNESCO.

Paton, D. & Bishop B. (1996). Disasters and communities: Promoting psychosocial well-being. In D. Paton and N. Long (Eds.) *Psychological aspects of disaster: Impact, coping, and intervention.* Palmerston North, Dunmore Press.

Chapter 3

NATURAL HAZARDS

C.E. GREGG AND B.F. HOUGHTON

INTRODUCTION

Natural hazards are those components of naturally occurring events such as hurricanes, earthquakes, and floods capable of threatening people and the things people value. Despite considerable expenditure to mitigate their impact, the economic losses and the numbers of people affected by natural hazards continue to escalate (Alexander, 1993; EM-DAT, 2004; Tierney, Lindell, & Perry, 1999; Tobin, 1999). Furthermore, factors such as the extent of development, gross domestic product, and availability of resources to undertake and implement mitigation, preparedness and response strategies influence societal choices regarding the implementation of strategies capable of mitigating natural hazard consequences. These strategies include engineered structures, building codes, land-use planning, insurance, and warning systems, but public policy is at the heart of each of these. This chapter examines natural hazards from the context of their characteristics, impacts on society and how people respond to meet the challenges of hazard events. We illustrate these issues with examples drawn from events worldwide.

Physical scientists have traditionally focused on models of the physical aspects of natural hazards to understand why disasters occur. For example, natural hazards have been characterized in terms of their frequency, magnitude, intensity, speed of onset, and duration, together with their spatial and temporal distributions. However, there is

19

increasing interest in understanding the role of human-use systems
(Tobin & Montz, 1997) in the outcomes of natural hazard processes.
Most disasters require human input, ranging from bad planning decisions to inadequate mitigation, preparedness and response. One
approach to reducing community losses from natural hazards involves
the development of sustainable communities (Beatley, 1998) that
avoid or reduce exposure to natural hazard events to acceptable and
manageable levels. This requires the integration of ideas involving the
physical processes of natural hazards, with the human-use system, and
moral beliefs about how we should live on the Earth.

The number of declared disasters arising from natural hazard events
is increasing worldwide. Figure 3.1 illustrates the increasing number of
federally declared disasters in the USA alone. These events have
exacted, and in some cases continue to exact, a staggering and sober-
ing toll from communities everywhere. The last decade of the twentieth century was the most costly decade in history and the year 1995
was the single most costly year ever; the Kobe earthquake in Japan

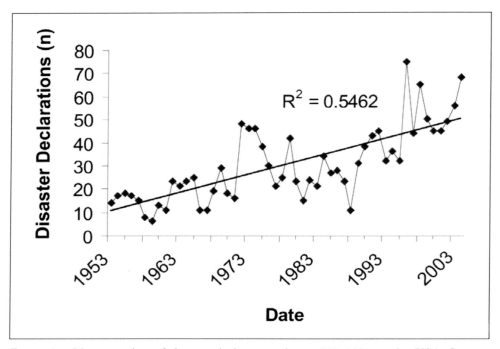

Figure 3.1. Mean number of disaster declarations from 1953–2004 in the USA. Source:
Federal Emergency Management Agency (2004).

cost an estimated $120 billion alone (Tierney et al., 1999). The December 26, 2004 earthquake and tsunami in Southeast Asia caused estimated fatalities in excess of 200,000 (the death toll from the tsunami continues to change, even in April 2005, as affected countries reassess the number of missing and dead). The increasing toll of natural disasters reflects conditions such as increasing population numbers and densities, expanding development, and the increasing value of the resources we place in harm's way. The influences of other dynamic conditions, such as global climate change, are more debatable.

In simple terms, people have built all too often in excessively dangerous places and there are inequities in who has had to pay the price. A discouraging observation in hazards research is the repeated impact of the same hazards on the same areas; in each case requiring outside assistance. The latter remains an impediment to sustainability because people have still not uniformly been held accountable for their actions (i.e., knowingly and intentionally building in hazardous places).

TERMINOLOGY

The broad field of hazard and disaster studies is being occupied increasingly by professionals representing social and physical sciences, psychology, geographers, planning, and emergency management. In this multidisciplinary field, terms such as *hazard* and *disaster* are used highly inconsistently to an extent where this is a barrier to effective communication of ideas between researchers and practitioners in the field and even with the public who ultimately depend on the quality, consistency and clarity of information provided. Indeed, Quarantelli (1998) devoted an entire book to discussing the various ways in which the term *disaster* has been used in the literature. Tobin and Montz (1997) have briefly described the evolutionary development of the term *hazard*.

In this paper, the term *hazard* is defined as "a natural process that could potentially threaten the things that people value" (e.g., human life, developed property, plants, animals, water, soil, and so on). Note, however, that we placed no reference to scale or the magnitude of the hazard. Our usage of the term *disaster* varies only because we draw upon examples of disasters described by other people who commonly used different criteria to establish if a damaging event was classified as a disaster. Notwithstanding, a disaster can generally be inferred to represent an event from which communities cannot cope with impacts using their own resources, thus necessitating a call for national or international assistance. There is considerable debate in the literature over what constitutes a disaster, and considerable sums of money may be at stake. For example, in the United States, federal proclamation of a disaster may involve economic aid for disaster response, recovery, and post-disaster mitigation (pre-disaster mitigation for the next event) of the order of hundreds of thousands to billions of dollars.

CHARACTERISTICS OF NATURAL HAZARDS

Understanding of the scale of hazard activity is limited by the relatively short time period during which hazards have been recorded. For example, written records for most natural hazards span only a few hundred years or less, yet this duration is seldom sufficient to observe the full range and peak magnitudes and intensities of hazard activity. This means that for some events we have not seen the largest possible hazards. Take for example the eruption of the Bishop Tuff, from Long Valley caldera, California. Thick deposits from that eruption 760,000 years ago devastated 2,200 km^2, and we have not witnessed anything like this eruption in modern times; the 1991 eruption of Mount Pinatubo in the Philippines, the second largest eruption of the twentieth century, devastated an area of only about 400 km^2 (Newhall & Punongbayan, 1996). Furthermore, hazard characteristics may change as a result of events like global warming, environmental degradation, human land use and tectonics, for both long and short-time scales.

There is a very broad range of natural hazard processes, but most natural hazards originate from either meteorological or geological events; a few hazards are grouped as hydrological and extra terrestrial events (Tobin & Montz, 1997). Table 3.1 shows the relationship between selected events and their component hazards. Events such as hurricanes produce multiple hazards while other events may produce a single hazard. Currently, we know a great deal about the characteristics of many hazards, but a task ahead involves the integration of all hazards into models that explain these characteristics and other factors such as risk, vulnerability and community resilience. This is necessary because most areas face risk from multiple hazards and multiple types of event, and primary hazard events can trigger a string of other secondary and tertiary hazards arising from physical, biological and technological sources. For example, many people survived the M9.5 earthquake in Chile in 1960, the largest yet recorded, but became fatalities in the tsunami that followed the earthquake (Atwater et al., 1999). This pattern was repeated in the 2004 M9.3 earthquake in southeast Asia. Here, we briefly examine some of the fundamental physical characteristics of natural hazards.

Frequency

The frequency of a natural hazard refers to how often the hazard is repeated during a specific period of time and the term is usually linked

TABLE 3.1. LIST OF SOME NATURAL HAZARDS ASSOCIATED
WITH SPECIFIC EVENTS AND CATEGORIES OF EVENTS.

Category	Event	Hazards
Meteorological	Hurricane/tropical cyclone	High winds, heavy rain, flooding, storm surge, tornadoes, coastal erosion
	Other storms	High winds, heavy rain, flooding, storm surge, tornadoes, coastal erosion, lightening, frost, hail, ice, snow, blizzards, snow avalanche, rockfall
	Cold and heat waves	Extreme temperatures
	Lightening	Electrical discharge, Wildfire
	Drought	Wildfire, salination
Geological	Earthquake	Ground shaking, ground rupture, ground cracking, liquefaction, landslides, tsunami
	Volcanic eruption	Tephra fall, pyroclastic density currents, lava flows, volcanic gases and aerosols, ground cracking, landslides, lahars, tsunami
	Landslide, mass failure	Rockfall, tsunami, subsidence, ground cracking
Hydrological	Flood events	Erosion, landslides, high water levels
	El Nino and La Nina	Drought, flooding, frost, landslide

Modified after Tobin and Montz (1997).

to events of specific magnitude or intensity. Knowing the return period of past hazard events aids in predicting the timing of future events.
The traditional approach to calculating frequency has been to take the
total number of events and divide this by the total number of years
over which the events occurred. For example, earthquakes have damaged San Salvador city in El Salvador severely 15 times between A.D.
1700 and 2001 (Harlow, White, Rymer, & Alvarez, 1993). This corresponds to a frequency of about 0.05 (i.e., the probability of occurrence
in any one year is 0.05; or on average one damaging earthquake every
20 years).

The limited availability of good data sets for many areas of the
world increases error in estimates of hazard activity. There exists good
data sets of hazard activity on regional scales, but global compilations
are less common. Notwithstanding, on a global scale, EM-DAT (2004)
data show that floods and storms dominated disaster frequencies on
regional (e.g., in the U.S.A. and Australia) and global scales during the
period 1900-2003 (Figure 3.2). Other hazards account for less than 14
percent of disasters. However, developing an accurate global database
of disaster data for contemporary time periods, let alone the early and

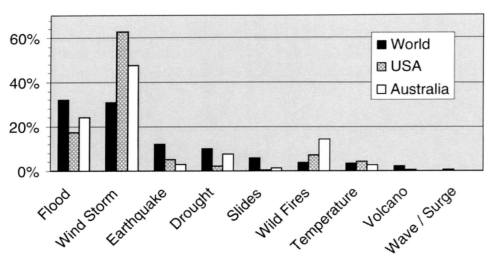

Figure 3.2. Percentage contribution of nine types of hazard events to the overall percentage of
disasters occurring worldwide and in selected regions [Australia and United States (USA)]
between 1900 and 2003. For example, flood disasters account for 32% of the total number of
disaster declarations around the world, but floods only account for 18% in the USA and 24%
in Australia. Source: EM-DAT (2004).

mid-twentieth century, is difficult and inevitably fraught with error, so the data must be treated with caution. For example, a cross-check of the EM-DAT database with U.S. Federal Emergency Management Agency (FEMA) data for disaster frequency across all hazards in the United States reveals some inconsistencies. The EM-DAT data base indicated that a total of 964 disasters occurred in the United States during the period 1900–2003, whereas FEMA show 1504 major disasters during the period 1953–2003 alone (FEMA, 2004).

Magnitude

The magnitude of hazard events largely involves scientific estimates of the size of an event, although there is considerable variation in how magnitude is measured within and across specific hazards. Magnitude is sometimes used interchangeably with intensity, but there is a difference. Magnitude focuses on physical processes and is unrelated to impacts on the human-use system; estimates frequently use some form of energy scale, recorded for the full duration of the event. For example, the Richter and Seismic Moment earthquake magnitude scales seek to measure the magnitude or amount of energy released in an earthquake. Earthquakes have only one magnitude, although estimates based on different techniques will differ to some extent. In contrast, estimates of the magnitude of volcanic eruptions refer purely to the volume or mass of erupted products.

Intensity

Intensity is used in two ways in the context of natural hazards - as a direct measure of rate (e.g., as energy per unit time) or indirectly linked to estimates of damage. The modified Mercalli earthquake scale and the Fujita tornado scale are two scales that use building damage to estimate intensity. Such scales reflect social and engineering factors as well as the force of the hazard, e.g., the presence or absence of steel reinforced concrete, shear walls, hurricane clips and so on. In contrast, the intensity scale for volcanic eruptions is based on the mass eruption rate in kg s^{-1}. These conceptual differences between the earthquake, tornado, and volcano scales illustrate the difficulty in reconciling magnitude, intensity, and destructiveness measurements between event types.

Duration

The duration of natural hazard events varies considerably from seconds to decades and is a critical factor in planning issues. For example, on one end of the spectrum are events with very short durations, such as earthquakes, tornadoes, landslides, avalanches, and flash floods. The obverse is droughts, slope creep, heat and cold waves, El Nino and some floods and volcanic eruptions. Planning for events of long duration is particularly problematic. Take for example, the lahar hazard at Mount Pinatubo in the Philippines, where annual rain-induced remobilization of unconsolidated pyroclastic material from earlier eruptions in 1991 has caused more direct and indirect damage on communities, crops and infrastructure downslope than did the eruptions (Newhall & Punongbayan, 1996). Another important consideration is the link between intensity and duration. For example, Simkin and Siebert (2000) showed that the median duration of 3301 volcanic eruptions was seven weeks. However, 42 percent of 252 highly explosive eruptions reached their peak intensity within the first day and 52 percent within the first week. Events that peak early may hamper response and recovery efforts through prolonged activity.

Precursory Period and Reaction Time

It is desirable to distinguish between the potential lead time a hazard may provide through precursory activity and the time required for the hazard to adversely affect an area once the hazard has developed. Precursory period is the time between detection of precursory activity and the onset of hazard activity. *Precursory period* has historically been referred to as warning time. An example of precursory period is the time delay between the beginning of volcanic tremor (i.e., a type of high frequency, low amplitude seismicity associated with magma moving underground) and the surface eruption of the magma. *Response time,* in comparison, is the difference in time between the beginning or first detection of the hazard (e.g., the formation of tsunami) and the time the hazard begins to impact adversely upon an area (e.g., tsunami to reach a coastal community). Response time has historically been referred to as "speed of onset" although speed of onset has also been linked to the rate of escalation of peak intensity.

Precursory period and reaction time have major implications for the design and maintenance of mitigation, preparedness, and response measures. For example, the precursory period and reaction times for some hazards are so short that officials will have no time to influence protective behavior for areas at risk. Earthquakes, for example, may provide only a few seconds of precursory activity, or none at all, while the reaction time for earthquakes may be of the order of seconds to tens of seconds.

Three other time scales can be considered here. These include:

1. Escalation time: the period of time between onset and climax of an event.
2. Duration: the total length of time during which an event occurs.
3. Recovery time: the period of time before normal life and land use can be resumed.

Spatial Distribution

Most natural hazards are confined to specific regions, although some hazards have global effects. For example, volcanic eruptions and earthquakes are highly concentrated at the boundaries of tectonic plates worldwide, and tornadoes are confined mostly to the United States and Australia. Tobin and Montz (1997) emphasized that the study of natural hazards needed to focus on the relationship between magnitude and intensity and space. For example, for a large earthquake, ground shaking may be felt over wide regions, but extensive damage will be limited largely close to the epicenter and where geologic conditions amplify the damaging effects of shaking, or where structures have not been strengthened to reduce shaking. Similarly, most volcanic hazards (e.g., pyroclastic density currents, lava flows, and ballistic blocks) are local phenomenon on scales of kilometers to tens of kilometers, but large eruptions that produce abundant gas and fine ash in high plumes have regional to global effects (Mills, 2000).

Figure 3.3 illustrates the relative distributions of natural disasters in five regions (e.g., Oceana, Europe, Africa, the Americas and Asia). These data cannot be construed to represent directly the relative magnitudes or intensities of hazard events because similar hazards occurring in different areas may impact each area differently. Figure 3.3 suggests that Asia accounts for some 21 percent of each category of natural disasters, thus underscoring a vulnerability to hazard activity. Many diverse physical and human factors must be considered to explain the inequities of distribution of disasters in the various regions.

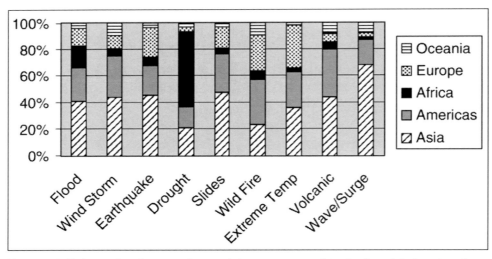

Figure 3.3. Relative distributions of natural disasters reported in the five global regions from 1900–2003 (n = 8,057). Asia experienced 68% of disasters related to waves/surge, while Africa experienced 58% of disaster-related drought. Asia accounted for 39% of all the 8,057 disasters reported, Americas (27%), Africa (15%), Europe (13%), and Oceania (6%). Source: EM-DAT (2004).

What are the spatial distributions of fatalities and economic loss? Figure 3.3 shows that Asia and the Americas accounted for two-thirds of all disasters, and Figure 3.4a suggests that these regions also bear the burden of higher economic losses. Figure 3.4b shows that Asia clearly bears the burden of most disaster fatalities; fatalities in Asian disasters accounted for a staggering 85 percent of the total disaster fatalities for the years 1900–2003. A recent report from the International Federation of Red Cross and Red Crescent Societies (2001) under-scored that this inequity persists to the present day–they reported that of the reported 665,598 people killed by natural disasters during the ten-year period from 1991–2000, 83 percent were in Asia. The recent earthquake and tsunami in Southeast Asia claimed over one-quarter of this amount in just a few hours.

Glickman, Golding, and Silverman, (1992) showed that in 1945–1986 the pattern of fatalities differs from that shown in Figure 3.4b when disaster fatalities are plotted against millions of population. However, the reinsurance company Munich RE reported from analy-sis of EM-DAT data on floods, earthquakes, tropical cyclones and drought that Asia bore the greatest loss in terms of most lives lost and

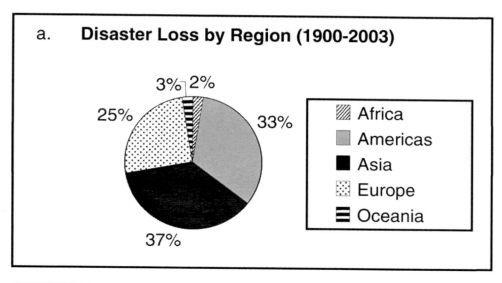

a. **Disaster Loss by Region (1900-2003)**

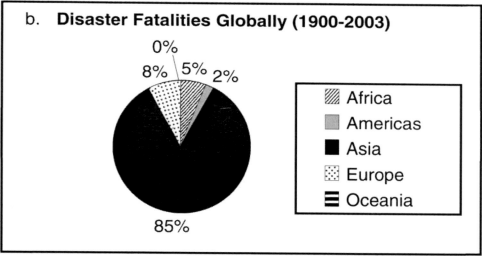

b. **Disaster Fatalities Globally (1900-2003)**

Figure 3.4a,b. a. Relative distribution of natural disaster economic losses reported in five global regions from 1900–2003. Asia, Europe and the Americas account for 95% of total losses, while Africa and Oceania account for 5%. Total worldwide losses were over $US912 billion (not adjusted). b. Relative distribution of fatalities in natural disasters reported from 1900–2003. The total number of disasters reported was 8,057 and the total number of fatalities was about 20.2 million. Source: EM-DAT (2004).

most lives lost per million of population for all hazards except drought (United Nations Development Program, 2004). A higher death rate per million of population in Africa was attributed to other factors besides drought (e.g., conflict, war, famine, etc.).

The spatial distribution of impacts has also been modeled on the relative extent of development in various nations. For example, when the world is subdivided into three groups of human development (i.e., low, medium, and high development), the International Federation of Red Cross and Red Crescent Societies (2001) reported that nations of low human development (LHD) bear the brunt of fatalities, but less economic costs. In contrast, nations of medium human development (MHD) were reported to have the most people affected by disasters (possibly a consequence of China and India being classified as MHD countries), and nations of high human development (HHD) bear the brunt of economic costs.

Other researchers have used losses as a function of gross domestic product (GDP) as a means of defining scales of disasters. For example, the International Federation of Red Cross and Red Crescent Societies (2001) reported that estimated world-wide losses of US$190 billion in 1995 represented 0.7 percent of the global GDP. In contrast, they estimated that the cost of the 1999 earthquake in Turkey was equivalent to 7 to 9 percent of Turkey's annual GDP and the impact of Hurricane Mitch (1998) on the Honduran economy was estimated to be equivalent to a staggering 75 percent of Honduras' annual GDP.

Temporal Distribution

A few hazards (meteorological and hydrological) tend to have specific temporal distributions and these help in their prediction. These hazards include tropical cyclones, tornadoes, floods and wildfire. Temporal distributions are primarily seasonal, but some hazards have diurnal distributions (e.g., thunderstorms, lightening, hail, tornadoes). The El Nino Southern Oscillation, on the other hand, may occur over much broader cycles of the order of years. In contrast, seasonality has traditionally been thought to have less, if any, influence on geological hazards such as volcanic eruptions and earthquakes. Notwithstanding, Cochran, Vidale, and Tanak (2004) found a correlation between the occurrence of shallow thrust faults and the occurrence of the strongest tides.

Secondary Hazards

Often the occurrence of one hazard will spawn secondary hazards. These include, for example, lahars generated from the fallout of hot volcanic material that melts ice and snow and tsunamis or landslides generated from earthquakes. Secondary technological or environmental hazards arising from natural hazards may involve the release of petroleum products, industrial chemicals and solvents, bio-hazardous materials and waste-water. Natural hazards may also trigger outbreaks of disease.

MITIGATING NATURAL HAZARDS

By definition, the term *mitigate* means to soften or to make less harsh (Neufeldt, 1994); to *mitigate* has no temporal meaning. However, the hazard-community has modified this term. Mitigation refers to projects instituted well in advance of events that reduce susceptibility to loss from hazard activity. This mode of thinking arises from changes in public policy for coping with hazard events and disasters. Traditionally, governments have responded to disasters by sinking large amounts of money into post-disaster response and recovery. The contemporary focus is on providing money for mitigation well in advance of hazard events to prevent or minimize the potential for hazards to cause disasters (Godschalk, Beatley, Berke, Brower, & Edward, 1999).

The use of engineered strategies to reduce the impacts of natural hazards has been largely applied by developed countries that have had the resources to do so. While this has led to reductions in fatalities in developed countries, the influence of mitigation strategies on the economic impacts of hazard events is less encouraging, as economic losses have continued to escalate. One recent example of cost-effective mitigation involves the protection of tourist facilities on Mount Etna volcano, Sicily. Barberi, Brondi, Carapezza, Cavarra, and Murgia (2003) reported that the successful construction of barriers to divert lava flows had a cost-benefit ratio of 1:20. Concern for mitigation on an international level is increasing (Munasinghe & Clarke, 1995), which is no surprise, given the role of developed nations in helping bear the financial costs of disaster recovery and reconstruction of those developing nations where mitigation measures are less common or absent. For example, the 2004 tsunami in southeast Asia has motivated international plans to build a global tsunami monitoring and warning capability (U. S. Office of Science and Technology and Policy, 2005).

Reducing the adverse effects of hazard events on property and safety can be done through a variety of strategies. These strategies include early warning systems, engineered measures designed to hold back or divert a hazard, building codes that require buildings to withstand the forces of hazards and land-use planning that isolates areas susceptible to hazard activity. Furthermore, insurance against damage from natural hazards is a means of distributing losses across communities or organizations (Kunreuther & Roth, 1998). Kunreuther (2000) explained how concerns over insolvency or significant loss of surplus, raised by insurers and re-insurers of natural hazards, could be alleviated by other policy instruments, and how the adoption of cost-effective measures for loss reduction will require enforced building codes and financial incentives (e.g., long-term loans tied to an insurance policy). Insurance can serve as a cornerstone for public-private partnerships (Kunreuther, 2000), the latter of which are seen as essential components of contemporary mitigation planning and sustainable development.

Warning Systems

Warning systems are intended to detect and monitor hazard activity and provide an early alert to officials and the public so that protective actions can be taken. This helps avoid disaster by minimizing the adverse hazard effects. Warning systems are complex, involving detection, monitoring and notification of and response to hazard activity.

The development of effective warning systems is a multidisciplinary process, and involves input from a wide range of specialists, including, but not limited to, physical science, engineering, information technology, emergency management, media, risk communication, and social science. There exists a wide range of technologies for warning systems across a range of hazards and the interested reader is referred to Sorensen (2000) who reviewed the last 20 years of history of hazard warning systems in the United States. Sorensen defined effective warning systems as those that integrated scientific monitoring and detection with an emergency organization that utilizes warning technologies that accommodate social design factors that facilitate the rapid issuing of alerts and notification to the public. Sorensen reported that for most hazards there had not been much improvement in warning systems, and that improvements were more positive for hazard prediction and forecast than integration.

An important general finding in warning system research is that a single warning concept will not be effective in equally serving the requirements of all hazards (Gregg, Houghton, Paton, Johnston, & Yanagi, 2005; Mileti & Sorensen, 1990). This is an important consideration for areas at risk from multiple hazards. For example, warning systems must ensure that official warning messages motivate the desired public response for both those events requiring immediate response (e.g., earthquakes, local tsunamis, tornadoes) and events that allow for time to react (e.g., distant tsunami, hurricanes).

Another consideration is to what extent governments should invest limited financial resources on high-tech prediction, forecast and warning systems versus other mitigation and preparedness measures such as building codes. For example, (Normile, 2004) discussed how early warning systems in Japan, Mexico and Taiwan detect seismic P-waves preceding more damaging S-waves, which lag behind the former by several seconds over distances of a few hundred kilometers, to provide seconds of early warning to distant areas. Opponents argue resources are better spent on strengthening vulnerable infrastructure rather than providing a few seconds of warning. In the case of the recent tsunami calamity in Asia, the presence of a warning system would have reduced losses, but to what extent will remain uncertain. For example, even in Hawaii, where tsunamis have been devastating historically and a public warning system has been tested monthly for decades, Gregg et al. (2005) found that levels of public understanding of the meaning of the warning system remains low (12%) and is essentially not much better than levels of understanding measured in Hilo, Hawaii during the 1960 tsunami that destroyed much of downtown Hilo (Lachman, Tatsuoka, & Bonk, 1961). This underscores the idea that warnings systems must integrate mechanical and social components if they are to be effective in reducing risk. In the case of the latter, this involves educational outreach that is tailored to meet the needs of individual communities (Gregg, 2005; Lindell, 1994).

Engineered Mitigation

The construction of structures such as dams has played a significant role in hazard mitigation, even when decisions to build such structures have involved factors other than reducing risk from natural hazards (e.g., China's Three Gorges Dam will serve to control deadly flooding, as well as provide electricity, and a transportation route to China's interior). Structural mitigation measures such as dams, levees, sea walls, etc often induce development of vulnerable land and potentially increase catastrophic risk in the event of a major failure, as opposed to decreasing risk. For example, measures may protect against a 100-year event, yet fail catastrophically in a 500-year event. Hundreds of levees failed when rivers flooded the mid-western United States in 1993 showing how vulnerable society is when it builds within hazard zones protected by engineered structures. Sheaffer, Roland, Davis, Feldman, & Stockdale (1976) reported that two-thirds of national losses from flooding result from events that exceed the performance limits of engineered works assumed by most people to ensure their personal safety.

Building Codes

Building codes can reduce the adverse impacts of hazards. For example, hurricane clips may prevent roofs from detaching from buildings during the high winds of passing tropical cyclones and thus prevent rain damage. However, as with engineered structures, building codes have their limitations. Godschalk et al. (1999) reported that in the wake of Hurricane Andrew, which struck South Florida in 1992, officials realized that strict building codes would not prevent serious damage. Furthermore, earthquake codes are typically designed to prevent buildings from collapsing, not to maintain structural integrity of the building and ensure habitability after a large earthquake. This policy increases human survival rates in earthquakes, but is less effective in reducing the economic impact. Furthermore, building codes are the offspring of public policy, and policy is vulnerable to inequity in its application across the breadth of society, and may be ignored or not enforced (Beatley, 1990; Godschalk et al. 1999).

Land-Use Planning

The principles of land-use planning are becoming increasingly integrated into natural hazard strategies. Burby, Deyle, Godschalk and Olshansky (2000) stated that land-use planning is the single most promising approach to achieving sustainable hazard mitigation. The idea behind land-use planning is to favor maximizing the utility of development while minimizing risk. This can include avoidance of hazardous areas, land-use zoning restrictions that maintain low population and building densities in high hazard areas, or relocation of existing at-risk development. The concept of sustainable development includes establishing specific levels of well-calculated and sustainable risks arising from the community's interaction with hazard activity.

Building sustainable communities through land-use planning can be a difficult, slow process. For reasons related to employment, land productivity, aesthetics, and land affordability, people often choose to reside and work in areas of high hazard. For example, people commonly wish to build close to water (rivers, lakes, and oceans) and yet are reluctant to agree to measures such as minimum set-backs that protect development against coastal erosion, storm surge, and flooding. Individuals tend to favor preservation of single property owner rights over the long-term benefits of mitigation.

Sustainable communities require shifts in this mode of thinking and often relocation of major development. In the short-term, the latter is an untenable scenario in most instances. This necessitates the development and implementation of specific protective strategies until more effective strategies such as relocation can be exercised. For example, traditional approaches to reducing the impacts of overland flooding once involved the use of engineered structures and building codes, but since the early 1960s there has been a move toward resettlement of at-risk communities in the United States. Still, much existing development lies within hazardous areas (Thomas & Mitchell, 2001), and where communities at risk cannot be relocated to safer areas, engineered mitigation structures, building codes, warning systems and adoption of other preparedness and response measures provide the only form of protection, while risk can be distributed through acquisition of insurance.

Public Policy

Public policy exerts an extreme influence over all aspects of risk reduction strategies. For example, policy such as New Zealand's Resource Management Act 1991 (amended in 2003) placed tight controls on the granting of building consents for land subject to a range of hazards and established liability for damages from hazard events where construction was knowingly and intentionally carried out in at-risk areas. Other policy such as the Disaster Mitigation Act of 2000 in the USA has fostered a move toward government subsidies of pre-disaster mitigation projects rather than response and recovery expenditure. These policies reflect the concept of long-term mitigation planning and are steps toward the development of a more realistic policy that reflect our understanding of natural hazards. However, as discussed, acceptance of policy is not equally distributed across the populations concerned and may be ignored or not enforced (Beatley, 1990; Godschalk et al. 1999).

CONCLUSION

Natural hazards are often highly variable in their physical, temporal and spatial characteristics. This variability, and the high number and complexities of hazards, explains why models that integrate understanding of individual hazards and risk reduction strategies from the range of hazard events are slow in developing. There are, however, some broad similarities in hazard characteristics and how to mitigate, prepare for, and respond to hazard events. These similarities need to be explored, applied in models, and considered in the context of how lessons learned from one hazard may be applied to other hazard events. An even greater challenge for the scientific community is to integrate models of natural hazards with those related to environmental and technological hazards and terrorism. Such work is vital in simplifying emergency management agencies' task of providing services for all hazards, which transcend boundaries that have traditionally confined scientific researchers to subfields of hazard.

Natural hazard events are extremely costly, but the reason for this is as much poor land-use decisions and insufficient, weak, and unenforced public policy as it is the magnitude of the physical hazards. The success of risk reduction strategies is a combination of physical, social-psychological, economic, cultural, environmental, and political factors. Policies are needed that require seller-disclosure of the range of natural hazards and buyer acknowledgement that state and federal economic aid will be unavailable if either developed property is knowingly and intentionally purchased after disclosure of hazards or if land is knowingly and intentionally developed after disclosure. Presently, hazard disclosure laws are not all-inclusive and are loosely constructed.

Despite the wide ranging estimates of losses from hazards and dis-asters, Cutter (2001) reported that we really do not know how much hazard events cost annually. Quantifying loss from natural hazards, especially indirect loss, is difficult. What we know, however, is that natural hazards cost society too much (in terms of loss of property and human suffering), given the state of knowledge of the physical aspects of the hazards and our improving understanding of the interaction between natural hazards and the human-use system. It is between these two areas where better linkage is needed and only through con-tinued integration of models for hazards and the human-use system will we begin to understand the most efficient and effective ways to reduce the rising toll of disasters.

REFERENCES

Alexander, D. (1993). *Natural hazards.* New York, NY: Chapman and Hall.

Atwater, B. F., Cisternas V, M., Bourgeois, J., Dudley, W. C., Hendley II, J. W., & Stauffer, P. H. (1999). Surviving a tsunami: Lessons from Chile, Hawaii and Japan. *US Geological Survey Circular, 1187,* 20.

Barberi, F., Brondi, F., Carapezza, M. L., Cavarra, L., & Murgia, C. (2003). Earthen barriers to control lava flows in the 2001 eruption of Mt. Etna. *Journal of Volcanology and Geothermal Research, 123,* 231–243.

Beatley, T. (1990). *Managing reconstruction along the South Carolina Coast: Preliminary observations on the implementation of the Beachfront Management Act.* Boulder: University of Colorado, Natural Hazards Research and Applications Center.

Beatley, T. (1998). The vision of sustainable communities. In R. J. Burby (Ed.), *Cooperating with nature: Confronting natural hazards with land-use planning for sus-tainable development* (pp. 233–262). Washington, DC: Joseph Henry Press.

Burby, R. J., Deyle, R. E., Godschalk, D. R., & Olshansky, R. B. (2000). Creating hazard resilient communities through land-use planning. *Natural Hazards Review, 1*(2), 99–106.

Cochran, E. S., Vidale, J. E., & Tanak, S. (2004). Earth tides can trigger shallow thrust fault earthquakes. *Science, 306*(5699), 1164–1166.

Cutter, S. L. (Ed.). (2001). *American hazard scapes: The regionalization of natural hazards and disasters.* Washington, DC: Joseph Henry Press.

EM-DAT (2004). *The OFDA/CRED international disaster database–*www.em-dat.net*–* Université Catholique de Louvain - Brussels - Belgium.

Federal Emergency Management Agency. (2004). *Total major disaster declarations (1953–2003).* Washington, DC.: Federal Emergency Management Agency.

Glickman, T. S., Golding, T., & Silverman, E. D. (1992). *Acts of God and man: Recent trends in natural disasters and major industrial accidents.* Washington, DC: Resources for the Future.

Godschalk, D. R., Beatley, T., Berke, P., Brower, D. J., & Edward, J. K. (1999). *Natural hazard mitigation: Recasting disaster policy and planning.* Washington, DC: Island Press.

Gregg, C. E. (2005). *Natural hazards in Hawaii: Some studies of awareness, risk perception and preparedness.* Unpublished doctoral dissertation, University of Hawaii, Honolulu.

Gregg, C. E., Houghton, B. F., Paton, D., Johnston, D. M., & Yanagi, B. (2006). (in press). Tsunami warnings: Understanding in Hawaii. Natural Hazards.

Harlow, D. H., White, R. A., Rymer, M. J., & Alvarez, S. (1993). The San Salvador earthquake of 10 October 1986 and its historical context. *Bulletin of Seismological Society of America, 83*(4), 1143–1154.

International Federation of Red Cross and Red Crescent Societies. (2001). World disasters report. Retrieved November 12, 2004, from http://www.ifrc.org/public at/wdr2001/chapter8.asp

Kunreuther, H. (2000). Insurance as cornerstone for public-private sector partnerships. *Natural Hazards Review, 1*(2), 126–136.

Kunreuther, H., & Roth, R. S. (Eds.). (1998). *Paying the price: The status and role of insurance against natural disasters in the United States.* Washington, DC: Joseph Henry Press.

Lachman, R., Tatsuoka, M., & Bonk, W. J. (1961). Human behavior during the tsunami of May 23, 1960. *Science, 133*(3462), 1405–1409.

Lindell, M. K. (1994). Perceived characteristics of environmental hazards. *International Journal of Mass Emergencies and Disasters, 12,* 303–326.

Mileti, D. S., & Sorensen, J. H. (1990). *Communication of emergency public warnings: A social science perspective and state-of-the-art assessment* (No. ORNL-6609). Oak Ridge: Oak Ridge National Laboratory.

Mills, M. J. (2000). Volcanic aerosol and global atmospheric effects. In B. H. H Sigurdsson, S. McNutt, H. Rymer, & J Stix (Eds.), *Encyclopedia of volcanoes* (pp. 931–943). San Diego: Academic Press.

Munasinghe, M., & Clarke, C. (1995). *Disaster prevention for sustainable development.* Washington, DC: International Decade for Natural Disaster Reduction and World Bank.

Neufeldt, V. (Ed.). (1994). *Webster's new world dictionary of American English* (Third College Edition). New York, NY: Macmillan.

Newhall, C. G., & Punongbayan, R. S. (Eds.). (1996). *Fire and mud eruptions and lahars of Mount Pinatubo, Philippines.* Seattle: University of Washington Press.

Normile, D. (2004). Earthquake preparedness: Some countries are betting that a few seconds can save lives. *Science, 306*(5705), 2178–2179.

Quarantelli, E. L. (1998). *What is a disaster? Perspectives on the question.* London: Routledge.

Sheaffer, J. R., Roland, F.J., Davis, G.W., Feldman, T., & Stockdale, J. (1976). *Flood Hazard Mitigation through Safe Land Use Practices.* Prepared for the Office of Policy Development and Research, U.S. Department of Housing and Urban Development. Chicago: Kiefer & Associates.

Simkin, T., & Siebert, L. (2000). Earth's volcanoes and eruptions: An overview. In B.

H. H Sigurdsson, S. McNutt, H. Rymer, & J. Stix (Eds.), *Encyclopedia of volcanoes* (pp. 249–261). San Diego: Academic Press.

Sorensen, J. (2000, May). Hazard warning systems: Review of 20 years of progress. *Natural Hazards Review,* 119–125.

Thomas, D. S. K., & Mitchell, J. T. (2001). Which are the most hazardous states. In S. L. Cutter (Ed.), *American hazard scapes: The regionalization of hazards and disasters* (pp. 115–155). Washington, DC: Joseph Henry Press.

Tierney, K. J., Lindell, M. K., & Perry, R. W. (1999). *Facing the unexpected: Disaster preparedness and response in the United States.* Washington, DC: Joseph Henry Press.

Tobin, G. A. (1999). Community resilience: The holy grail of hazards planning. *Environmental hazards, 1,* 13–26.

Tobin, G. A., & Montz, B. E. (1997). *Natural hazards: Explanation and integration.* New York, NY: Guilford Press.

U. S. Office of Science and Technology and Policy. (2005). Fact sheet: *Plan for an improved tsunami detection and warning system.* Retrieved April 30, 2005, from http://www.ostp.gov/html/TsunamiFactSheet.pdf

United Nations Development Program. (2004). *Reducing disaster risk: A challenge for the future.* New York, NY: John S. Swift Co.

Chapter 4

LIFELINES AND URBAN RESILIENCE

DAVID JOHNSTON, JULIA BECKER AND JIM COUSINS

INTRODUCTION

The destructive Asian tsunami on December 26, 2004, reminded the world of the devastating force of nature, both in its power to take lives and to destroy the infrastructure of communities. One way to reduce the susceptibility of communities to loss from hazard consequences is to create a community that is sustainable and resilient. Sustainable and resilient communities are organized in such a way that the effects of disasters are minimized and the recovery process is quicker (Tobin, 1999). As part of developing community resilience, it is necessary to consider and account for the robustness of community's infrastructure (with respect to a natural event). A community's infrastructure provides services, utilities and linkages which allow society to function. The term "lifelines" is commonly used for this infrastructure and can be defined as the systems or networks which provide for the circulation of people, goods, services and information, upon which health, safety, comfort and economic activity depend (Platt, 1991). Lifelines are the means whereby a community supports its day-to-day activities and include mechanisms used to respond to emergencies.

During and after hazard events, "lifelines" are vulnerable to disruption and/or damage. The extent and type of disruption and damage will differ depending on what has occurred. Lifelines systems are often large, complex and interdependent. Therefore, the failure of one system (or part of it) causes repercussions in other systems and increases a community's vulnerability further. This point is highlighted in the following case studies from New Zealand, which explore the impacts of four separate hazard events.

CASE STUDY 1

Impacts of Volcanic Ash Falls From the 1995–1996 Eruptions of Ruapehu

The largest historical eruption of Ruapehu, New Zealand, took place between September 1995 and August 1996 (Johnston, Houghton, Neall, Ronan, & Paton, 2001). Ash falls had the most widespread impact, with eruptions spreading ash over much of the North Island of New Zealand (Figure 4.1). The most disruptive ash falls covered more than 30 000 km2 and affected more than 20 communities. Luckily, no

Figure 4.1. The 1996 Ruapehu eruption dispersed ash over much of the North Land, New Zealand. Photo: David Johnston.

communities received more than a few millimetres of ash.

The 1995–1996 Ruapehu eruptions impacted upon infrastructure and lifelines in a variety of ways. The following paragraphs outline some of the effects of the ash falls.

Water supplies. Contamination of water supplies from ash was a common concern and many communities initiated special or enhanced monitoring of their water supplies. The city of Rotorua, 140 km northeast of Ruapehu, almost ran out of water when a resident washed ash into a power transformer just after the ash fall, resulting in an explosion which cut electricity to water pumps. Residents' efforts at ash clean-up almost drained the supply and the local council imposed a hosing ban until the power supply was restored to the water supply headworks.

Transportation. Air transportation was widely affected. New Zealand's Civil Aviation Authority issued more than 2000 "Volcanic Ash Advisories" in 1995 and 1996. These restricted air spaces (e.g., precluding aircraft flying in cloud or at night within these zones due to the inability of aircraft radar to detect ash clouds) during eruptive episodes because of drifting ash and sulphur dioxide haze, resulting in cancellation of many flights and rerouting of others away from the exclusion zones. Airlines report that restrictions caused a major disruption to operations and created additional workload. As the exclusion zones changed constantly, regular briefings for pilots were required and rerouting added extra distance to flights, increasing fuel costs and flight times. This caused down-line problems with catering schedules, baggage handling and passengers connecting to other flights. Up to 13 airports were affected at times, causing flow-on effects well beyond these immediate locations.

During and after ash falls, visibility on roads was commonly reduced. Closures of State Highway One, adjacent to the volcano, occurred on three occasions in 1995. Each of two closures in October, 1995 was due initially to reduced visibility and later to a slippery rain-wetted ash-sludge on the road surface. This required removal before safe-driving conditions could be restored. These road closures disrupted thousands of travellers, although alternative routes were available.

Electricity transmission. Falls of volcanic ash and mud caused shorting of high-voltage electrical power lines close to the volcano. This caused voltage fluctuations and problems for electrical equipment throughout the North Island. For example, fluctuations in supply tripped the emergency power 200-km to the south at Wellington Hospital causing nonessential services to be shed. Included in this, by error, was a water pump in a block containing dialysis machines. Thermal power stations to the north were started to ensure security of the system. After ash falls, electricity generation and supply companies routinely cleaned ash from affected substations.

Volcanic ash removal. No communities received more than a few millimetres of ash, but several were forced or chose to initiate clean-up operations to remove ash from buildings and streets. The cost of the clean-up operation in Rotorua alone was estimated at $NZ 53,500 and included cleaning of the central business district, cleaning road-side curbs and channels in all urban areas, and cleaning cesspools in urban and rural areas.

The 1995–1996 Ruapehu eruptions highlighted the vulnerability of infrastructure to even small amounts of volcanic ash. These eruptions caused similar physical effects to the previous major eruption in 1945, but had considerably greater social and economic impacts (Johnston et al., 2000). In the intervening 50 years the vulnerability of New Zealand communities to eruptions from Ruapehu has increased due to an increased population, a more developed and diversified local econ-omy, higher visitor usage of the national park around the volcano, and a more technologically advanced infrastructure. Resilience of infra-structure and lifelines to future volcanic eruptions would be enhanced with the preparation of volcanic contingency plans, community edu-cation about what to do in a volcanic eruption, and a general empha-sis on appropriate community and infrastructure development.

CASE STUDY 2

Impacts of Flooding on Gas Supplies in February, 2004

In February, 2004 New Zealand suffered one of the worst storm events in historical times, with extreme weather and flooding affecting much of the lower North Island and upper South Island. At the height of the storm over 2,300 people were evacuated and over 9,300 km of roads closed. In the Manawatu-Wanganui area, 25 bridges were either destroyed or seriously damaged (Ministry of Civil Defence Emergency Management, 2004). One of these bridges, crossing the Pohangina River near Ashhurst, carried a high pressure gas pipeline, which is operated by the National Gas Corporation (NGC). Luckily, the line was not cut when a section of the bridge washed out, but left suspended in the strong flowing Pohangina River (Figure 4.2).

On February 16, 2004, NGC was forced to isolate and depressure the impacted section for safety reasons. In doing so, supplies were disrupted to all communities to the east as far as Hawke's Bay. Gas loads were shed by ceasing supply to all but essential users and residential customers. One of the major casualities was a massive vegetable processing plant in Hastings (Watties), which was forced to suspend operations for several days. Due to the urgent need to reestablish gas supplies, engineers and contractors immediately began work on recovery operations.

Figure 4.2. Damage to the Pohangina River Bridge as a result of the February, 2004 floods. Note the still uncut gas pipeline to the right of the bridge. Photo: David Johnston.

The impacts of flooding on gas supplies highlights the unpredictability of hazardous events on infrastructure and interdependence between lifelines. In the case of the gas pipeline over the Pohangina River, widespread gas outages occurred, because the competency of the gas line was dependent on the structure of the damaged bridge. Lifeline resilience can be achieved when such interdependencies are recognized and accounted for before an event occurs.

CASE STUDY 3

Impacts of a Moderate Earthquake– 1987 Edgecumbe, New Zealand

The 1987 Edgecumbe earthquake was a moderately large earthquake of magnitude 6.6 (Figure 4.3). In New Zealand we can expect an earthquake of that size or greater once every three years. However, since 1987, earthquakes have been either more than 200km deep or centered in very isolated places. The three largest of magnitude 7 or more were located offshore.

The 1987 earthquake was centered near the small town of Edgecumbe (population about 3000). Edgecumbe was strongly shaken, as were the nearby Bay Milk Factory, Edgecumbe electricity substation, the Tasman Pulp and Paper plant and the Caxton Paper Mill. The towns of Kawerau (population 6,000) and Whakatane (12,000) were moderately shaken, and the city of Tauranga (90,000) was lightly shaken.

As can be seen in Table 4.1, losses totalled $374 million (in $1987) (Butcher, Andrews, & Cleland, 1998). Somewhat unusually for a New Zealand earthquake, the losses were dominated by damage to industrial facilities rather than residential properties. The damage to lifelines, and its consequences, are discussed next.

Water supply. The degree of damage depended on the strength of shaking. In Edgecumbe there was extensive damage to both the main supply pipes and the reticulation system. Most breakages were joint failures in brittle, asbestos-cement mains, and connections to the mains. The water supply was also contaminated for several days. In Kawerau, there were two breaks in the main supply pipeline plus other minor damage, while in Whakatane there was minor damage only.

Figure 4.3. Twisted rail lines caused by the 1987 Edgecumbe earthquake.

The water supply to Edgecumbe was totally lost, and repairs took eight days. As a temporary measure, potable water was provided by milk tankers. Repair of the Kawerau system was probably completed within less than 24 hours. The Whakatane supply was not disrupted.

TABLE 4.1. REPORTED LOSSES FROM THE 1987
EDGCUMBE EARTHQUAKE (FROM BUTCHER ET AL., 1998).

Item	Loss ($m 1987)
Non-domestic buildings, contents, plant & equipment	255
Business interruption	56
Dwellings and contents	28
Preliminary repairs to Matahina Dam	10
Flood protection and drainage	7
Welfare	5
Farms & orchards	4
Electricity transmission & distribution	3
Telephone system	2
Roads & bridges	2
Sanitary drainage	1
Water supply	1

Roads, rail and bridges. Landslides blocked the all main roads into the district, and the 2m vertical offset of the Edgecumbe fault blocked one subsidiary road near Edgecumbe. The fault trace also crossed at least one other road but the offset was not large enough to cause closure. There was much minor cracking of roads as a result of liquefaction and lateral spreading. Although this meant that caution was needed in several locations, no complete closures were required.

There was extensive but mostly relatively minor damage to about 60km of rail track. Close to the epicentre, there were distortions of up to 2m horizontally and 1m vertically, the latter where the track was intersected by the Edgecumbe fault. A locomotive was overturned near Edgecumbe.

Subsidence of road and rail bridge approaches was common. A laminated rubber bearing was displaced at one road bridge, and timber

piers were distorted at two rail bridges. Overall the level of damage
was relatively minor.

The three major routes into the epicentral area were reopened four,
19 and 25 hours after the earthquake. Other repairs were carried out
gradually over the following four years. Rail movements were halted
for nine days. Complete repair to lines took 44 days. Two road bridges
were closed–one a minor bridge near Te Teko (subsequently reopened
to all traffic 50 hours after the earthquake) and the other a major highway bridge near Whakatane (reopened to all traffic six hours after the
earthquake).

Electricity. There was extensive damage to older (pre-1968) transformers and switchgear in the Edgecumbe substation, plus a lesser
degree of damage to the Kawerau substation. Power supply to the
region was totally lost. Main transmission lines were livened within 24
hours, but feeder lines were then disconnected for safety reasons.
Restoration of connections to customers took one week, inspections of
appliances a further three weeks.

Sanitary Drainage. Sewers in Edgecumbe (brittle asbestos-cement
and earthenware pipes) were severely damaged. Damage to pumping
stations was mostly minor, with an important exception being the rupture of an inlet pipe to the main pumping station for Whakatane. The
Edgecumbe sewerage system was completely disabled. As a temporary measure "Portaloos" were placed at strategic locations around the
town for communal use, and were required for about 20 days. Full
repair of the system took nearly 12 months. Five years later there were
still overflow problems during periods of heavy rain. Repair of the
Whakatane system took three months, and during that period untreat-
ed sewage was discharged into the Whakatane River. The capacity of
the system was limited for a few days.

Stormwater. Extensive damage occurred to the stormwater system,
including buckling of kerbs and channels and misalignment of man-
holes and sumps, however it appeared that the system continued to
function.

Telephone. Damage to the telephone system was relatively minor,
but a lack of emergency generators at some exchanges meant that
capacity was reduced by 25–50 percent as a result of loss of power
supply. Significant underground cable damage was caused during
repairs to other lifelines services. As is usual after significant earthquakes there was severe line congestion for the first few days after the

earthquake. Normal service was restored within about two weeks.

Gas Supplies. Gas supply and distribution systems survived the earthquake and remained fully operational. Most significantly, the high-pressure supply pipeline was not damaged by fault offset at either of the two locations where it intersected the Edgecumbe fault. The supply pipe was made of ductile steel, and the distribution pipes of ductile plastic. As a precaution, the pressure of the high-pressure feed was lowered for a period until the integrity of the main supply pipeline could be confirmed. Gas remained available to those customers who were in a position to use it.

Matahina Dam. Matahina Dam is a hydro dam on the Rangitaiki River about 15km upstream of Edgecumbe. It is a moderately large earth/rock dam, with a crest length of 350m and height of 85m. As a result of the earthquake, the center of the crest settled about 100mm and moved 270mm downstream. Although the dam did not fail, and probably was not considered to be at risk, spillway gates were opened as a precaution and the lake level was drawn down about 2.5m. Residents downstream noticed the rise in river levels. Fear of catastrophic failure spread rapidly, and as a result there was spontaneous evacuation of several small settlements and schools.

Stopbanks and farm drainage systems. Damage to stopbanks along the three major river and drainage systems within the Rangitaiki Plain varied from minor to major, depending largely on the quality of the stopbanks. A more serious form of "damage" was a tectonic down-thrusting of one to 2m that accompanied the fault rupture process and affected about 25 percent of the Rangitaiki Plain. At the time no over-topping or flooding resulted from either the damage to the stopbanks or the tectonic down-thrusting. Reinstatement of flood protection levels and drainage systems was relatively costly and took about five years.

The 1987 Edgecumbe Earthquake was not a major earthquake disaster because, (a) the earthquake was only moderate in magnitude, and (b) only small towns were affected by strong shaking. Although full repairs took as much as five years for some items of infrastructure, most services were restored to basic functionality within at most a few days.

Because of the prompt restoration of most services, we can conclude that in terms of infrastructure and lifelines, there existed a degree of resilience for an earthquake of this magnitude. Aspects of this resilience may be transferable to other small towns in New Zealand experiencing similar types of earthquake.

CASE STUDY 4

Impacts of a major earthquake–1931 Hawke's Bay

With a magnitude of 7.8, the 1931 Hawke's Bay Earthquake (centered on the cities of Napier and Hastings, New Zealand), was definitely a large earthquake, indeed almost a great earthquake (Figure 4.4). Shaking damage in both cities was severe, post-earthquake fires destroyed much of the commercial center of Napier, and more than 250 people were killed (Callaghan, 1933; Conly, 1980; McGregor, 1989; Wright 2001). This has been acclaimed as New Zealand's deadliest historical earthquake (Dowrick, 1998).

Our perceptions of the Hawke's Bay Earthquake are dominated by three features. The first was the wholesale collapse of substandard buildings, mostly constructed from unreinforced brick, but also one poorly designed and constructed concrete building (a Nurses home adjacent to the Napier Hospital). Partial or complete collapse of buildings was the cause of nearly all of the casualties.

The second feature of the earthquake was the fire that started afterwards. In all, there were 15 separate ignitions on the day of the earthquake, four in Napier (commercial buildings), four in Hastings (commercial buildings), one in Port Ahuriri (warehouse), one at Pakipkai (freezing works), three at Wairoa (two houses, freezing works) and two at Mohaka (one house, hotel). Most fires in Hastings were prevented from spreading either because the ignited building was well separated from others, or because water was available for fire-fighting, albeit after a short delay.

In Napier, however, it was several hours before adequate water could be accessed, and in that time the fire had spread from building-to-building and grown to an uncontrollable size. Unfortunate wind shifts were one important factor in the spread, another was the collapse and "opening-up" of many brick-clad buildings. The fire was eventually halted by a combination of wide streets, open parkland, water, and tenacious fire-fighting.

The third notable feature was widespread tectonic uplift of land to

Figure 4.4. Napier waterfront as a result of liquefaction caused by the 1931 earthquake. Photo: Alexander Turnbull Library.

about 1m. It had both negative and positive consequences. The negative included the drainage of the Ahuriri Lagoon and consequent loss of a major local fishing resource, and the loss of port facilities at Port Ahuriri. The positive included the gaining of valuable land that now supports housing, industry, farming, and the Napier Airport.

With respect to lifelines we start with outlining the damage to the water services, supply of drinking water and disposal of waste water. It was lack of these that arguably caused greatest hardship to the people of Napier and Hastings.

Water supply. Water supply pipes in Napier were so badly broken that all water had drained from the city's reservoirs within about 15 minutes of the earthquake. An immediate consequence of the drainage was that there was not enough water for fire-fighting, with the result that the four fires in central Napier were able to spread through 11 city blocks. The financial loss from the destruction of those 11 blocks equaled the entire cost of repairing all other damage from the earthquake. Drinking water was initially in very short supply, but it transpired that the city's artesian bores had not been damaged by the earthquake and a limited supply of water was soon restored. Because there was no reticulation, the supply remained limited for many weeks. The local baths were made available for communal washing.

Sanitary Drainage. Sewers in Napier and Hastings were shattered by the earthquake and unusable. As a consequence of this, hygiene became a major concern, with the result that most women and children were evacuated from Napier and Hastings. Within five days of the earthquake 5,000 people had been evacuated, nearly 20 percent of the population.

The lack of sewers was perhaps a more important factor than the reduced water supply. Reinstatement became a priority issue with the result that significant progress had been made within one week, and within six weeks water and drainage had been restored to 75 percent of the houses of Napier.

Roads, rail and bridges. With one exception, all roads linking Napier and Hastings with the rest of New Zealand were thoroughly blocked by landslides in steep country; by cracking in flat, soft, soils; or by damage to bridges. The exception was the road south towards Wellington which, though badly damaged, remained negotiable with care. The local roads of the Hawke's Bay plain remained in a useable state.

Rail lines to the north and south were closed by buckling of rails, slumping and cracking of embankments, especially in areas of soft ground, and by slumping of approaches to bridges. About 60 km of line was affected. The line to the north was incomplete and extended no further than 10 km from Napier.

Slumping of bridge approaches was common and several bridges were damaged. The main road bridge across the Wairoa River was destroyed, as was a road bridge linking Hastings and Havelock North. As a result of the transportation disruptions, relief efforts and evacuations were considerably hampered for the first and most critical few days after the earthquake. The rail line from the south was reopened after three days, and essential full repairs were complete within one week. Reopening of the road north took more than three weeks.

Shipping. Wharves were very badly damaged by slumping of backfill, and there were unknown (at the time) changes in water depth. As a result of the damage, shipping movements reduced and, ultimately, a new port had to be constructed. Recreational facilities had to be moved and reconstructed.

Electricity. Power was supplied to the Hawke's Bay area from the Mangahao power station to the south and the Waikaremoana power station to the north. Both supplies passed through a large substation at Taradale, a few kilometres west of Napier. The feed from the north was disrupted by a collapsed tower, and the transformers at the Taradale substation were displaced. The electric power supply was completely cut, which removed the hazard of electrocution, but hindered night-time rescue efforts, the provision of hospital services, communications, and the relief effort overall.

Telephone. With respect to telephone systems, many poles tilted, some collapsed, wires became tangled and exchange equipment was damaged. The Napier post office was destroyed by fire. Telephone communication with the rest of New Zealand was completely cut for 24 hours, leaving rudimentary radio links as the only means of communication. A basic level of service was restored within three days, using a local school for both post and telegraphic services.

Gas Supplies. The gas mains in both Napier and Hastings were badly damaged and repairs to the mains took one week in Hastings and two months in Napier. Luckily, gas did not contribute to the burning fires. In Napier, the engineer at the gas works was aware of the potential danger and closed off the mains as soon as the shaking had subsided.

Stopbanks and drainage systems. After the earthquake, there was extensive slumping and fissuring of stopbanks protecting low-lying land adjacent to Napier and Hastings. Tectonic uplift caused alterations in drainage patterns. Fortunately, the weather remained fine until the bulk of the repair work had been completed, and so the consequences of the damage were minimal. It became necessary, and ulti-

mately highly beneficial, however, to divert the Tutaekuri River. Prior
to the earthquake the Tutaekuri meandered from south to north along
the side of Napier, and provided a serious barrier to growth of the city.
After the earthquake it was feasible to cut a direct channel to the sea
to the south of Napier. Subsequent drainage and reclamation provided much-needed land for development to the west of Napier.

The 1931 Hawke's Bay Earthquake was a major disaster. It created
significant destruction and disruption to lifelines. The consequences
were so bad that for a time there was serious discussion about aban-
doning the Napier site. However, the decision was made to rebuild,
the reconstruction provided much needed employment in a time of
severe economic depression, and the new land fortuitously provided
by tectonic uplift served to alleviate a chronic shortage of building
space in Napier.

The Hawke's Bay earthquake is a good example of how lifelines can
be badly affected in a big earthquake, and can be used as a case study
to predict what the effects of a future earthquake might be. In addition,
as we saw with the Ruapehu eruption example, the population and
infrastructure of the Hawke's Bay, and indeed New Zealand as a
whole, have rapidly expanded in the years since the last big earthquake, making the lifelines perhaps more vulnerable to an event of a
similar size and nature. Undertaking a lifelines assessment study of the
area (e.g., Hawke's Bay Engineering Lifelines, 2001) can address these
infrastructural vulnerabilities, and suggest mitigation measures which
will contribute to creating a more resilient community.

ASSESSING LIFELINE VULNERABILITY

In the past two decades projects in the USA, Australia, and New
Zealand have been initiated to address the issue of the vulnerability of
"lifelines" to natural hazards. In New Zealand in the early 1990s, the
Wellington Earthquake Lifelines Study (Hopkins, Lumsden, & Norton,
1993) examined the impacts of a major earthquake on the engineering
lifeline services (water, drainage, electricity, transportation etc.) in the
Wellington region. The Christchurch Engineering Lifelines Study
(1994) extended the range of hazards considered to include earthquakes, snow and wind storms, flooding and tsunamis. Both studies
used a similar methodology, following the steps shown in Figure 4.5.

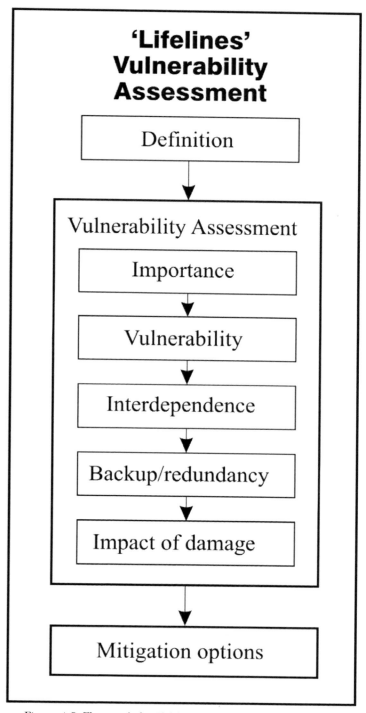

Figure 4.5. Flow path for "lifelines" vulnerability assessment.

All these projects follow the general risk management approach outlined in the Australian/New Zealand Risk Management Standard (4360) (2004).

A key feature of many of these projects was the wide involvement of engineers and managers from utility organizations, including local authorities, and private and public companies. The vulnerability methodology which follows is based on the general approach developed by several projects mentioned above. The initial objective of the methodology was to enable a number of agencies to assess their vulnerability to hazards that would affect more than one utility at the same time, and to identify appropriate mitigation measures. Much of this work can be completed by a series of workshops involving utility companies. A brief planning guideline for these workshops is outlined in Table 4.2.

TABLE 4.2. UTILITIES WORKSHOP: PLANNING GUIDELINES.

Utilities workshop: planning guidelines

Pre-workshop

1. Send out notes to participating utilities.

2. Develop two or three scenarios in which to base the workshop on.

3. Produce overlays of utilities on scenario hazard maps.

4. Get participating utilities to fill in vulnerability charts for the key components of their systems. If they are not able to, complete this task for them prior to the workshop.

Workshop

Phase 1 - Vulnerability assessment

• Get each participating utility to give a briefover of their system and describe their assessment of the impact of the scenarios.

Phase 2 - Interdependence assessment

• Pair each utility with each other and get them to ask each other "how does the loss of our service affect operation of your service?"

• Repeat this for every combination.

• Put results into an interdependence matrix.

continued

TABLE 4.2. UTILITIES WORKSHOP: PLANNING GUIDELINES–*Continued*

Phase 3 - Mitigation options

- Using the vulnerability charts and interdependence matrix explore mitigation options and see which options have the greatest impact on reducing the overall vulnerability.

- Use this exercise to identify key gaps in knowledge both in terms of the vulnerability and consequences of the scenarios.

Phase 4 - Action plans

Scope out a forward path address:

1. Mitigation options.

2. Gaps in knowledge about the hazard, consequence and ways of mitigating the hazards.

Scope

Many types of hazards have the potential to impact on lifelines. The following lifelines are suggested but others may be considered.

- Transport - air, road, rail, water
- Electricity
- Gas
- Water
- Sewerage and stormwater systems
- Communications–e.g., telecommunication networks, cell phone sites, radio transmitters
- Critical facilities–e.g., medical centers, civil defense offices, fire, police and emergency vehicle stations, emergency shelters.

Due to the size and complexity of certain lifeline systems not all components of each will be considered. Rather, the selection of system components is intended to be representative of the broad types that make up the system. Vulnerability assessments can been undertaken at two levels:

- a uniform hazard analysis–analyzes the vulnerability of each utility to the hazards based on known probabilistic information
- a scenario hazard analysis–analyzes the vulnerability of all utilities to a clearly defined hypothetical event exemplifying the most
  likely worst case scenario for each hazard

Methodology

In order to facilitate and communicate effectively to the different
participating organizations during a lifelines assessment project, task
groups can be established made up of organizational representatives
that have commonality or similarity of purpose. The following task
groups are suggested:

- hazard task group–to establish and define the actual hazard information and impacts to the utilities.
- utility task groups–representatives can be divided into subtask
  groups based on their sector type:
  - transport
  - energy (electricity, gas)
  - communications
  - civil (water, sewerage, stormwater)
  - critical facilities

Each of the task group participants should:

- analyze the impacts of the (already) identified hazards on their
  own lifeline utility
- provide insight into the performance of their task group sector as
  a whole.

The vulnerability assessments in this study follow the path outlined
in Figure 4.5 and have been adapted from previous studies.

At Risk Components

The first step is to define what components of a lifeline system is at
risk from the hazards identified. To do this, each system and its components are mapped in two ways:

1. geographic maps to show the location of key components of a life-lines system
2. system maps to show the interrelationships between lifeline system components in a schematic way.

Most infrequent natural hazard phenomena (such as volcanic eruptions and earthquakes) are extremely complex and rarely follow the exact pattern of past events. Therefore, pure quantitative assessments (such as that applied to engineering risk) are not always practical. In order to make semi-quantitative assessments, individual components may be assessed on a vulnerability chart using scores listed in Table 4.3.

TABLE 4.3. VULNERABILITY CHART KEY.*

Importance

Scale from 1 to 5 assessing the importance of the component to the operation of the system. The support % includes the operation of back-up systems. Scale 1 to 5.

  1 supports <10 % of the system

  2 supports 10-25 % of the system

  3 supports 25-50 % of the system

  4 supports 50-75 % of the system

  5 supports 75-100 % of the system

Vulnerability

Inoperative

Each component assessed for its likelihood of becoming inoperative in each ash thickness category. Scale 0 to 3.

  0 Not susceptible to being rendered inoperative

  1 Low likelihood of being rendered inoperative

  2 Moderate likelihood of being rendered inoperative

  3 High likelihood of being rendered inoperative

*These scores are entered on the Vulnerability Chart (Table 4.1) for each assessed component.

continued

TABLE 4.3. VULNERABILITY CHART KEY–*Continued*

Damage

Each component assessed for its likelihood of being damaged in each ash thickness category. Scale 0 to 3.

   i) Discrete components

       0 Not susceptible to damage

       1 Low likelihood of damage

       2 Moderate likelihood of damage

       3 High likelihood of damage

   ii) System Segments

       0 Not susceptible to damage

       1 Low likelihood of damage

       2 Moderate likelihood of damage

       3 High likelihood of damage

Interdependence

The dependency on other components or systems to be operational. Scale 0 to 3

   0 No dependency

   1 Low dependency

   2 Moderate dependency

   3 Total dependency

Back-up or redundancy

Does the component or system have back-up systems and/or is there redundancy in the system?

Impacts of damage

The consequence of a component being damaged. Scale 0 to 3.

   0 No impact

   1 Low impact

   2 Moderate Impact

   3 High Impact

Analysis Process

The analysis process has five stages, as outlined below:

1. **Importance**–Each component of a system is assessed for its importance to the system (ranked from 1 to 5).
2. **Vulnerability**–The vulnerability of each component to hazards is assessed. Components may become inoperative due to disruption from interdependent services or as a result of mitigation actions but may not necessarily be damaged. It is therefore important to separate the vulnerability of a component to becoming inoperative, from its vulnerability to being physically damaged.
3. **Interdependence**–This can be assessed using an interdependence matrix (See Table 4.4, which has been completed as a guide only). Dependency is ranked from 0 to 3. By adding the rows a measure of importance can be calculated; adding the columns gives a measure of total dependency. The sum of dependency and importance is referred to as the priority factor.
4. **Backup or redundancy**–Does the component or system have back-ups and/or is there redundancy in the system? (yes/no). If yes, what is the capacity of the back-up system?
5. **Impact of damage**–Impact or consequence of the damage and/or failure and the ability of the system to function is assessed:
   - *High impact*–The element is vital and its continued unavailability would cause substantial impact on ability of the system to operate.
   - *Moderate impact*–The element is important and its continued unavailability would cause an impact on ability of the system to operate if it remained inoperative for greater than 24 hours.
   - *Low impact*–The element is nonessential but its failure may reduce the efficiency of the system. Its continued unavailability would cause an impact on ability of the system to operate if it remained inoperative for greater than a week.
   - *No impact*–The system can function for an extended time without this element.

Mitigation Measures

Once the vulnerability of a system has been assessed and vulnerable elements have been identified, mitigation strategies can be developed. Three types of approaches can be used:

1. Policy and management measures that reduce the likelihood of damage and/or failure;
2. Engineering design measures that reduce the vulnerability of the system; and
3. Preparedness, response and recovery planning to deal with the consequences of the event.

TABLE 4.4. INTERDEPENDENCE MATRIX.

Depends on	Water Supply	Gas Supply	Sewerage	Storm Water	Mains Electricity	Standby Electricity	VHF Radio	Telephones	Roads	Rail	Air transport	Fuel Supply	Fire Fighting	Air-conditioning	Total Importance
Water Supply		*	1	*	*	*	*	*	*	*	*	*	3	2	6
Gas Supply	*		*	*	*	*	*	*	*	*	*	*	*	*	0
Sewerage	*	*		*	*	*	*	*	*	*	*	*	*	*	0
Storm Water	*	*	*		*	*	*	*	*	*	*	*	*	*	0
Mains Electricity	2	1	2	2		*	2	3	*	1	3	2	*	3	21
Standby Electricity	3	1	3	3	*		1	3	*	*	3	2	*	2	21
VHF Radio	3	3	3	2	3	*		2	2	2	3	*	3	*	26
Telephones	2	1	1	*	1	1	2		*	1	1	1	2	*	13
Roads	2	2	2	2	3	2	1	2		2	3	2	3	1	27
Rail	*	*	*	*	*	*	*	*	*		*	*	*	*	0
Air Transport	*	*	*	*	*	*	*	*	*	*		*	*	*	0
Fuel Supply	3	1	1	1	*	3	1	2	3	2	3		3	*	23
Fire Fighting	*	*	*	*	*	*	*	*	*	*	2	1		*	3
Air-conditioning	*	*	*	*	2	2	*	3	*	*	2	*	*		9
Equipment	3	3	3	2	3	3	3	3	3	3	3	2	3	3	40
Total Dependence	18	12	16	12	12	11	10	18	8	11	23	10	17	11	
Priority Factor	24	12	16	12	33	32	36	31	35	11	23	33	20	20	

Note: 3 = High Dependence
      2 = Moderate Dependence
      1 = Low Dependence
      * = No Dependence

Priority Factor = Importance + Dependence

Mitigation options should be evaluated in terms of the risk reduction and the benefits or opportunities created. In selecting any appropriate option or options, the cost of implementation must be balanced against the benefits derived from it (Figure 4.6). At a community level a broad range of hazard mitigation tools are available including:

1. public education;
2. development regulations;
3. policy for critical and public facilities;
4. land and property acquisitions;
5. building codes and standards; and
6. research (Burby, Deyle, Godschalk, & Olshansky, 2000).

However, the decision on which combination of tools to use with respect to the natural hazard risk remains a challenge for organiza-

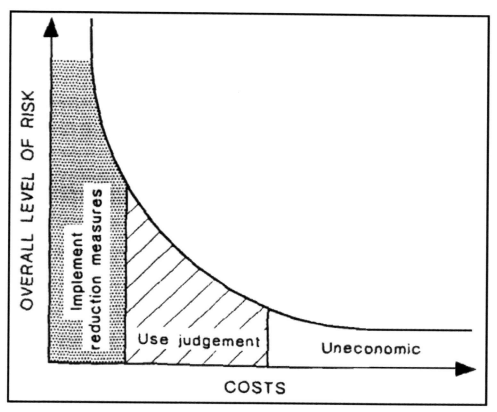

Figure 4.6. Cost or risk reduction measures (from Australian/New Zealand Standard 1995).

tions, local authorities and its citizens. Several recent reviews have explored the steps necessary to achieve effective mitigation of hazards and the barriers to effective hazard mitigation. The Australian/New Zealand Risk Management Standard (4360) (2004) provides a good starting point to organizations wishing to reduce their risk and improve their resilience to natural and man-made hazards.

THE CONTRIBUTION OF LIFELINES STUDIES TO URBAN RESILIENCE

Creating a community resilient to natural disaster is best achieved by using an approach which focuses on the general sustainable development of a community, while also including specific strategies that have been proven as useful for mitigating against natural hazards.

Infrastructure is a crucially important issue for communities, and it is constantly employed in our day-to-day lives. We constantly use electricity, gas, transportation, telephones, water systems, sewerage systems, and more—the list is endless. When a natural event is imposed upon infrastructure, as in the case studies that have been discussed, our "lifelines" can break down leaving a community vulnerable.

One approach which can reduce the vulnerability of infrastructure and contribute to increasing the resilience of a community is to undertake a lifelines assessment study. Such a study allows a community to identify what hazards are likely to occur, which parts of the infrastructure system are vulnerable, how they are vulnerable, and what measures can be taken to mitigate the vulnerabilities. Using and applying the results of study such as this, in combination with good sustainable community development principles, can contribute to a more resilient urban environment in the face of future natural events.

REFERENCES

Australian/New Zealand Standard. (1995). *Risk Management.* AS/NZS 4360, 32 p.
Australian/New Zealand Standard. (2004). *Risk Management.* AS/NZS 4360, 30 p.
Burby, R. J., Deyle, R.E., Godschalk, D. R., & Olshansky, R. B. (2000). Creating hazard resilient communities through land-use planning. *Natural Hazards Review, 1*(2), 99–106.
Butcher, G., Andrews, L., & Cleland, G. (1998). *The Edgecumbe earthquake—A review of*

the 2 March 1987 Eastern Bay of Plenty earthquake. Christchurch, New Zealand: University of Canterbury, Centre for Advanced Engineering.

Callaghan, F. R. (1933). The Hawke's Bay earthquake–General description. *New Zealand Journal of Science and Technology, 15*(1), 3–37.

Conly, G. (1998). *The shock of '31. The Hawke's Bay earthquake.* Auckland, NZ: Reed Publisher.

Dowrick, D. J. (1998). Damage and intensities in the magnitude 7.8 1931 Hawke's Bay, New Zealand, earthquake. *Bulletin of the New Zealand National Society for Earthquake Engineering, 31*(3), 139–163.

Hawke's Bay Engineering Lifelines. (2001). *Report of the Hawke's Bay engineering lifelines Project* (HBRC Plan No. 3065). Napier: Hawkes Bay Regional Council.

Hopkins, D. C., Lumsden, J. L., & Norton J. A. (1993). Lifelines in earthquakes: A case study based on Wellington. *Bulletin of the New Zealand National Society for Earthquake Engineering, 26*(2), 208–221.

Johnston, D. M., Houghton, B. F., Neall, V. E., Ronan, K. R., & Paton, D. (2000). Impacts of the 1945 and 1995-1996 Ruapehu eruptions, New Zealand: An example of increasing societal vulnerability. *Geological Society of America Bulletin, 112,* 720–726.

McGregor, R. (1989). *The great quake. The story of the 1931 Hawke's Bay earthquake.* Napier, NZ: Regional Publications.

Ministry of Civil Defence Emergency Management. (2004). *Review of the February 2004 flood event.* Wellington, New Zealand: Ministry of Civil Defence Emergency Management.

Platt, R. H. (1991). Lifelines: An emergency management priority for the United States in the 1990s. *Disasters, 15*(2), 172–176.

Tobin, G. A. (1999). Sustainability and community resilience: The holy grail of hazards planning? *Environmental Hazards, 1,* 13–25.

Wright, M. (2001). *Quake–Hawke's Bay 1931.* Auckland, NZ: Reed Publishing.

Chapter 5

HAZARD MITIGATION: A PRIORITY FOR SUSTAINABLE COMMUNITIES

ROBERT O. SCHNEIDER

INTRODUCTION

The fostering of sustainable communities in the face of an extreme hazardous event places emergency management in a wider framework than traditionally acknowledged by many of its professional practitioners. In fact, it places the emergency management function at the very center of community development decision making.

In the United States, largely in response to the rising costs associated with natural disasters during the 1990s, it has been suggested that the primary objective of emergency management should be to mitigate hazards in a sustainable way to slow the trend of increasing and catastrophic losses. Hazard mitigation not only became a new theme among some American scholars and practitioners, it was increasingly connected to broader issues such as environmental stewardship, community planning, and sustainable development (Britton, 1999). The fostering of local or community sustainability in the face of hazard events became viewed as integrally connected to the broader process of community planning and development (Beatley, 1995; Mileti, 1999; Schneider, 2002).

The linkage of hazard mitigation to the concept of sustainable community development became a new and increasingly popular trend in emergency management. But the practical effectiveness of the emergency management profession in efforts to implement sustainable hazard mitigation in practice was sporadic at best (Mileti, 1999). Likewise, the dedication of policymakers to mitigate hazard impacts before disasters strike and their ability to plan and implement mitigation programs remained very much in question (Godschalk, Berke, Brower, & Kaiser, 1999). Notwithstanding these very real and practical problems, the linkage of hazard mitigation to sustainable development holds tremendous potential for the reformulation of emergency management.

This chapter will explore the development of a linkage between sustainable hazard mitigation and U.S. emergency management policy and practice over the past two decades. In so doing, it will provide a more complete definition of the contemporary emergency management function and attempt to suggest a broader, more proactive, and increasingly vital role for it in the communities it serves. Our discussion will begin with an analysis of the concept of sustainable development and its logical and necessary linkage to emergency management. A brief overview of recent trends in the field will demonstrate that the movement in the U.S. toward a "new" emergency management focused on sustainable hazard mitigation, begun in the 1990s, holds tremendous potential. This analysis will include a brief summary of the basic principles and techniques that have come to be associated with sustainable hazard mitigation. We will conclude by noting challenges posed by recent events that may distract emergency management in the U.S. from its new focus on sustainable hazard mitigation.

SUSTAINABILITY: A NECESSARY LINKAGE

Defining sustainable development is a challenge. The primary reason for this is that the concept of sustainable development has become an overarching tent into which several groups and stakeholders have projected their hopes and aspirations. The concept was first used by environmentalists who, in assessing the problems associated with protecting ecosystems, realized that these tasks were connected to the lives of the largely poor populations that lived in and around sites of environmental concern (Kates, 2003). The interaction of the environment with development, the connection between the human condition (economic, health, nutrition etc.) and the sustainability of communities, and the linkage of human to environmental sustainability, led environmentalists to identify the concept of sustainable development as the vital center where everything intersects.

The United Nations Conference on Environment and Development in Rio de Janerio in 1992 signified, to some extent, the growing global acceptance of sustainable development as a goal. The goal of broad-based development that is equitable, participatory, environmentally sustainable, and that balances human and environmental needs with economic growth, has become a shared concern in scientific and political communities throughout the world (Kusterer, Ruck, & Weaver, 1997). The fact that this goal seems to be more urgently expressed by and on behalf of the developing world, and that it is of less immediate salience among some wealthier nations, may explain why it remains a broad goal but has proven difficult to implement.

The linkage of sustainable development to emergency management, like its linkage to environmental sustainability, is both logical and inherent. In general, whether in reference to environmental degradation, disease, or natural hazards, the majority of major threats faced by human civilization are manmade. They stem from humanity's overwhelming success at dominating and/or transforming the world around it. They also are connected to decisions that humanity makes about development, including and especially those decisions that relate to economic development and the constructed environment. Whatever the source of the threat, humanity is most often better at responding to a crisis once it is recognized and defined than it is at recognizing crisis in the making. The capacity to anticipate and prevent crisis is the crux of the matter not just in emergency management, it is important in all human endeavors and is directly related to all community development decision making. Sustainable development requires, at a minimum, the possession and use of knowledge relevant to building communities that can anticipate and/or prevent crisis. It encourages using knowledge to intelligently set goals, provide indicators and incentives, examine alternatives, design innovation, establish effective institutions, encourage good decision making, and take appropriate action. This includes the ability to anticipate and prevent crisis.

Sustainable development includes, by definition, the development of disaster resilient communities. Hazard mitigation and sustainability are linked in a very practical way. A brief analysis of these two concepts demonstrates this connection very clearly.

The concept of hazard mitigation begins with the realization that most disasters are not unexpected. Most disasters are the predictable result of interactions among the physical environment, the social and demographic characteristics of human communities in that environment, and the specific features (buildings, roads, bridges, and other features) of the built environment (Mileti, 1999). This is to say that the magnitude of future disasters and the risks to life and property associated with them may be reduced with advanced planning. Effective mitigation can also substantially reduce the cost of disaster response and recovery. Hazard mitigation takes the form of advanced action designed to reduce the long-term risk to human life and property from natural and manmade hazards. Especially with regard to natural hazards such as hurricanes, floods, or earthquakes, the prospects for meaningful and successful mitigation are very high indeed (Godschalk et al. 1999).

There are two basic types of hazard mitigation for natural hazards. These are structural mitigation and nonstructural mitigation, also often referred to respectively as hard and soft mitigation. Structural (or hard) mitigation is the easiest to understand. It includes the strengthening of buildings and infrastructure exposed to hazards by a variety of means (building codes, improved engineering and design, improved construction technologies and practices, etc.). The fundamental purpose of structural mitigation is to increase resilience and damage resistance.

Nonstructural or soft mitigation is also important. Nonstructural mitigation includes directing development away from known hazard or high-risk locations through land use plans and regulations, relocating to safer areas existing developments that have sustained repeated damage, and maintaining the protective features of the natural environment (i.e., sand dunes, forests, vegetated areas that absorb and reduce hazard impacts). Nonstructural mitigation also includes addressing the special needs of at-risk populations. This includes housing and economic needs as well as other quality of life issues. The poor populations of the world are frequently those that face the greatest risk. While often much more difficult to implement politically, nonstructural mitigation has significant value in risk and cost reduction (Godschalk et al., 1999).

The value of hazard mitigation has been recognized and incorporated into U.S. disaster policy. The Robert T. Stafford Disaster Relief and Emergency Assistance Act, passed by the U.S. Congress in 1988, was designed to encourage comprehensive disaster preparedness and hazard mitigation. At the heart of this law was a set of hazard mitigation requirements for local governments to help reduce disaster losses and risks. Section 409 of the Stafford Act in fact requires the preparation of state and local disaster mitigation plans as a condition for receiving federal disaster assistance. These plans are supposed to be developed prior to a disaster and should be regularly reviewed and updated. In practice, unfortunately, many localities developed plans in post-disaster situations to qualify for federal money. As such they had no application as mitigation plans and were driven by reaction to an immediate disaster without any comprehensive planning for the future (Godschalk et al., 1999).

The intent of the Stafford Act, if not its actual implementation, was on target. It recognized that the ultimate purpose of hazard mitigation efforts is best realized when they result in a shift in emphasis from a disaster or event driven system to a threat and a policy driven system. This is to recognize that hazard mitigation is proactive and not reactive. A proactive approach to hazard mitigation requires that the framework shift from reacting or responding to individual disasters or hazards to a focus on living within an ecological system with foreseeable variations. It emphasizes the implementation of practices that result in the development of resilient communities. In other words, it emphasizes a linkage between hazard mitigation and sustainability.

Sustainability in the context of emergency management means, at a minimum, that a locality can tolerate and overcome damage, diminished productivity, and reduced quality of life that may result from a hazardous event or occurrence and that it can do so without significant outside assistance (Mileti, 1999). It means that the community's economic and social institutions will continue and that a recovery from the immediate disaster and return to normality is assured. But such an outcome does not happen without planning.

To achieve sustainability in the face of hazard or disaster threats, a community must choose where and how its development proceeds. Each locality or community must evaluate its environmental resources and hazard risks, choose the future losses it is willing to bear, define the losses that are unacceptable, and ensure that all community development decisions and actions adhere to these goals.

Planning for sustainable communities, in the framework articulated here, is directly connected to community planning, including planning for economic development. It links social, economic, and environmental concerns to the process of hazard mitigation. Hazard mitigation, in turn, includes the promotion of sustainability as a key component. Community planning and development must insure that economic and political decision makers operate with a full awareness of the risks posed to people and property by disasters. Reducing vulnerability must be done in relation to all community goals such as reducing poverty, providing jobs, promoting a strong economy, and generally improving people's living conditions. Community decision making and development policy, in turn, must include anticipation of and solutions to the risks associated with potential hazards that may threaten a community.

Hazard mitigation is, at the heart of things, the function that links sustainability, planning, development, and emergency management together in the process of building disaster-resilient communities. The logic of this linkage broadens the emergency management function significantly and leads to an increasingly vital role for it in community planning and development. This linkage has come to be recognized, in theory if not always in practice, in the United States (Federal Emergency Management Agency, 2000). An examination of the recent evolution of emergency management practice in the U.S. demonstrates the validity of this statement.

FROM THE OLD TO THE NEW EMERGENCY MANAGEMENT

An examination of emergency management literature in the United States suggests that there has been a shift from an "old" event driven, response-oriented system to a "new," more strategic, and mitigation-oriented approach. Some of this shift was a response to the escalating cost of natural hazards to taxpayers. Mega disasters such as Hurricane Andrew in 1992 or the Midwest flooding in 1993 accelerated this trend. Floods, for example, are the most serious disasters in the U.S. in terms of lives lost, people and communities affected, property loss, and frequency of occurrence. Between 1966 and 1985 direct losses from floods grew from $2.2 billion per year to $5 billion per year (Cigler, 1996). Throughout the decade of the 1990s, natural disasters in the U.S. continued to increase in terms of both damage costs and frequency.

In the more serious disaster scenarios experienced in the U.S. since 1989, disaster losses of up to more than $1 billion per week have been experienced (Federal Emergency Management Agency, 1997). Between 1989 and 1994 alone, natural disasters cost the U.S. treasury more than $34 billion (Federal Emergency Management Agency, 1997). It has been estimated that the actual dollar value of property loss from natural hazards and disasters in the U.S. from 1975–1994 was $500 billion. While there is some variation in estimates, the average annual loss is between $6 and $10 billion (Mileti, 1999). There is agreement that the future will be more hazardous and even more expensive.

Until the 1990s, the amount of public money spent before a disaster (i.e., to prepare for and alleviate disaster vulnerability) was a small fraction of that spent after disasters. But the disaster-related experiences and the rising costs incurred during this period soon did contribute to a new emphasis on hazard mitigation. A new perspective on disasters emerged that emphasized that vulnerabilities are created by human actions and decisions (Anderson, 1995). Increasingly hazardous situations came to be seen in the context of the interface between extreme hazard events and vulnerable populations, and the vulnerability of populations came to be seen as the result of decisions and choices associated with community planning and development. But the emphasis on hazard or disaster mitigation that accompanied this new perspective ran counter to the experiences and assumptions associated with the "old" emergency management.

Let us examine the portrait of the "old" emergency management. Until quite recently, the strategic motivation for the emergency management profession arose from the challenges of responding or reacting to specific and immediate disasters rather than from the recognition of opportunities and the implementation of long-term planning. It had long been demonstrated that emergency management issues were of low salience in most states and communities (Wolensky & Wolensky, 1990; Wright & Rossi, 1981). In fact, the literature often noted indifference or outright opposition to disaster preparedness (Kreps, 1991). Public officials and public administrators in local communities, we were often told, did not fully comprehend the nature of the emergency management function. A basic assumption, still somewhat prevalent, is that emergency management is primarily a response function and a concern only for first responders. Other public officials remain uninvolved and assume that they need not learn much about the field (Grant, 1996).

By 1979, with the formation of the Federal Emergency Management Agency (FEMA), the national orientation almost exclusively emphasized the disaster preparedness and emergency response functions. FEMA was designed to consolidate the federal agencies with responsibilities in these areas and provide a single point of contact for state and local governments seeking preparedness, response, and recovery assistance. The development of the emergency management function at the local level is a rather recent development and grew out of federal legislation, such as the Emergency Planning and Community Right to Know Act of 1986, that emphasized and provided federal support and federal mandates for more thorough disaster planning and preparedness at the local level.

Even with a growing number of federal initiatives assigning more disaster preparedness functions to local governments, emergency management did not quickly become a priority at the local level. Unless a specific hazard was more or less immanent, sustained governmental interest and public support at the local level was difficult to sustain (Perry & Mushkatel, 1984). Policymakers and stakeholders alike tended to underestimate hazard potentials. They were often inclined to see hazard occurrence as having a low probability and had thus been reluctant to impose limitations on private property, unwilling to bear the costs of hazard preparedness, and altogether ambivalent toward hazard mitigation (Grant, 1996). Emergency management remained a low priority, often resented as an unfunded federal mandate, and a responsibility often seen as being somewhat at odds with more important tasks such as economic development. These attitudes unfortunately shaped and restrained the early development of the emergency management profession in local communities across the country.

From its earliest days, the emergency management function in the U.S. suffered as a result of low political support and scarce resources. In many local jurisdictions it became an added or part time responsibility for an already overburdened local official such as a fire chief. Often the individuals appointed to local emergency management directorships had little professional training or experience relevant for the job. A 1990 analysis summarized the obstacles that local governments had to overcome in order to implement effective emergency management agencies as follows:

1. The diversity of hazards in many communities;
2. The technical complexity of regulatory, planning, and response efforts;
3. The low salience of emergency management as a public issue;
4. The historic and culturally ingrained resistance to regulation and planning, especially at the local level;
5. The lack of strong political and administrative advocates for emergency management;
6. The uncertainty of risk, i.e., doubts about whether programs will ever be needed;
7. The jurisdictional confusion of a complex federal system and an even more complex division of authority among state and local governments;
8. And, the economic and political milieu that is inhospitable to government in general and new public programs in particular (Waugh, 1990).

By the late eighties and early nineties, this portrait added up to narrow or limited appreciation of the emergency management function. As a result of low salience, poor training, and lack of support, the focus of the emergency management professional tended to be narrow, disaster specific, technical, and limited to very specific tasks. This is beginning to change. It is beginning to change, in part, as a result of a new emphasis that emerged during the 1990s. This involved the elevation of the concept of hazard mitigation to the level of a national priority.

James Lee Witt, President Clinton's FEMA Director, undertook the task of applying the Clinton "reinventing government" initiative to reinvent FEMA (Sylves, 1996). Based on the blueprint provided in Osborne and Gaebler's (1992) *Reinventing Government,* the Clinton Administration compelled federal agencies to undertake self-assessments and to articulate strategies for applying the entrepreneurial spirit and tapping into free market sources to improve efficiency and the service delivery capacity of the federal government (Osborne & Gaebler, 1992). The result in FEMA, under Witt's leadership, was a significant transformation of emergency management in the United States.

The National Performance Review reports produced by FEMA during the "reinventing government" initiative refined its mission and defined new national priorities for emergency management. Attempting to give FEMA a clearer mission, Witt went beyond the more traditional emphasis on the preparedness and response approach of the past to emphasizing a sharper and better defined focus on reducing risks (Sylves, 1996). Building on the logic of the Stafford Act of 1988 and the experiences of the late eighties and early nineties, FEMA went on to articulate a new emphasis on hazard mitigation.

Mitigation must become a recognized national priority. Although mitigation makes good sense, it often isn't a priority for communities. Establishing mitigation as a primary foundation for emergency management will decrease demands for response to disasters. Buildings, homes, and infrastructure that are built better, withstand hazards better (Federal Emergency Management Agency, 1993).

The plan produced by Witt called for the implementation of disaster mitigation planning by state and local governments. This included federal funds to assist communities in developing mitigation plans and the requirement of evidence of state achievement of mitigation standards as a condition for FEMA release of federal mitigation funds (Sylves, 1996).

With the new focus on hazard mitigation and sustainability, emergency management in the United States could be said to have begun to be thought of in broader terms than ever before. It is an increasingly common premise that the aim of managerial work in the public sector is to create public value (Moore, 1995). This is to suggest that public managers, including emergency managers, utilize scarce public resources that have value in alternative uses. The challenge is to maximize the value attained through these resources. Managerial success may thus be interpreted as proactively initiating and reshaping public enterprises in ways that increase their value to the publics they are intended to serve (Moore, 1995).

One need not delve too deeply into the discussion of public value to see that, in the linkage of emergency management to the broader task of sustainable community development, there is a broad and potentially dynamic connection between emergency management and community development that holds the potential for enhancing the public value of emergency management to the communities it serves. The challenge is to recast emergency management as a participant in the broad nexus of institutional and public actors who influence the process of community planning and development. Sustainable development is the key to this nexus. The development of a "new" emergency management profession is perhaps the most important step required for the "new emergency management" to be successfully implemented (Schneider, 2004).

If, as suggested in this analysis, emergency management is a critical part of the process of sustainable community development, the profession must come to see itself in a new context. Emergency managers must see themselves as participating with all political and social institutions in a coordinated effort. The primary focus must be on the building of sustainable communities as the fundamental public value to be served by the emergency management function. But the question remains how, in performing their specific tasks, can emergency managers organize their work to serve this public value?

As a first step, emergency managers must be trained and prepared to articulate and develop a role for themselves as a participant in the local consensus building effort in their community and to perceive themselves as working on a common agenda with other community institutions and leaders. All relevant public and private stakeholders, as defined in the context of sustainable development, must be brought into the emergency management planning process. Emergency managers, in turn, must be brought in as stakeholders to the network of community leaders and policymakers involved in community planning and development activities.

A second step, to be accomplished as the emergency management function is integrated into the process of community planning, is the definition of the technical components in each phase of the function (risk assessment, mitigation, preparedness, response, and recovery) as a part of a holistic system. This entails, as the most fundamental ingredient, the integration and consistency of all technical components with integrated policies and programs related to disaster mitigation and sustainability within the community. Hazard or disaster mitigation, in essence, must be the preeminent task that ties emergency management into the value of sustainability and defines its role in the context of community planning and development. It must therefore be elevated to the level of first or primary responsibility for the emergency manager. It must also be elevated to the level of an essential or necessary component in all community planning and development activity.

A third or final step necessary for the new emergency management to succeed as a component in sustainable development is the linkage of all public policies within the community to the concept of sustainability. All policies necessary to promote the sustainability of communities, including emergency management policies, must be linked or integrated in the process of community planning. The end product of emergency management must be understood as fundamentally connected to all facets of community life in a coordinated effort to promote sustainability.

To accomplish the three steps briefly outlined above, emergency management needs to move from the traditional tendency to be reactive and disaster specific. It must broaden its orientation beyond efficient disaster response and recovery operations. Everything we have discussed requires that emergency managers be more proactive by emphasizing hazard mitigation. This ultimately means they must work to become networked in partnerships that involve all community leaders associated with the concept of sustainable development. This is to suggest that they must become public actors in the context of a broader involvement in community planning. To make the necessary and persuasive case to community leaders, to build networks of support groups and stakeholders, to establish the strategic linkages with other community leaders and institutions necessary to bring about this transformation, technical skill alone is insufficient. The training and education of emergency managers needs to be refocused on the skills relevant for a more strategic emergency management.

Increasingly, it would seem, advanced educational training at the undergraduate and graduate level is required for all emergency managers. The sort of training associated with public administration generally, including advanced training in leadership, organizational behavior, strategic planning, analytical methods, and public policy, has never been more urgently needed. The challenge of articulating a broader role for emergency management, its vital linkage to the building of sustainable communities, and its need to emphasize mitigation all suggest that a more proactive professional is needed. The vital tasks of networking and building relationships within the community of decision makers, the ability to recognize the opportunities for successful hazard mitigation in the broader task of sustainable development, and the need for strategic thinking and leadership all demand that the education of the emergency management professional take on a new priority and that it represent a broader range of competencies than the technical skills associated with the field.

Finally, the professional training of all public management professionals should include a basic foundation in emergency management. Graduate and undergraduate programs alike should provide more training that reflects the linkage between hazard mitigation, community planning, and sustainable development. This does not mean that all public administrators should be cross-trained as emergency managers, but rather that emergency management should be a component of their professional education. It should include a focus on the value of mitigating hazards in a sustainable way as a critical and necessary component to community planning and development generally.

Professional training must broaden the understanding that the assessment of hazard potentials and the mitigation against their potential impact is connected to the making of a series of choices that impact the economic, physical, and social well-being of the community. Given the efforts to refocus emergency management on sustainable hazard mitigation, it is not surprising that the need for such training has been increasingly recognized as a priority in the United States.

At a very basic level, disparities still exist in local emergency management capabilities across the U.S. According to the National Academy for Public Administration (NAPA) (1993), these disparities are directly connected to the lack of emergency management knowledge and the lack of understanding of intergovernmental problems in emergency management. One of NAPA's major recommendations has been to advocate major improvement in emergency management education and training. On a more advanced level, the linkage of emergency management to sustainability and the emphasis on hazard mitigation has accelerated the need for education and training. FEMA has, in response to this need, initiated a higher education project to promote the creation of emergency management programs in colleges and universities. Below is a statement of FEMA's goal with respect to higher education.

One goal of FEMA is to encourage and support the dissemination of hazard, disaster and emergency management-related information in colleges and universities across the U.S. We believe that in the future emergency managers in government, business and industry will come to the job with college education that includes a degree in emergency management. We also believe that in order to build disaster resistant and resilient communities a broad range of college students and professionals need courses that introduce them to hazards, disasters, and what to do about them (FEMA, 2003).

It is encouraging to note that there is a healthy growth of new undergraduate and graduate degree programs in emergency management.

These are designed not only to provide an understanding of the principles and practices of emergency management, but they represent a growing emphasis on hazard mitigation as well. These programs are interdisciplinary in nature. The emergency preparedness and response phase draws heavily from sociological research findings on human and organizational response to disasters. Hazard mitigation and recovery portions of the curriculum draw heavily from the urban planning discipline. Geography, environmental science, and public administration are also contributing disciplines (Reddy, 2000).

PRINCIPLES AND TECHNIQUES OF SUSTAINABLE HAZARD MITIGATION

By the end of the 1990s, the principles and techniques of hazard mitigation were fairly well-established and broadly known in the United States. They begin with a focus on comprehensive emergency planning or comprehensive emergency management (CEM). CEM reflects a switch in the orientation of emergency management, especially during the 1990s and the James Lee Witt regime at FEMA, from preparation for a single hazard or narrowly defined set of hazards toward an all hazards approach. CEM calls for an integrated approach to the management of emergency programs and activities with each element or program fitted into an inclusive framework that encompasses all hazards at all levels of government. It applies to all risks, natural and manmade, and coordinates local, state, and federal actions across the four stages of emergency activity (mitigation, preparedness, response, and recovery).

Hazard mitigation, as we have seen, is focused on the goal of sustainable communities. Disaster planning before a disaster strikes, and/or a planned recovery process after a disaster, can serve as a catalyst for creating more sustainable communities. Resistance to disaster is thus a critical characteristic of a livable and sustainable community. In the past decade, as sustainable hazard mitigation has become a national priority in the U.S., it has been tied to six basic principles (Mileti, 1999).

First, a guiding principle of sustainability is that human activities in any community should maintain and, if possible, enhance environmental quality. In other words, to contribute to sustainability, hazard mitigation efforts must be linked to natural resource management or its protection.

Second, sustainable communities must define and plan for the quality of life they want for themselves and for future generations. The quality of life, defined in terms of income, health, crime, pollution, disaster, and other risks, is a critical component in the building of sustainable communities. Hazard mitigation planning should be conducted in the context of all other community planning relevant to enhancing the quality of life.

Third, sustainable communities foster local resiliency to and responsibilities for disaster. Each community must take responsibility for identifying, in a comprehensive fashion, its environmental resources and its exposure to hazard risk. This it does not only to prepare to respond to a disaster (remember local governments are usually the first responders), but also to implement the necessary steps to reduce damage and withstand any disaster without significant loss of productivity or quality of life.

Fourth, sustainable communities are tied to vital local economies. This principle suggests that local hazard mitigation must include a diversified local economy that is not easily disrupted by disasters. Sustainable communities are also the product of community planning that insures disaster costs are not shifted to other communities, to at-risk populations within a community, to the atmosphere, or to future generations. This implies effort to calculate hazard risks accurately, distribute their costs fairly, and most importantly the determination to take into account the impact of economic decisions about growth, energy, employment, housing, etc. in relation to sustainability.

Fifth, a sustainable community preserves ecosystems and resources to insure that the cost of today's advances, or the risks they produce, are not passed to future generations. Hazard mitigation in sustainable communities never delays or postpones reasonable action only to pass on increased risk or inevitable disaster costs to future generations.

Finally, the sixth principle of sustainable mitigation emphasizes a consensus building approach involving all people who have a stake in the outcome of hazard mitigation planning activities. The information that can be generated and distributed through this process, the ideas and the sense of ownership that may grow out of broad participation, outweigh the very likely outcome that consensus may be hard to reach. The practical necessity of placing hazard mitigation on the planning agenda of every public and private entity in the community can only contribute to the shaping of a community-wide consensus building effort that elevates sustainability as a primary goal in the broader work of community planning and development.

Just as these six principles have come to be identified with the goal of sustainable hazard mitigation, so too the basic techniques utilized in natural hazard mitigation are well known. These include land use planning, building codes, insurance, warnings, engineering, and new technological approaches (Mileti, 1999). Let us very briefly review these six basic mitigation tools. In so doing, we will emphasize the minimizing of losses form hazards and the connection of hazard resilience to sustainability.

Land use planning involves more efficient use of space. It essentially means development and redevelopment decisions are connected to the preservation or restoration of natural protective features in the community. It also means that disaster resilience is an essential component of local development policy.

Local governments have utilized land use policy in hazard prone areas, but with mixed results. Some have suggested that the absence of federal policy on land use and development in hazard prone areas is a weakness.

Building codes have been widely used to strengthen the built environment in the face of natural hazard risks. Local governments in the U.S. have enacted fairly comprehensive building codes to regulate new construction, and these codes have increasingly reflected hazard mitigation. The model building codes that are readily available and utilized by state and local governments have become more prevalent than custom-drafted codes. These model codes are of excellent quality, but there has been some concern about the quality of the enforcement of these codes. The general concern is that inconsistent or inadequate enforcement efforts have resulted in building codes being less effective than desired. Nevertheless, the awareness that disaster resilient construction is a critical component in sustainable community planning is widespread.

Insurance redistributes losses rather than reducing them. For this reason, it is not really a mitigation measure. But insurance may minimize the disruption that follows a disaster. More to the point, it may encourage people to adopt risk reduction strategies by creating incentives to mitigate as a means of obtaining rate discounts or lower deductibles.

U.S. flood control policies have emphasized flood insurance, requiring it under some circumstances, in the hope that it would be an effective nonstructural option in the nation's floodplain management. The National Flood Insurance Program was designed to save the government money by using premiums paid by floodplain occupants to fund flood-related disaster assistance. The mandatory flood insurance purchase requirements associated with this program have not always been effectively enforced. Also, critics suggest that insurance may provide individuals with a disincentive to protect their properties against flood damage. The assumption that losses will be covered may work against the initiation of mitigation strategies.

Improvements in prediction, forecast, and warnings are measures that may reduce the loss of life and the injuries associated with natural disasters. They do not necessarily reduce loss to infrastructure or private property. Long-term warnings that identify a threat years or decades off may have an impact on sustainable hazard mitigation as decision makers will have the information and the time they need to design disaster resistant communities. The challenge is to insure that decision makers will take long-term warnings seriously and be proactive in responding to them.

Improvements in the built environment, made possible by good engineering practices, are essential to building sustainable communities. Carefully engineered buildings and structures are not, in themselves, the total answer. To the degree that improved engineering technology encourages more expensive development in high-risk locations, it may lead to a false sense of security rather than real mitigation. Still, engineering codes in the U.S. have evolved to include planning for all natural hazards.

There are a variety of developments in hazard relevant technologies that are available to aid emergency managers in mitigation efforts. Geographic information systems (GIS) have many applications for example. GIS may be used to estimate damage to infrastructure, provide risk information to aid in community land use planning and in building planning, simulate disaster damage to aid in planning, and aid in environmental planning. Computer-mediated communication, remote sensing, decision support systems, risk analysis, all have developed rapidly and show great promise for use in disaster preparedness and mitigation planning.

While technology has advanced, the willingness of some communities to utilize it or their perceived inability to afford it are challenges to be met and overcome. Certainly the potential for GIS and other technological applications in emergency management seems almost unlimited.

The six techniques discussed here are among the most basic and widely used hazard mitigation tools available to a community. Resistance to disaster is a critical characteristic of sustainable communities. It is only through mitigation, planning before a disaster strikes, that sustainability may be achieved. By integrating the concepts of sustainable development into each phase of disaster or hazards planning (mitigation, preparedness, response, recovery), communities can take effective action to eliminate loss of life/property and sustain economic vitality. Hazard mitigation planning, in the context of comprehensive community planning, can help create a safe and sustainable community.

With the progress made in hazard mitigation in the U.S. over the past two decades, and with the growing sophistication of both the principles and techniques associated with sustainable mitigation, it may be tempting to suggest that the effort to make hazard mitigation a national priority has succeeded. To a degree, it has. But we must conclude this analysis with a caution that recent events may interrupt this progress.

CONCLUSION: A NEW CHALLENGE TO
SUSTAINABLE HAZARD MITIGATION

With the aftermath of September 11, 2001 and the creation of the Department of Homeland Security (DHS), it is tempting to suggest that emergency management has attained a new level of significance in the U.S. national consciousness. Indeed, the emergence of the profession and the creation of FEMA itself owe much to the national defense mania of the Cold War era. But, if the past is any indication, the national security concerns that periodically increase public awareness and political attentiveness to the emergency management function do not result in a broad commitment of new resources to the full array of possible disasters. Indeed, it might even be suggested that the current national security focus holds as much potential to distract the emergency management profession as it does to increase its operational scope and effectiveness.

The creation of the DHS has created a new focus. The U.S. government has reorganized emergency management under the umbrella of its anti-terror efforts and increased appropriations to respond to the threat of terrorism. FEMA, and state and local emergency management structures across the nation, are integrated into the DHS. The authority previously given to the FEMA director is now vested in the DHS Secretary. Not only may the stature and authority of FEMA be reduced in this new arrangement, it is equally possible that the effectiveness and operational abilities of FEMA staff and programs may be compromised (Bullock & Haddow, 2004).

Emergency management programs and functions have been folded into DHS. With this reorganization, and larger budget allocations targeted for homeland security, there is reason for concern about the continuity of traditional programs (Waugh, 2004). The concern is that resources may be diverted or prioritized for counterterrorism. New DHS personnel are bound to be less interested in and unfamiliar with the language, methodologies, and practices of emergency management. The capacity of government at all levels to deal with natural and technological hazards may be negatively impacted by the diversion of the attention of national policymakers and DHS to other concerns. Within the DHS structure, it already appears that minimal attention is being paid to matters other than terrorism-related concerns (Waugh, 2004).

The U.S. emergency management system has been underfunded, at all levels, for decades. With some potential for new federal appropriations to local governments connected to terrorism, and the primary emphasis on terrorism at the national level, it is very likely that local emergency management will be consumed with terrorism-related initiatives and activities (Bullock & Haddow, 2004).

The rush by American political leaders to create a new terrorism response structure is most understandable and not in dispute here. But this development has ignored the fact that a very effective federal structure already existed. There may have been no need to build an entirely new infrastructure. The existing emergency management structure had the capacity to treat any type of emergency or disaster *and* would have allowed for incorporation of the special needs related to terrorism (Bullock & Haddow, 2004).

Post 9-11 discussions have recycled many disaster myths that the emergency management profession long ago rejected, including the belief in widespread panic and the assumptions that accompany that belief (Dynes, 2003). Likewise, the new focus on terrorism repeats the event specific focus of the old emergency management. Terrorism, and primarily in the context of the DHS focus on consequence management or post-event issues, has placed a great deal of the focus on first responders and law enforcement and far too little on reducing the impact of events (mitigation) and prevention (Bullock & Haddow, 2004). This may, in other words, skip over or ignore much of the progress made in the field of emergency management over the past two decades.

Ideally, as the U.S. emergency management system shifted its focus to preparing for and responding to terrorist events, it was not meant to be at the expense of its capacity to deal with natural and technological hazards in the context of an all hazards approach. But there is concern that this is what has happened. During the Cold War, for example, FEMA spent 75 percent of its financial and human resources on preparing for nuclear war. State and local governments, seduced by the prospect of FEMA funding for defense related projects, followed suit. This contributed to some retardation in state and local capacity to respond to natural disasters (Bullock & Haddow, 2004). To focus on one threat, terrorism, at the expense of attention given to more frequent and widespread threats, would risk abandonment of the all hazards approach with its emphasis on hazard mitigation. Clearly, greater thought and evaluation might have found a way to treat the serious threat of terrorism within the broad and increasingly effective emergency management framework already established.

The U.S. emergency management system has been built around generic all hazards programs. Over the past two decades, its emphasis has been on building disaster resilient and sustainable communities, and its procedures and techniques have been made adaptable to all hazards. It provides a unifying approach, a common language, and an established operational framework for all emergency managers and public officials (Waugh, 2004). The emphasis over the past decade on sustainable hazard mitigation has arguably shown great promise for reducing the impacts and costs of disasters. The question is, has 9-11 changed that trend and slowed the potential for progress? With an event specific orientation, and its emphasis on response and law enforcement, U.S. terrorism policy may hold the potential to distract emergency management from the work of over two decades that has made sustainable mitigation the cornerstone of U.S. emergency management policy.

REFERENCES

Anderson, M. (1995). Vulnerability to disaster and sustainable development: A general framework for assessing vulnerability. In M. Munasinghe & C. Clark (Eds.), *Disaster prevention and sustainable development: Economic and policy issues* (pp. 41–59). Washington, DC: The World Bank.

Beatley, T. (1995). Planning and sustainability: A new (improved?) paradigm. *Journal of Planning Literature, 9,* 383–395.

Britton, N. R. (1999). Whither emergency management? *International Journal of Mass Emergencies and Disasters, 17*(2), 223–235.

Bullock, J. A., & Haddow, G. D. (2004). The future of emergency management. *Journal of Emergency Management, 2*(1), 19–24.

Cigler, B. A. (1996). Coping with floods: Lessons from the 1990s. In R. T. Sylves & W. L. Waugh (Eds.), *Disaster Management in the U.S. and Canada* (pp. 191–213). Springfield, IL: Charles C Thomas.

Dynes, R. (2003). Finding order in disorder: Continuities in the 9-11 response. *International Journal of Mass Emergencies and Disasters, 21*(3), 9–23.

Federal Emergency Management Agency. (1993). *National performance review report.* Washington, DC: Author.

FEMA. (1997). *Report on Costs and Benefits of Natural Hazard Mitigation.* Washington D.C. Federal Emergency Management Agency Mitigation Directorate.

Federal Emergency Management Agency. (2000). *Planning for sustainability: The link between hazard mitigation and livability.* Washington, DC: Author.

Federal Emergency Management Agency. (2003). *FEMA's EMI higher education project.* Retrieved March 3, 2004, from http://training.fema.gov/emiweb/edu/index.asp

Godschalk, D. R., Berke, T., Brower, D. S., & Kaiser, E. J. (1999). *Natural hazard mitigation: Recasting disaster policy and planning.* Washington, DC: Island Press.

Grant, N. K. (1996). Emergency management training and education for public administrators. In R. T. Sylves & W.L. Waugh (Eds.), *Disaster management in the U.S. and Canada* (pp. 313–325). Springfield, IL: Charles C Thomas.

Kates, R. (2003). Making the transition. Interviewed by B. Harris in *Government Technology, 16*(14), 10–15.

Kreps, G. A. (1991). Organizing for emergency management. In T. E. Drabek & G. J. Hoetmer (Eds.), *Emergency management principles and practices for local governments* (pp. 30–54). Washington, DC: International City Managers Association.

Kusterer, K., Ruck, M. T., & Weaver, J. H. (1997). Achieving broad-based sustainable development: Governance, environment, and growth with equity. Hartford:

Kumarian Press.

Mileti, D. (1999). *Disasters by design: A reassessment of natural disasters in the United States.* Washington, DC: Joseph Henry Press.

Moore, M. H. (1995). *Creating public value: Strategic management in government.* Cambridge: Harvard University Press.

National Academy for Public Administration. (1993). *Coping with catastrophe: Building an emergency management system to meet people's needs in natural and manmade disasters.* Washington, DC: Federal Emergency Management Agency.

Osborne, D., & Gaebler, T. (1993). *Reinventing government: How the entrepreneurial spirit is transforming the public sector.* New York: Addison-Wesley Publishing Company.

Perry, R. W., & Mushkatel, A. H. (1984). *Disaster management: Warning, response, and community reaction.* Westport, Ct: Greenwood Publishing Group Inc.

Reddy, S. D. (2000). Introducing emergency management curriculum into public affairs. *Journal of Public Affairs Education, 6*(3), 183–192.

Schneider, R. O. (2002). Hazard mitigation and sustainable community development. *Disaster Prevention and Management, 11*(2), 141–147.

Schneider, R. O. (2004). An overview of the new emergency management. *Journal of Emergency Management, 2*(1), 25–29.

Sylves, R. T. (1996). Redesigning and administering federal emergency management. In R. T. Sylves & W. L. Waugh (Eds.), *Disaster management in the U.S. and Canada* (pp. 5–25). Springfield, IL: Charles C Thomas.

Waugh, W. L. (1990). Emergency management and the capacities of state and local governments. In R. T. Sylves & W. L. Waugh (Eds.), *Cities and disaster: North American studies in emergency management* (pp. 221–237). Springfield, IL: Charles C. Thomas.

Waugh, W. L. (2004). The all hazards approach must be continued. *Journal of Emergency Management, 2*(1), 11–12.

Wolensky, R. P., & Wolensky, K. C. (1990). Local government's problems with disaster management: A literature review and structural analysis. *Policy Studies Review, 8,* 703–725.

Wright, J. D., & Rossi, P. H. (1981). *Social sciences and natural hazards.* Cambridge: ABT Books.

Chapter 6

ASSESSING SOCIAL RESILIENCE

PHILIP BUCKLE

INTRODUCTION

This chapter is based in part on my own experience in planning and managing disaster relief and recovery programs in Victoria, Australia and on my research with Graham Marsh and Syd Smale investigating local perception of risks, local capacity to withstand disasters, implementation of vulnerability and resilience assessment programs and the development of community capability. It became obvious to me, professionally, that disaster relief and recovery programs for both natural and nonnatural disaster could only be developed where there was a good understanding of the losses and needs and strengths of individuals, families and communities. Of course, this is more or less easy enough to achieve after a disaster when needs may be identified through damage and needs assessment surveys. But planning requires similar assessments before the damage has occurred and this can be best achieved through vulnerability and resilience assessments. These assessments, therefore, are central to effective planning and management. They indicate what the goals of planning are, what the outcomes to be driven for actually are, that is, to reduce exposure to risk and to increase capacity to manage risk.

Resilience and vulnerability are central concepts in understanding the nature of disasters, their impacts and consequences and methods of dealing with the potential for loss. However, neither concept has been exhaustively explored (despite a clear need for intellectual rigour and conceptual clarity), although much more attention has been given to vulnerability than to resilience. This methodological immaturity is reflected in the plethora of definitions (see, for example, Weichselgartner, 2001) which is both a symptom of confusion and a cause of confusion and ambiguity.

In this chapter I offer several lists setting out the qualities of resilience and vulnerability as a step towards a matrix for identifying resilience. These lists constitute different dimension of resilience and vulnerability, though it is only by considering all of these dimensions, more or less simultaneously, that we can build a comprehensive picture of vulnerability. The usual way of achieving this is by developing a matrix, well-regarded by hazard analysts and risk assessors as an analytical tool. But even matrices may inadequately reflect the complexity of the interactions between the many factors that define how people and social institutions behave towards each other and across social domains. Even within homogeneous communities or small areas the nature and type of interactions can be so complex and dynamic that mapping even the most significant interactions can difficult.

This complexity may defeat an effort to systematically set out the linkages, dependences and networks of resilience and vulnerability. An attempt is, however, justified at least because previous assessments have been linear and static and have not taken into account the multi-layered and continuously changing nature of social interaction. Anderson and Woodrow (1998) identified the need to describe vulnerabilities and capacities. They prepared a matrix with vulnerability and capacities each measured against physical/material, social/organisational and motivational/attitudinal axes. They acknowledge that reality is even more complex. They also allow for gender, disaggregation by other differences such as wealth, and they acknowledge the need to conduct these analyses at different time periods (to build up a picture of change and they acknowledge that this sort of analysis can be applied at different scales, village, neighborhoods, districts and so on.

What this analysis does not do, but I admit achieving this is problematic, is to indicate how different levels interact with each other, how subsystems interact with each other, and how elements of subsystems interact between and across subsystems.

DEFINITIONS

There are several definitions of resilience, and its' de facto corollary, vulnerability and in practical terms the fine distinctions between these definitions are not always helpful when it comes to the practicalities of assessing "real world" resilience.

Emergency Management Australia's (1998) glossary defines resilience as a "measure of how quickly a system recovers from failures" (p. 94), and vulnerability as the "degree of susceptibility and resilience of the community and environment to hazards. The degree of loss to a given element at risk or set of such elements resulting from the occurrence of a phenomenon of a given magnitude and expressed on a scale of 0 (no damage) to 1 (total loss) (p. 114).

The United Nations International Strategy for Disaster Reduction (United Nations, 2005) offers more comprehensive definitions. Resilience is defined as the capacity of a system, community or society potentially exposed to hazards to adapt, by resisting or changing in order to reach and maintain an acceptable level of functioning and structure. This is determined by the degree to which the social system is capable of organizing itself to increase its capacity for learning from past disasters for better future protection and to improve the effectiveness of risk reduction measures. Vulnerability they define as the conditions determined by physical, social, economic, and environmental factors or processes, which increase the susceptibility of a community to loss from hazard impacts. Coping capacity is defined as the means by which people or organizations use available resources and abilities to face adverse consequences that could lead to a disaster. Importantly, they argue that this involves managing resources, both in normal and hazardous times. Thus, strengthening coping capacities facilitates building resilience to withstand the effects of natural hazards. Finally, they define community capacity as the combination of all the strengths and resources available within a community, society or organization that contribute to reducing the level of risk, or the effects of a disaster. Capacity can include the physical, institutional, social or economic resources and means, as well as skilled personal or collective attributes such as leadership and management that a community can bring to bear on managing hazards. Capacity may also be described as capability.

A point to note about these definitions, and they are included as being representative of most definitions, is that they refer to "community" as a large social group but do not refer to the individual, whereas most lists refer to groups of vulnerable people, but not to individuals or communities. The intent of giving these examples is to show that resilience is a multifarious concept that can apply to the capacity to withstand loss, the capacity to prevent a loss occurring in the first place, and the capacity to recover from a loss if it occurs. Vulnerability, on the other hand, is a measure of what losses may occur and how severe they may be.

To conclude this section it does need to be pointed out that vulnerability and resilience are linked logically but are not necessarily opposite ends of a spectrum. A person or community may be both vulnerable and resilient at the same time. For example, a person who has built a house on a flood plain is vulnerable to flooding, but may have a degree of resilience, through adequate insurance that can help them recover from the loss. The capacity to recover from the loss, resilience, is independent of vulnerability. Resilience and vulnerability do not cancel each other out to arrive at a neutral state. They complement rather than confront each other.

WHO IS RESILIENT, WHO IS VULNERABLE?

Although not dependent there is some concordance between resilience and vulnerability and we may assume, for practical purposes, that if a person or group has a high vulnerability then they have a low resilience. The following is a list of vulnerable groups of people (Marsh, 1999):

1. Aged (particularly the frail) being less mobile, often poor, often isolated
2. Very young, dependent on others, lacking the capacity to care for themselves
3. Disabled (mental and physical) requiring assistance from other people or agencies for normal daily support
4. Poor/People with limited resources to meet essential needs
5. Nondominant Language speakers who may have difficulty accessing information and services
6. Indigenous groups who may be socially marginalized and poor

7. Socially isolated who may lack support physically and emotionally
8. Physically isolated with difficulty accessing services and information
9. Seriously ill who require high levels of support just to meet daily needs
10. People dependent on technology-based life support systems who also require high levels of daily support
11. Large families who have to manage multiple needs within one household
12. Single parent families with limited resources and low coping capacity
13. People with limited coping capacity who can be made highly vulnerable by the addition of small amounts of additional stress or loss
14. People with inadequate accommodation who are already in significant need
15. Those on holiday and traveling (particularly those in tent and caravan resorts) who are not familiar with local circumstances and assistance
16. Tourists from overseas who are not familiar with local conditions and who are far from their support networks.

It must be remembered also, that a person can belong to more than one of these groups where one vulnerability may exacerbate another. Lists such as these are often taken in practice to suggest that people who do not fall into one of the identified groups are not vulnerable and are therefore resilient. As I shall discuss later this is not the case. Vulnerability and resilience are neither mono-dimensional nor polar. A person, group, or community is neither vulnerable nor resilient but on a number of different axes, such as housing, income security, psychological coping capacity, and they may be assessed as being more or less vulnerable **and** resilient to particular threats. It is possible to exist in both states at the same time, because a person or group is composed of a tightly-bound skein of different attributes.

Not belonging to one of these groups does not mean that a person is not vulnerable in some circumstances. The European tourists killed and injured by the Indian Ocean Tsunami in 2004 would, in most cases, not have fallen into any of these categories but they were still vulnerable. Their relative wealth, health, or youth did not necessarily protect them from the ravages of the tsunami and its consequences.

LEVELS OF SOCIAL RESILIENCE

Studies of resilience and vulnerability have almost invariably focussed on the individual as the unit of assessment as is indicated in the previous list. However, people do not exist solely as individuals. Social behavior results in them forming groups, behaving collectively and interacting across different levels of social grouping. These levels include:

1. Individual
2. Family
3. Tribe or clan
4. Locality or neighborhood
5. Community
6. Social associations such as clubs and faith congregations
7. Organization (such as a bureaucracy or a private sector firm)
8. Systems such as environmental systems and economic systems.

As well, resilience may be assessed for even broader areas such as region and nation. At these levels the aggregation of detail gives a very coarse resolution, although this may be adequate for policy purposes.

These categories are not exclusive. An individual may belong to several groups. For example, a person lives and exist in their own right as an individual, they may be a member of a family, they may belong to a number of groups and associations such as a church congregation, a local environmental group, a sporting club and similar, and they belong also to the wider community.

It is not just the individual that is the focus of resilience and vulnerability. Families and larger groups, up to and including whole communities, may possess capacities and weaknesses that render them more or less susceptible.

There are many post-disaster examples of groups of people, some formal volunteer groups (e.g., the Red Cross), others centred on churches and others on groups such as football clubs (not normally linked with community volunteer activity), providing support to particular individuals and families. In many cases whole communities come together, often for many weeks or months, to work together in communal projects where the output is owned by no one but shared by everyone.

Even more interesting are emergent groups that arise apparently spontaneously after events to provide mutual aid to their members. Predicting when and how these groups will arise, and what stimulates their occurrence is very difficult but has something to do with communities that are stable, have a sense of identity and have no substantial splits or enmities within them.

Equally community activity can be directed at prevention and preparedness work such as supporting volunteer fire-fighters brigades, fund raising for emergency services and prevention works such as maintaining flood protection works.

The important point about this section of the discussion is that families, groups and communities do possess internal dynamics that indicate a level of autonomous capacity to act and be acted upon and therefore exist as entities semi-independent of their constituent, individual members. It is not possible to have a community with no individual members but it is not nonsensical to talk of the same community that has so changed over time that it has a totally new complement of members, none of whom belonged originally. In this sense communities are quasi independent entities and while they cannot in substance own assets (in law this is less clear) they do have control over some assets (e.g., community halls) and they can "possess" intangible assets such as networks and values that facilitate daily individual life.

DIMENSIONS OF RESILIENCE AND VULNERABILITY

Impacts and Needs

Whilst there will be wide variations in the types of community impacts and the needs arising as a result, the following list sums up the areas of significant impact, but not in any necessary order of priority:

- Life and Injury (1,2, 3)
- Physical Health/Wellbeing (1,2, 3)

- Mental Health/Wellbeing (1,2, 3)
- Home/Shelter (1,2, 3)
- Safety and civil security (1,2, 3)
- Food (1,2, 3)
- Potable Water (1,2, 3)
- Sewerage and public health systems (4,5)
- Information about services an support (1,2, 3)
- Access to services and support (1,2)
- Income security/economic opportunity (1,2, 3)
- Social links, social networks and social support (1,2, 3)
- Community owned assets (4,5)
- Community "owned"/shared intangibles (such as values, aspirations, communal activities) (4,5)
- 1 = individual directly affected, 2 = 1st order indirect impacts on small groups, 3 = 2nd order indirect impacts on community, 4=direct impacts on community, 5 = 1st order indirect impacts on individuals

This is not a simply a list of types of losses but an indicative list of vulnerabilities; what people and communities have to lose. The converse of this list is that resilience may be subdivided into the capacity to withstand loss in these areas or to recover from this loss.

This, too, is a not untypical list but it does need some explication. Some impacts apply only to individuals directly (such as injury), indirectly to small groups (where for example, the injury of one family member affects others) and less directly still to the wider community (the shared cost of health care for the injured person). Some of these impacts are related to community assets (shared by all but owned by no one) directly and less directly to individuals (where say a water supply system is damage)

Lists such as that set out above are valuable as aide-memoires but they are never complete and can always be added to, but their real danger is in breeding excessive confidence that the task of analysis has been completed when it is always in progress.

Elements that Support Resilience at an Individual Level: A Functional Assessment

The resilience of a person or group may be assessed on the basis of how well they "own" and can "manage" the following attributes:

Information and advice on preparedness and assistance measures and how to access them, the normal bio-psychosocial reactions which can be expected and how people can deal with these reactions in themselves, members of their family and their community, and how to make sense of the event in terms of its cause and fitting it into their "view" of the world can be provided.

Resources include financial resources, which can be their own, insurance, or from other sources, to apply to prevention, preparedness and recovery measures. Resources also include physical goods, such as alternative accommodation, essential household items, alternative transport systems, tools and other items.

Management capacity embraces having the time and opportunity to manage appropriate resilience generating activities, as well as the physical capacity, which may include the support of other people, machinery, or support where there is a particular need. It also includes access to services and other support systems such as building services, financial services, counselors, and interpreters.

Personal and community support includes particularly post event personal support, such as outreach services, personal advisers and counselors, specialist support services, advocates and gatekeepers and community support, for example, community development officers.

Involvement refers to linkages with other people, with a wide network of family, friends and acquaintances shown to be critical in supporting and sustaining resilience. Involvements also means consultation in developing disaster management programs and encouragement in generally making a contribution to policy and program development.

These five attributes are not just relevant to individuals or even families. They apply equally to community groups. These, in a sense, have an identity separate from any particular individual or group. They also have attributes and processes, such as networks, community ceremonies, a "culture," history, potential and desired futures, that is different to the attributes of an individual. Resilience is an organic relationship between individual, group and community in the context of a hazard.

As I and others (Buckle, Marsh & Smale, 2001a) have pointed out, the traditional characterizations of particular groups of people, such as the aged, as being resilient or vulnerable does not tell us which people in a particular situation may be vulnerable. This is because people or groups will have a specific mix of vulnerabilities and coping strategies that depend on their circumstances and the context of the hazard and its interaction with the persona and group. These lists, therefore, have an indicative value at best.

The value of a functional approach is that it defines resilience and vulnerability as characteristics that can be reduced or enhanced with observable and measurable effects. We cannot address vulnerability reduction or resilience development on the basis of characteristics such as age or gender. These may provide strong pointers to how and when and what type of action should be taken. They may indicate priorities. But, in the end, we cannot change a person's age or gender. What we can do is to improve their access to resources, to improve their health status, to empower them and to give them access to equitable treatment. However, in stating this we do recognize that empowerment is not an easy process, particular when the most vulnerable, the least resilient, are often those least able to cope generally and who may also be isolated from mainstream resources.

A limitation and danger of lists of characteristics of resilience and vulnerability is that they may instil a false confidence and may lead planners and managers to treat the list not as an aide-memory but as a definitive statement which may lead to unjustified confidence and complacency that the problem has been solved.

Elements that Support Resilience at Community Level

Resilience and vulnerability are not just characteristics that affect individuals but also groups and communities.

- **Knowledge of hazards** and of community characteristics essential in developing and maintaining capacity to avoid or reduce the impacts of disasters.
- **Shared community values**; this includes a positive sense of the future, a commitment to the community as a whole and agreement, broadly, on community goals. This does not exclude diversity, but does exclude competitive and antagonistic goals and values.
- **Established social infrastructure**, this attribute includes information channels, social networks and community organizations

(e.g., churches, sporting clubs).

- **Positive social and economic trends** include a stable or growing population and a viable economy, both contributing to sustainability. Positive trends and sustainability assist the community to deal with adverse conditions.
- **Partnerships** between agencies, community groups and private enterprise or any combination facilitates innovation, shared knowledge, experience and resources.
- **Resources and skills** can be generic attributes (e.g., management or financial skills, human resource potential). These can be measured by their cost, availability and ease of access.

In research in Australian communities, we were repeatedly told that key matters could be resolved to half a dozen issues (Buckle, Marsh, & Smale, 2003, pp. 15–16):

1. The need for empowerment of local people and their communities so that planning, decision making and action were neither "top-down" nor "bottom-up" but a combination of these that reflected a genuine partnership.
2. There is a need for local leadership especially where there is population decline or economic decline (which is often accompanied by the loss of local leaders) or where the population is changing rapidly or, as in many rural areas, the population is aging and there is a net loss of young people.
3. There is a need for a focal point, a center where residents, local leaders, agency, business and government representatives can meet. This center also has a symbolic value as an area of trust and mutual support rather than as a combative arena and where isolation, mistrust and misunderstanding can be broken down. This is paralleled by a need for inclusiveness in processes of planning and decision making along with a feeling of ownership in these processes and their outcomes by all people who have an interest in them.
4. Trust in the municipal and government authorities and in the private sector is critical; there is a need for high levels of trust and social capital within networks and across networks with an active program to restrict conflict and to generate mutual respect and understanding.

5. There is an important need to develop and maintain networks and to do this between networks as many are isolated from other networks.
6. There needs to be effective and open and accessible communication processes in which all stakeholders may participate.

In general, there exists a set of principles for community capacity building and nurturing resilience that can be summarized as follows (Buckle, 2003, pp. 42–46). Local communities and organizations must be managed according to principles of good governance (legal authority, transparency, accountability, inclusiveness and agreed priorities). This addresses the extent to which programs and the policies they reflect conform to contemporary standards and to community needs and aspirations. Adequate resourcing of resilience-building programs is often overlooked with the result that resources are inadequate to fully complete programs. Resources are more than money and include skills and knowledge. Any capacity-building program needs to ensure that there is integrated development of social, economic livelihoods, environmental and cultural dimensions to community life. All programs need to be self-sustaining, not just in the sense of their having a positive effect on their environment, but also with regard to generating future resources and their capacity to interact successfully with other programs.

Change is inevitable and inherent in social life, resilient communities and the programs on which they are based need to incorporate mechanisms for change and adaptation, these mechanisms include community consultation, monitoring, audit and feedback. Any program needs to meet goals of effectiveness that include a positive cost benefit ratio, efficiency and involving sustainable partnerships.

RESILIENCE IS CONTEXT SPECIFIC

Resilience and vulnerability are not inherent characteristics of a particular individual, group or locality. They indicate relationships between appropriate skills, resources and knowledge and the risks generated by an actual hazard.

The context may be time dependent; people may be more or less vulnerable depending on the time of day, time of the week, or the time of year. For example, earthquakes may be more threatening to life if they occur at night when people are in their homes, but bushfires are less likely to cause damage to homes if people are at home and can defend their property (and know how to do so). Droughts, floods, bushfires and cyclones are seasonal and so is exposure and vulnerability to these.

Hazards have different characteristics in terms of damage potential, rapidity of impact, duration, extent of area affected, frequency and warning time. These factors vary between hazard types, and even between the same hazard occurring at different times. The potential for harm therefore varies also with the type of hazard.

These are two dimensions, time of occurrence and type of hazard, that, together with the characteristics (resilience and vulnerability) of the person or group at risk, that make resilience and vulnerability contingent on local circumstances. Wisner (2004) indicated some different typologies of vulnerability assessment but favors a contextual approach. I agree that resilience and vulnerability can only be properly understood as constructs (not as inherent attributes) that arise from a particular set of circumstantial social, economic, political, historical and cultural conditions and to understand the cause and consequences of a particular vulnerability or capacity.

DIMENSIONS OF RESILIENCE

What I have offered so far is a series of lists relevant to a discussion of resilience and vulnerability. I want now to emphasize that the assessment of resilience prior to the event is extremely problematic given the complex interaction of the capacities of the individual, the community, the various impacts and needs caused by disasters and the significance of context in ascertaining resilience. It is therefore questionable whether resilience is ever predictable in advance except on a very coarse scale.

Any assessment must take into account that in theoretical and practical terms, resilience is not the opposite end of a spectrum to vulnerability. Assessments and rankings of vulnerabilities will only ever be an approximation, and given the complexity of this problem this is not necessarily a bad thing, at least in practical terms. What this does alert us to is the need to assess resilience at the finest level we can and to assess it not against the individual or community who are not in themselves naturally resilient or vulnerable, as these qualities are context dependent, but against particular states of that individual and to balance vulnerability against capacity. So, for example, a rich person is much less vulnerable to loss of a home (because they have assets to restore losses) than a poor person who is asset poor, but both may be equally vulnerable psychologically.

ASSESSING RESILIENCE

Assessing resilience and vulnerability is difficult given the complex and dynamic nature of people and the communities and societies to which they belong. The complexity generated by the various permutations of factors discussed here means that they may not be possible to predict except in a very general sense.

It becomes a point of argument whether it is helpful, say, to categorize the "elderly" as vulnerable or whether it is unhelpful. I suppose that if a person is elderly and is vulnerable also this is a helpful categorization if it leads to support and action. It is less helpful if one is elderly and not vulnerable, at best it may stigmatise a person and at worse it may generate an uninformed but constraining and imposed benevolence and may lead to a loss of dignity as a person is assumed to be needy when they are not. It may be, however, harmful if an incorrect categorization leads to other people who are vulnerable receiving less support than to which otherwise they would have been entitled.

What I suggest is that a "functional" approach be taken where vulnerability and resilience are assessed on the basis of the ability of a person or group or community to work towards and to attain certain basic goals, such as the capacity to manage their own affairs, to have access to appropriate and appropriate levels of resources, including food, water, shelter, health care, education and cultural activity, social inclusion and information and access to other necessary and desirable services. This approach can also be applied to groups and communities. Can they meet their goals in the face of specified systemic shocks or disasters.

Even this is not likely to yield detailed results as local circumstances, by definition, will vary from area to area, over time and from one situation to another. Situational or contextual assessment is therefore needed, where local, immediate circumstances are taken into account to assess capacity and vulnerability. Only after situational assessment can an accurate view be achieved of capacities, vulnerabilities, strengths and weaknesses, needs and assets. This, in turn, provides a framework for developing appropriate mitigation, remedial and support mechanisms. Such an approach can yield useful and useable results. It is practical and can be applied to planning and management. The choice of scale can change and at larger scales the results may be applied to whole districts or regions or even countries, though the lack of sensitivity due to scaling issues will limit the applicability of the results to broad programme and policy considerations.

As Wisner, Blaikie, Cannon & Davis (2004) indicate there are many checklists or aide-memoires and they have their place as tools in the process of assessing vulnerability and resilience but they do not explain how people and groups becomes or remain or move out of vulnerability and resilience. The drivers of such change are structurally political, economic and cultural forces that expose people to processes and events (such as floods and wildfires). These events and processes in themselves are not harmful, it is only when humans and their institutions and artefacts are exposed to them in close proximity that a risk is generated. Avoiding proximity to wildfires, floods and so on is constrained by lack of choice and lack of resources (lack of political status, poverty etc.) and the risk can in a real sense be said to be generated by external forces that exist independently of the "hazard."

RESILIENCE AND VULNERABILITY
TO WHAT, WHEN, AND FOR WHOM

Resilience and vulnerability arise from the circumstances in which an individual find themselves. This "finding" may involve a degree of compulsion as general social, economic and political dynamics and structures constrain the opportunities of many people, especially the poor and the marginalized. Of course, resilience and vulnerability can also be owned by families, groups and communities. This is a critical dimension, especially as individuals exist within, interact with, and exert influence on their social environment. So resilience or vulnerability at one level may directly or indirectly influence resilience or vulnerability at other levels.

Lists and matrices are useful tools, but we need tools and methods to evaluate dynamic interactions within and between these various social domains. But this is a significant challenge to assess need and capacity in the full complexity of their social, economic and political circumstances.

Finally, we need to move away from simply categorizing resilience and vulnerability according to peoples' demographic status (e.g., aged or the young, or any other group). It is important to identify how they are resilient and the circumstances that generate and reduce vulnerability and generate and sustain resilience. We need to identify those attributes about which we can do something, such as poverty or knowledge, for we cannot do anything about aging, either accelerating it or slowing it down.

REFERENCES

Anderson, M. B., & Woodrow, P. J. (1998). *Rising from the ashes: Development strategies in times of disaster.* London: Intermediate Technology Publications.

Buckle, P. (2000). *Assessing resilience and vulnerability in the context of emergencies: Guidelines.* Melbourne: Department of Human Services.

Buckle, P., Marsh, G., & Smale, S. (2000). New approaches to assessing vulnerability and resilience. *Australian Journal of Emergency Management, 15,* 8–14.

Buckle, P., Marsh, G., & Smale, S. (2001a). *Assessment of personal & community resilience & vulnerability* (Project 14/2000). Mt Macedon, Australia: Emergency Management Australia.

Buckle, P., Marsh, G., & Smale, S. (2001b). *Assessing resilience & vulnerability: Principles, strategies & actions guidelines emergency management Australia* (Project 15/2000). Mt Macedon, Australia: Emergency Management Australia.

Buckle, P., Marsh, G., & Smale, S. (2003). *The development of community capacity as applying to disaster management capability* (Project 14/2002). Mt Macedon, Australia: Emergency Management Australia.

Emergency Management Australia. (1998). *Australian emergency management glossary.* Canberra, Australia: Commonwealth of Australia.

Marsh G., Smale, S., & Buckle, P. (1999). Report on community impact issues following possible major prolonged disruptions to utilities or possible Y2K situations. Melbourne: Department of Justice, Victoria, Australia.

United Nations. (2005). United Nations international strategy for disaster reduction. Retrieved January 9, 2005, from http://www.unisdr.org/eng/library/lib-terminology-eng%20home.htm.

Weichselgartner, J. (2001). Disaster mitigation: The Concept of vulnerability revisited. *Disaster Prevention and Management, 10*(2), 85–94.

Wisner, B. (2004). Assessment of capacity and vulnerability. In G. Bankoff, G.

Frerks, & D. Hilhorst (Eds.), *Mapping vulnerability: Disasters, development and people* (pp. 194–205). London: Earthscan.

Wisner, B., Blaikie, P., Cannon, T., & Davis, I. (2004). *At risk: Natural hazards, people's vulnerability and disasters.* London: Routledge.

Chapter 7

NATURAL HAZARD RESILIENCE: THE ROLE OF INDIVIDUAL AND HOUSEHOLD PREPAREDNESS

DOUGLAS PATON, JOHN MCCLURE, AND PETRA T. BÜRGELT

INTRODUCTION

The definition of resilience adopted in this book describes it as a capacity to draw upon personal and social resources to manage the consequences of disasters. During the period of disaster impact, people may be isolated from external assistance and have limited, if any, access to normal community and societal resources and functions for several days. Under these circumstances, their capacity to adapt will reflect their level of preparedness (e.g., knowledge of hazard impacts, the protective measures and resources they put in place to assist their adaptation) and their capacity for self-reliance (Lasker, 2004; Paton, 2003; Smith, 1993).

Protective measures (e.g., securing fixtures and furniture, securing a house to its foundation) can reduce the risk of damage and injury. Other resources (e.g., stored food and water, a household emergency plan) facilitate coping with the temporary disruption that accompanies hazard activity. Given that disasters can strike with no or very little warning, unless prepared in advance there will be neither time nor opportunity to acquire the requisite knowledge or resources during the period of impact. Despite the attention and financial resources devoted to its achievement, the goal of ensuring sustained levels of adoption of protective measures in communities susceptible to hazard consequences has proved elusive.

It has become increasingly apparent that neither living in areas susceptible to hazard impacts nor just providing people with information on hazards and their consequences exercises a significant influence on preparedness (Burger & Palmer, 1992; Duvall & Mulilis, 1999; Gregg et al., 2004; Lasker, 2004; Lindell & Perry, 2000; Lindell & Whitney 2000). By drawing upon their recent work (Cowan, McClure, & Wilson, 2002; Hurnen, & McClure, 1997; Johnston et al., 2005; McClure, Allen, & Walkey, 2001; McClure, Walkey, & Allen, 1999; McIvor & Paton, in prep; Paton, Kelly, Bürgelt & Doherty, in press; Paton, Smith & Johnston, 2005; Paton & Bürgelt, 2005) the authors account for this by discussing how people interpret their relationship with the civic, social and natural environments, and make decisions about the adoption of protective measures accordingly.

Constructing Reality

People are not passive recipients of information. Symbolic interactionism (Blumer, 1969) suggests that people actively and constantly interpret stimuli from the environment while interacting with the elements in that environment, and integrate the interpretations through a process of reflection with already existing mental models. People thus construct the meaning of the things they interact with and then act towards them in ways consistent with these meanings.

How people interpret the world (reality) differs from person to person, changes over time, depends on context, and reflects the unique experiences they have accumulated during their lives (Bowers, 1988). The diversity of this experience means that when people interact with the environment they take different objects into account and interpret and integrate them differently (Blumer, 1969). In addition, since individuals constantly assimilate new experiences, their sense of self, their interpretations and their actions constantly evolve over time, with this process defining how people adapt to new conditions (Denzin, 1992). The ultimate function of interpretations is to adapt as well as possible to changes in the environment.

However, peoples' interpretations and actions are always contextual and influenced by the social structures they encountered in everyday life (social context) (Blumer, 1969). The social structure affects how people act, because it defines situations in which people act, and "supplies a fixed set of symbols which people use to interpret their situation" (Blumer, 1969, p. 86). These conditions, which can become taken for granted, can either constrain or facilitate certain individual interpretations and actions. With regard to disaster preparation, this makes it important to accept that people interpret information in a context defined by their experience, beliefs and misconceptions about hazards, the actions proposed to mitigate their adverse consequences, the information available and its sources (Dow & Cutter, 2000; Lasker, 2004; Paton, 2003). Bostrom, Fischhoff, and Morgan (1992) noted that the interpretation of information can contribute to misunderstandings about hazards. They argue that if these misconceptions are not corrected, information will be neither received nor acted upon in the manner anticipated by disaster planners. This is becoming an increasingly important issue.

Communities are becoming increasingly diverse, resulting in the social context in which information is received being characterized by correspondingly varied experiences, beliefs, needs and expectations. A failure to accommodate this diversity can diminish the capacity of mass media information dissemination, which characterizes much contemporary risk communication, to facilitate the adoption of protective actions (Paton et al., 2005; Johnston et al., 2005; Paton & Bürgelt, 2005). These authors found that community members commonly perceived the disaster-related information presented to them as not specific enough. Consequently, it failed to help them understand either complex hazard issues or why specific actions on their part were required to mitigate them. Consequently, the information made available failed to motivate actions that would assist adaptation to hazard consequences. Problems can also arise if information fails to consider existing interpretive frameworks.

People have been found to overestimate their knowledge of what to do in the event of a volcanic eruption (Paton et al., 2000) and assume levels of preparedness that are discrepant with actual levels (Charleson, Cook & Bowering, 2003; Lopes, 2000). Overestimates of preparedness can also result from inferring from participating in training for more "routine" hazards (e.g., fire drills at school or work) a capacity to respond to more serious natural hazards (Gregg et al., 2004).

Differences about what constitutes adequate preparation have also been noted. Paton & Bürgelt (2005) found that residents' beliefs regarding sufficient preparedness for bushfires ranged from just mowing the lawn regularly to implementing multiple preparedness measures. They also noted differences in beliefs regarding when protective actions should be adopted. While some people habitually instigated actions at the commencement of the fire season, others put precautions, which could have been implemented earlier, in place only when faced with proximal factors—when dangerous weather conditions (hot, dry, and windy) and bush conditions prevailed, or when fire was perceived as a direct threat to their property. While information on protective measures is available during this period, opportunities for comprehensive protection are unlikely within the short time frame afforded by such beliefs about preparedness. Furthermore, the high levels of stress likely to prevail at this time may reduce the efficacy of such action. The point is, if people base their decisions on beliefs that existing levels are sufficient or wait until certain proximal cues are present in their environment, they are less likely to attend to risk information. Households that overestimate their preparedness for hazard events on any of these grounds will reduce their perceived risk, their willingness to attend to new information, and their perceived need for any additional preparation (Lopes, 2000; Paton et al., 2000).

Pre-existing meaning systems characterized by hazard-related anxiety can reduce peoples' willingness to attend to risk communication or act on it. If people manage their anxiety by insulating themselves from information that triggers feelings of anxiety, the likelihood that they will prepare will diminish (Duvall & Mulilis, 1999; Lamontaigne & LaRochelle, 2000; Paton et al., 2005).

People are not passive recipients of information, even when it is intended to inform them about significant issues in their environment. People make judgments about the information presented to them and actively interpret it within frames of reference that can differ systematically from their scientific and civic counterparts who develop and deliver risk messages. People interpret information in a context defined by their expectations, experience, beliefs and misconceptions about hazards, the actions proposed to mitigate their adverse consequences, and the sources of information (Dow & Cutter, 2000; Lasker, 2004; Paton, 2003), with people actively evaluating the relevance of information for them accordingly. This can result in their being disinclined to attend to information or to interpret it in ways that differ from that intended by civic agencies. Hence, to facilitate the adoption of protective measures, it is important to understand how people interpret their relationship with hazards and how they interpret hazard information.

If the interpretive mechanisms can be identified, this knowledge can be used to design risk reduction strategies to encourage the sustained adoption of protective measures. One approach that has proved promising involves conceptualizing how people interpret their relationship with hazards and the actions required to protect them as a social cognitive processes (Duval & Mulilis, 1999; Grothmann & Reuswig, in press; McClure et al,. 1999; 2001; Paton, 2003). Paton et al. (2005) demonstrated that the adoption of protective actions results from people successfully negotiating a sequential series of decisions that describe their relationship with a hazardous environment. Using this process as a framework, this chapter reviews issues that inform how people make decisions about whether or not to adopt protective measures. The components of this decision-making process are summarized in Figure 7.1. Discussion commences with consideration of factors that motivate people to prepare.

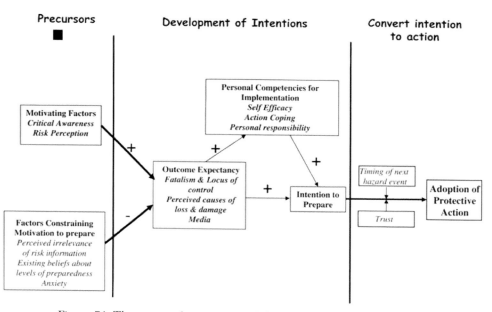

Figure 7.1. The preparedness process. Adapted from Paton et al. (2005).

STAGE ONE: MOTIVATION TO PREPARE

The preparation process commences when people are motivated to confront hazardous aspects of their environment. Two prominent motivators influencing preparing are threat/risk perception and critical awareness. It is to a discussion of these two factors that we turn now.

Risk Perception

Unless a person perceives a threat or risk associated with hazard activity it is unlikely that they will be motivated to deal with it. This is why encouraging the perception of a threat is often the focus of risk communication, with the use of this approach being based on the assumption that informing people of the threat posed by a hazard will result in their doing something about it. However, conveying information about the likelihood of hazard activity occurring and its consequences is not a straightforward process. Civic and scientific sources, who design risk communication programs, derive their judgments from relatively objective assessments of likelihood of occurrence and consequences. They typically assume that citizens will either do likewise or will accept their information at face value. This assumption is unfounded. Peoples' interpretation of risk may not share the relative objectivity that characterizes expert analysis. Rather, their understanding of and response to risk is determined not only by scientific information about risk, but also by the manner in which this information interacts with psychological, social, cultural, institutional and political processes. Reasons why peoples' estimates of risk can differ from their civic counterparts is illustrated by discussing how cognitive biases and social processes influence this discrepancy.

Firstly, risk perception can be influenced by people making judgments derived from comparisons with "other people" rather than on a more objective assessment of environmental threat. When asked to rate their preparedness relative to others within their community, individuals often believe themselves to be better prepared relative to the average for their community. This statistical anomaly, known as unrealistic optimism bias, means that while people may accept the need for greater preparedness, they perceive it as applying to others but not to themselves (Burger & Palmer, 1992; Paton et al., 2001). That is, they transfer risk to others within their community. If all members are making similarly biased assumptions about the distribution of risk within a community, the need for action will be attributed to others, with personal motivation to prepare being diminished accordingly.

Secondly, a discrepancy between expert and citizen estimates of risk can reflect citizens' tendency to overestimate the capacity of hazard mitigation strategies to eliminate a threat. This overestimation reflects the operation of an interpretive bias known as risk compensation (Adams, 1995). This process has also been known as levee syndrome. This construct describes how people maintain a balance between the perceived level of safety proffered by their environment and the level of risk manifest in their actions and attitudes. Thus, a perceived increase in extrinsic safety (e.g., the fact that hazard monitoring and structural mitigation are being undertaken by civic agencies) will decrease perceived risk, reducing motivation to prepare. For example, the dissemination of information on structural mitigation to the public (which assumes that peoples' behaviour will remain constant) has been linked to reduced levels of both perceived risk and preparedness in household, and an increased likelihood of citizens transferring responsibility for their safety to civic authorities (Hurnen & McClure, 1997; Paton et al., 2000).

Thirdly, relative to objective estimates, citizens' perceptions of risk can differ because they base their estimates on the relationship between hazard activity and personally salient issues. Bishop et al. (2000) and Paton et al. (2001) found that the level of risk attributed to salinity and volcanic ash hazards respectively was determined less by hazard characteristics per se and more by the extent to which hazard activity directly affected peoples' livelihoods. Information on the hazard itself may thus not be meaningful enough to motivate action.

Finally, the likelihood that expert and citizen estimates of risk will coincide depends on the degree to which citizens are actively involved in decision making about acceptable levels of risk and the strategies used to mitigate this risk (Paton & Bishop, 1996; Syme, Bishop & Milich, 1992). Risk communication strategies based on social justice principles increase the likelihood that citizens take responsibility for their own safety, thus increasing their motivation to act to safeguard themselves. Equity may also be an issue within families. Bushfire interviewees suggested that difference in opinions within families regarding imbalances in the trade-off between preparation costs (e.g., effort expended) and benefits (e.g., usefulness of measures) reduced motivation to prepare.

These issues must be accommodated in risk communications. Discussion with people in areas susceptible to earthquake and bushfire hazards suggest that risk communication would be rendered more effective if it engaged people in meaningful ways. A useful strategy is to elicit citizens' model of each hazard and correct identified misunderstandings. One way of implementing this strategy involves asking people to identify the activities they deem important for themselves and their family and structuring discussion around how protective actions could protect these important elements (Paton et al., 2001). It is also evident that citizens must be provided with specific information on the costs and benefits of actions, and that these must be reiterated following the introduction of new structural mitigation measures.

Critical Awareness

A second predictor of motivation is critical awareness—the extent to which people perceive hazard issues as important enough to think about them and to discuss them with others on a regular basis (Bagozzi & Dabholar, 2000; Dalton et al., 2005; Paton, 2003; Paton et al., 2005). The nature and frequency of discussion regarding disasters is linked to participation in community activities (e.g., membership of clubs or social action groups) (Bishop et al., 2000; Paton et al., 2001; Paton & Bürgelt, 2005). Critical awareness could be increased by inviting representatives of community groups (e.g., community boards, Greypower, Rotary, religious and ethnic groups) to review hazard scenarios regarding how to deal with the potential challenges, opportunities and threats they could pose for their members (Lasker, 2004; Paton, 2000). To expedite this process, it would be helpful to have knowledge of the content of these interactions.

Bushfire interviewees believed that sharing real-life stories of bushfire experiences helped distribute realistic knowledge about bushfires, their consequences, and how and why to prepare (Paton & Bürgelt, 2005). Participants in the earthquake focus groups believed that the relationship between community discussion and preparing was strengthened by the involvement of respected and knowledgeable community members. The importance of community leadership is evident from other sources (Dalton et al., 2005; Lasker, 2004), with the credibility of community leaders deriving from their knowledge and their ability to reconcile mitigation actions with peoples' needs and concerns. Tsunami focus group participants also believed that having access to someone knowledgeable about their situation, who would provide accurate information, and who could assist them to construct family emergency and evacuation plans in ways consistent with their needs was important (Johnston et al., 2005). However, because community members differ with regard to the perceived importance of hazard issues and their discussion, it is important to understand why some people actively discuss issues while others do not. One way of exploring this is in terms of peoples' attitudes and the social norms prevailing within a community.

While people hold attitudes to most of the issues that impinge upon them, they are not given equal importance. Rather, they are organized hierarchically according to their relative importance (Bagozzi & Dabholar, 2000; Hardin, & Higgins, 1996). Thus, even if people have a positive attitude to natural hazard risk reduction, this does not guarantee its translation into protective actions. For example, more salient beliefs regarding crime or health care issues may subjugate their natural hazard counterparts as determinants of action or some highly salient attitudes may preclude supporting certain mitigation strategies. The bushfire interview data revealed that, irrespective of their general attitudes to safety, people who held strong positive environmental protection attitudes found it difficult to support mitigation measures such as controlled burning or clearing that would result in destroying the environment they value. These examples reiterate other findings suggesting that attitude ambivalence moderates acting on intentions (Conner, Povey, Sparks, James & Shepherd, 2003).

The salience of hazard issues, the likelihood of their being topics of regular discussion, and the content of discussion can be influenced by social norms. The judgments people make regarding their actions is influenced by beliefs regarding how significant others would evaluate them if they were to support or adopt a mitigation measure. If they believe others would value such actions, the likelihood of adopting a protective measure is greater, and vice versa. For example, beliefs regarding what others would think and the social disapproval or legal actions that could accompany certain actions (e.g., clearing shrubs from around a property) resulted in people deciding not to adopt bushfire mitigation measures. However, shared beliefs regarding social responsibility and social reciprocity (e.g., to give back to the community and assist one another) were cited by others as factors supporting the adoption of protective measures. Thus, it is important to examine how people perceive problems relative to the views held by significant others.

Recent work provides empirical support for this view (McIvor & Paton, in prep). They found that attitudes and social norms regarding hazards influenced the formation of intentions to prepare for earthquakes. While attitudes had a direct effect on intention, the influence of subjective norms was mediated by peoples' beliefs in the ability of mitigation measures to actually reduce risk. This introduces a need to consider factors that could mediate the conversion of motivation into intentions to act.

Once motivated, people are then faced with a new series of issues about which judgments are required. This issue is discussed here in relation to decisions about two issues. The first concerns the relationship between the protective actions proposed and the person's beliefs about the capacity of these measures to reduce risk. The second involves peoples' beliefs about their competence to implement them. These issues are addressed in the next section.

STAGE TWO: FORMING INTENTIONS TO PREPARE

Progression to intention formation is a function of peoples' belief in the ability of mitigation measures to surmount hazard effects, and their belief in their competence to act and to resolve the demands associated with hazard effects (Paton, 2003; Paton et al., 2005). Paton et al. (2005) found that, in addition to its direct influence, critical awareness had an influence on intentions that was mediated by outcome expectancy. Similarly, Lasker (2004) concluded that, on its own, hazard salience resulted in 35 percent of respondents supporting protection planning. However, when salience and the perceived capacity of protective measures to reduce harm were combined, this increased to 89 percent. Duval and Mulilis' (1999) Person-relative-to-Event model also concluded that preparing was a function of the interaction between self-efficacy (people's assessment of their resources to enable an action) and response efficacy (perception of the efficacy of adjustment in protecting persons and property). Lindell and Whitney's

(2000) finding that response efficacy was a stronger predictor of preparedness than self-efficacy or perceptions of an earthquake's probability, severity and immediacy (i.e., risk perception) reiterates the importance of beliefs in the capability of protective action to reduce or eliminate adverse hazard consequences (Garcia, 1989; Farley, Barlow, Finkelstein, & Riley, 1993; Paton & Johnston, 2000) as a predictor of their adoption.

If the factors that influence perception of effectiveness can be understood, we will be in a better position to design effective intervention. In pursing this objective, discussion here considers how fatalism and locus of control, perceptions of the causes of loss and damage, and the media coverage of disaster influence the perceived effectiveness of mitigation measures.

Fatalism

Fatalism—the belief that the destructive effects of a hazard are inevitable—is a key predictor of people's failure to prepare for earthquakes (Turner, Nigg, & Paz, 1986). Fatalism relates to locus of control. Citizens with an internal locus, who believe that circumstances reflect their own actions, exert more control over their circumstances than those with an external orientation, who believe that circumstances reflect societal forces and chance factors such as fate (Strickland, 1989). People with an internal locus are more likely to prepare for tornadoes (Sims & Baumann, 1972), take out flood insurance (Baumann & Sims, 1978), and see earthquake damage as preventable (McClure et al., 1999; Simpson-Housley & Bradshaw, 1978).

External locus of control relates to learned helplessness in which people attribute negative events to uncontrollable causes, or generalize from genuinely uncontrollable events to other events that can be controlled, and so remain passive (Abramson, Seligman, & Teasdale, 1978; McClure, 1985). For example, many people assume that because earthquakes are uncontrollable, their devastating effects are also uncontrollable (Turner et al., 1986). However, while the events might be uncontrollable, the magnitude of the consequences can be influenced.

Consequently, preparedness could be enhanced by changing people's locus of control beliefs towards a more internal locus of control. However, this task is not straightforward, as these beliefs have firm cultural and psychological underpinnings. Fatalism and locus of control beliefs are not simply reversed by exposure to a factual message, but they can be modified when strategies target specific domains (Turner et al., 1986), and when the contingency between mitigating actions and positive outcomes is demonstrated (e.g., Strickland, 1989).

Turner et al. (1986) showed the value of focusing on specific situations by asking citizens if they thought anything could be done to help more vulnerable groups, such as people living in unsound buildings and children in schools. When citizens focused on these specific targets, they were less fatalistic and thought that preventive action would be helpful. Similar findings were obtained by Flynn, Slovic, Mertz, and Carlisle (1999). Likewise, when citizens' attention is shifted from the awe-inspiring aspects of the earthquake to specific groups and concrete actions, their outcome expectancy increases (Charleson, 1991; Smith, 1993).

However, there are limits to how much risk messages can produce these positive effects. People with a strong external locus of control believe that damage cannot be prevented, even where damage is demonstrably exceptional (McClure et al., 1999). They cannot see that the damage often reflects something about the damaged building. In such extreme cases, it is necessary to employ other motivational strategies and legislative requirements. These principles also apply with cultures and ethnic groups that have a more fatalistic orientation (Perry et al., 1981).

Interpreting the Causes of Loss and Damage

The concept of fatalism also relates to attribution theory, a framework that examines people's explanations of different outcomes. Attributions for damage reflect the complexity of people's causal models about hazards (cf., Bostrom et al., 1992; McClure et al., 1999). While expert models might include earthquake magnitude and proximity, soil type, building design, and so on, ordinary people commonly have relatively simple models of earthquakes. They typically perceive earthquakes as catastrophic events that inevitably produce major damage, regardless of what people do (Turner et al., 1986). They are less aware of factors that mediate the effects of earthquakes, and therefore see the outcomes as less controllable.

This view was reiterated by tsunami focus group participants. Being presented with information they found inadequate (i.e., to explain complex hazard consequences and their relationship with mitigation measures) made it more difficult both to form expectations about what happens when a tsunami strikes and to conceptualize the need for and relevance of protective measures. Being overwhelmed increased participant apathy, reducing the likelihood of their preparing. The participants believed that education that focused more on explaining how particular actions would mitigate specific consequences would motivate residents to prepare for tsunamis.

Education programs can reduce fatalism by explicitly elucidating the complex nature of natural hazards and their effects, and explaining how specific preparation measures reduce damage (e.g., earthquake damage is mediated by factors such as building construction). McClure et al. (1999) in a study of the relationship between peoples' hazard knowledge and outcome perceptions retrospectively showed that the complexity of people's models of earthquakes was positively related to their judgment that damage could be prevented. People made judgments about damage that was either distinctive (only one house in a street collapses) or widespread (all houses in a street collapse). Complexity was measured as the number of causes cited in open-ended explanations of the damage. With distinctive damage, people with simple and complex models judged the damage equally preventable. However, when damage was widespread, as predicted, people with simple models of earthquakes believed that there was little that could have been done about it, whereas people with complex models believed that damage could have been be reduced.

Hurnen and McClure (1997) examined whether citizens' knowledge of actions that mitigate earthquake damage (e.g., fastening walls to foundations with anchoring bolts) predicted their judgments of preventability. They found that participants with high earthquake knowledge were more prepared for earthquakes. Subsequently, each item in the earthquake knowledge scale was explained to participants, to clarify why each action influenced earthquake damage. Preventability judgments obtained before and after this procedure showed that participants judged the damage to be more preventable. McClure et al. (1999) and McClure et al. (2001) found that communication that emphasized the distinctiveness of earthquake damage more effective than that portraying widespread damage. In fact, warnings that portray severe, widespread damage in earthquakes will increase fatalism.

One source of information consistently implicated in conveying information in this way is the media.

Media Influences on Outcome Expectancy

Other critical attributions that influence preparing are the effect of different causal agents (consensus information) on other occasions (consistency information). With regards to these attributions, media coverage plays a crucial role. Most media reports of earthquakes ignore how different types of buildings perform, and provide little consensus and consistency information (Gaddy & Tanjong, 1987). McClure et al. (2001) presented scenarios that described a building that was damaged in a recent earthquake and stated how similar buildings had performed in other earthquakes. When the participants were subsequently presented with pictures of similar buildings that were badly damaged in other earthquakes, they attributed damage to the building's design. In contrast, when they were shown pictures with similar buildings that stood up well in other earthquakes, they attributed damage more to the earthquake. The finding that judgments about earthquake damage are affected by knowing how the same type of building behaves in other earthquakes might seem obvious to engineers and other experts. However, the uninformed fatalistic attitude of nonexperts tends to ignore these distinctions and many people assume that big earthquakes produce widespread devastation regardless of the design of structures. Unfortunately, media reporting tends to reinforce this impression.

Media coverage that emphasizes devastation reinforces peoples' belief that disasters are too catastrophic for personal action to be effective (Keinan, Sadeh & Rosen, 2003; Lopes, 1992), reducing outcome expectancy. When disaster occurs, news media usually portray scenes where the greatest damage has occurred (Gaddy & Tanjong, 1987; Hilton, Mathes, & Trabasso, 1992; Hiroi, Mikami, & Miyata, 1985), accentuating the magnitude and severity of damage. This point is illustrated by comments from a journalist arriving in Kobe after the major 1995 earthquake. "I was amazed how much of Kobe was still there. . . . I mean, I had watched hours and hours of TV in America about this earthquake, and I had no idea that there were houses and tall buildings still standing all over the city" (*International Herald Tribune,* February 2, 1995, p. 2).

Media could play a more positive role by reporting the differing performance of different types of buildings, and providing consensus and consistency information. Cowan et al. (2002) compared news reports written immediately after the 1995 Kobe earthquake with articles written a year later ("anniversary" articles). Reports written immediately after the earthquake emphasized widespread damage using headings such as: "Earthquake ravages Kobe." Those written a year later, however, focused on contrasts between the design of damaged and undamaged buildings and the lessons that could be learned from the earthquake, using headings like: "Lessons from Kobe." When these two types of reports were presented to two groups of participants (with all references to Kobe removed), the "anniversary" reports produced more controllable attributions for the earthquake damage than the "day after" reports. The more analytical articles lead to more adaptive views of earthquakes than the "catastrophe" reports written immediately after an earthquake. Consequently, the "generalized damage" information conveyed by news media can increase fatalism and lead people to attribute earthquake damage to uncontrollable causes. However, fatalism can be reduced if news media show that damage is distinctive, and if they portray scenes where buildings stand firm because of their good construction. Reports like the "anniversary" articles could be included in educational programs.

The above discussion suggests that outcome expectancy beliefs can be enhanced by presenting scenarios that increase the complexity of peoples' hazard models, demonstrating that hazard intensity and the damage they create are unevenly distributed and, with regard to damage, that loss is a function of the interaction between choices people can make (e.g., securing houses to their foundation, securing chimneys, water heaters and tall furniture) and hazard activity (e.g., shaking intensity). Demonstrating the reality of avoidable losses and how people can exercise control over these interactions increases outcome expectancy. Engendering a belief in the effectiveness of mitigation measures is important but not sufficient to ensure the formation of intentions to adopt protective measures.

Personal Competencies

If people confer upon the proposed protective measures a capacity to reduce risk, whether they progress to forming intentions is a function of their beliefs in their competence to adopt and/or implement them. Factors implicated in informing this role include coping style and self-efficacy judgments (Duval & Mullilis, 1999; Paton et al., 2005). An important aspect of coping style is peoples' capacity for problem solving and their ability to actively confront challenges. Self-efficacy has other implications for protective actions designed to mitigate the consequences of infrequently occurring hazards. The number and quality of action plans, and the effort and perseverance invested in risk reduction behaviors, is strongly dependent on one's self-efficacy judgments (Bennett & Murphy, 1997). Personal competencies that increase the likelihood of sustained action are especially important given the infrequency of the hazards people are being encouraged to prepare for.

If people are motivated to prepare, have high outcome expectancy, and are predisposed to confront problems, they are more likely to form intentions to prepare. However, the relationship between intentions to prepare and actual preparing can be moderated by several factors. These factors are considered in the next section.

STAGE THREE: CONVERTING INTENTION TO PREPAREDNESS

The formation of intention to adopt protective measures does not guarantee their conversion into action. This issue is discussed here by drawing on research on two factors that have been implicated in the process of converting intentions into preparedness; the time frame within which people estimate that the next hazard event will occur, and their level of trust in the sources of information.

Time Until Next Hazard Event

The likelihood of preparing is higher amongst those who believed that the next damaging hazard impact will occur within 12 months, and drops rapidly in those who anticipated it not occurring for several years (Paton et al., 2005). The importance of understanding this difference derives from the finding that very few people believe that a damaging hazard will occur within 12 months. For example, Paton et al (2005) found that only 6 percent of respondents believed that a damaging earthquake could occur within the next 12 months, and

Gregg et al. (2004) found that only 5 percent of residents in an area at high risk for lava flows believed it could occur within the next year. This perception could be counteracted by complementing the 'not if but when' message in risk communication with one advocating a "sooner rather than later" message.

Beliefs regarding timing could be influenced by how risk information is presented. The earthquake focus group had trouble interpreting what was meant by a 10-year or 50-year event, with this data typically being interpreted as a literal indication of when the next event will occur rather than as a statement of probability describing likelihood of occurrence on an annual basis. This would reinforce the presence of the beliefs reported in the previous paragraph regarding the need for action. If it is believed that events will not occur until some point in the more distant future, conversion of intention to action may be muted.

Trust

The adoption of protective measures is more likely when people trust the information source. The importance of trust in sources of information was endorsed by the tsunami and earthquake focus groups. The tsunami focus group described the source of their diminishing trust as stemming from the belief that civic and real estate agencies withheld information from residents because they placed concern for the impact on economic and business activity above residents' safety. Participants also believed that councils withheld information about tsunami hazards to minimize the possibility of their being criticized for what they have done, or not done, to manage the attendant risk. Trust can also be affected by citizens' beliefs that expenditure on hazard mitigation by civic agencies is unnecessary (Paton et al., 2001). Levels of trust can be affected by beliefs that the information provided is incomplete or inconsistent with views developed from peoples' independent search for information (e.g., using the internet, talking with other residents). These examples illustrate the perils of failing to engage community members in discussion about hazards and what to do about them.

Equity and fairness regarding the distribution of risk throughout different sectors of the community and members' involvement in decision making about acceptable levels of risk and risk reduction underpin community members' trust in civic sources (Lasker, 2004; Paton & Bishop, 1996). Syme et al. (1992) demonstrated that engaging community members about hazards with potentially devastating consequences significantly influenced their commitment to take responsibility for their own safety and to trust the source of information. By involving community members in decision making about risk and risk management, citizens were less inclined to want to "scapegoat" those responsible for emergency planning. This appeared to be due to greater community knowledge of the trade-offs involved in creating safer environments. Thus, levels of trust, satisfaction with communication, risk acceptance, and collective commitment to confront hazard consequences are increased by community engagement based on procedural justice principles.

CONCLUSION

The adoption of protective measures involves a complex reasoning process within which people make a series of decisions as they negotiate the relationship between them, environmental hazards, and the resources and actions required to protect themselves. Under these circumstances, facilitating preparing requires more than just making information available to people. It is crucial to provide information that meets the needs of people, that makes sense to people, and that assists their decision making in a context described by the interaction between information from scientific and civic sources and the psychological, social, cultural characteristics that frame peoples' needs, expectations, and beliefs. These relationships must be understood and accommodated in strategies designed to encourage the adoption of protective measures.

Given the sequential nature of the preparedness process, the effectiveness of intervention will be enhanced by using it as a guide to assist people to address issues about which decisions must be made (e.g., to discuss issues with others in their community, to accept risk, believe in the efficacy of mitigation measures, etc.) as they negotiate their relationship with a hazardous environment. It is also important that these strategies actively engage community members in ways that assist their making each decision. This would entail matching the decision support offered to the specific decisions required in each phase. For example, intervention to change outcome expectancy could involve presenting information that counters fatalism by illustrating how specific actions can mitigate risk from certain hazard effects. A different approach would be required to encourage more discussion within a community. Similarly, promoting change in core competencies such as self-efficacy and action coping will involve citizens in identifying and resolving problems in their community.

This is an area in which several interesting issues remain to be explored. This chapter focused on the adoption of protective actions. Future work must examine the possibility that "not preparing" represents the outcome of a discrete reasoning process (Paton et al., 2005) whose influence may have to be counteracted prior to attempting to encourage the adoption of protective measures. Additional work is also required to determine whether similar processes influence tasks with different protective functions. For example, do similar mechanisms underpin decisions to adopt protective (e.g., securing furniture and fittings, securing roofs to houses and houses to foundations, installing waterproof cladding) and self-reliance (e.g., storing food and water, preparing household emergency plans) measures? The possibility of their being influenced by different factors is supported by observations that the former tend to be less frequently endorsed by respondents than the latter. Given that protective measures will influence whether people survive the impact (e.g., if the house and its furniture is inadequately secured occupants may be killed or injured) they may not be in a position to capitalize on their self-reliance resources, this issue should be given a prominent place in future research agenda on preparedness. It is also important to audit preparedness to ensure that the data available is representative of actual preparedness behavior.

The effort expended on this task is important. The foundation of adaptive capacity is having the resources available to facilitate coping with the temporary disruption associated with the immediate impact of hazard activity and the beliefs and psychological competencies necessary to use them to confront the consequences of hazard activity. The adoption of protective measures and the competencies to use them are complimentary (Paton et al., 2001). While the social and psychological factors and competencies described in this chapter do increase the likelihood that people adopt essential protective measures, they also fulfill another function. They have a key role in predicting people's ability to actively and constructively confront and cope with adverse experiences and disruption to their lives posed by hazard activity. This role makes these factors important components of adaptive capacity.

REFERENCES

Abramson, L.Y., Seligman, M.E.P., & Teasdale, J.A. (1978). Learned helplessness in humans: Critique and reformulation. *Journal of Abnormal Psychology, 87,* 49–74.

Adams J. (1995) Risk, UCL Press, London.

Bagozzi, R.P.& Dabholar, P.A. (2000). Discursive psychology: An alternative conceptual foundation to Means-End Chain Theory. *Psychology & Marketing, 17,* 535–586.

Baumann, D.D., & Sims, J.H. (1978). Flood insurance: Some determinants of adoption. *Economic Geography, 54,* 189–196.

Bennett, P. & Murphy, S. (1997). *Psychology and health promotion.* Buckingham, Open University Press.

Bishop, B., Paton, D., Syme, G., & Nancarrow, B (2000). Coping with environmental degradation: Salination as a community stressor. *Network, 12,* 1–15.

Blumer, H. (1969). *Symbolic interactionism: Perspective and method.* Englewood Cliffs, NJ: Prentice-Hall.

Bostrom, A., Fischhoff, B. & Morgan, M.G. (1992). Characterizing mental models of hazardous processes: A methodology and an application to radon. *Journal of Social Issues, 48,* 85–100.

Bowers, B. (1988). Grounded theory. In B. Sarter (Ed.), *Paths to knowledge: Innovative research methods for nursing* (pp. 33–59). New York: National League for Nursing.

Charleson, A.W. (1991). Mitigation of Earthquake damage to household chattels and light office equipment. *Proceedings of the Pacific Conference on Earthquake Engineering, New Zealand, 1991,* 281–290.

Charleson, A.W., Cook, B. & Bowering, G. (2003). *Assessing and increasing the level of earthquake preparedness in Wellington homes.* Proceedings of the 7th Pacific Conference on Earthquake Engineering. Wellington, New Zealand Society for Earthquake Engineering.

Conner; M., Povey, R., Sparks, P., James, R. & Shepherd, R. (2003). Moderating role of attitudinal ambivalence within the theory of planned behaviour. *The British Journal of Social Psychology, 42,* 75–94.

Cowan, J., McClure, J., & Wilson, M. (2002). What a difference a year makes: How immediate and anniversary media reports influence judgments about earthquake. *Asian Journal of Social Psychology, 5,* 169–185.

Dalton, J.H., Elias, M.J. & Wandersman, A. (2005). *Community psychology.* Belmont, CA: Wadsworth

Denzin, N. K. (1992). *Symbolic interactionism and cultural studies: The politics of interpretation.* Oxford: Blackwell.

Dow, K & Cutter, S.L. (2000). Public orders and personal opinions: household strategies for hurricane risk assessment. *Environmental Hazards, 2,* 143–155.

Duval, T.S. & Mulilis, J.P. (1999). A person-relative to event (PrE) approach to negative threat appeals and earthquake preparedness: A field study. *Journal of Applied Social Psychology, 29,* 495–516.

Farley, J.E., Barlow, H.D., Finkelstein, M.S., & Riley, L. (1993). Earthquake hysteria, before and after: A survey and follow-up on public response to the Browning forecast. *International Journal of Mass Emergencies and Disasters, 11,* 305–322.

Flynn, J., Slovic, P., Mertz, C. K., & Carlisle, C. (1999). Public support for earthquake risk mitigation in Portland, Oregon. *Risk Analysis, 19,* 205–217.

Gaddy, G.D., & Tanjong, E. (1987). Earthquake coverage by the Western Press. *Journal of Communication, 36,* 105–112.

Garcia, E.M. (1989). Earthquake preparedness in California: A survey of Irvine residents. *Urban Resources, 5,* 15–19.

Gregg, C., Houghton, B., Paton, D., Swanson, D.A., & Johnston, D. (2004). Community preparedness for lava flows from Mauna Loa and Hualalai volcanoes, Kona, Hawaii. *Bulleton of Volcanology, 66,* 531–540.

Grothmann, T. & Reussweig, F. (in press) People at risk of flooding: Why some residents take precautionary actions while others don't. *Natural Hazards.*

Hardin, C.D. & Higgins, E.T. (1996). Shared reality: How social verification makes the subjective objective. In R.M. Sorrentino & E.T. Higgins (Eds) *Motivation & cognition, Volume 3, The interpersonal context.* New York: Guildford Press.

Hilton, D.J., Mathes, R.H., & Trabasso, T.R. (1992). The study of causal explanation in natural language: Analyzing reports of the Challenger disaster in The New York Times. In M.L. McLaughlan, M.J. Cody, & S.J. Read (Eds.) *Explaining one's self to others* (pp. 41–59) Hillsdale, NJ: Erlbaum.

Hilton, D.J., & Slugoski, B.R. (1986). Knowledge-based causal attribution. The abnormal conditions focus model. *Psychological Review, 93,* 75–88.

Hiroi, O., Mikami, S., & Miyata, K. (1985). A study of mass media reporting in emergencies. *International Journal of Mass Emergencies, 3,* 21–49.

Hurnen, F. & McClure, J.L. (1997). The effect of increased earthquake knowledge on perceived preventability of earthquake damage. *Australasian Journal of Disaster and Trauma Studies, 3,* 1–10.

Johnston, D., Paton, D, Crawford, G., Ronan, K., Houghton, B. & Bürgelt, P.T. (2005). Measuring tsunami preparedness in coastal Washington, United States. *Natural Hazards, 35,* 173–184.

Keinan, G., Sadeh, A. & Rosen, S. (2003). Attitudes and reactions to media coverage of terrorist acts. *Journal of Community Psychology, 31,* 149–165.

Lamontaigne, M. & La Rochelle, S. (2000). Earth scientists can help people who fear earthquakes. *Seismological Research Letters, 70,* 1–4.

Lasker, R.D. (2004.) *Redefining readiness: Terrorism planning through the eyes of the public.* New York, NY: The New York Academy of Medicine.

Lindell, M. K., & Perry, R.W. (2000). Household adjustment to earthquake hazard. *Environment and Behavior, 32,* 461–501.

Lindell, M.K. & Whitney, D.J., 2000. Correlates of household seismic hazard adjustment adoption. *Risk Analysis, 20,* 13–25.

Lopes, R. (1992). *Public Perception of Disaster Preparedness Presentations Using Disaster Images.* Washington, DC.: The American Red Cross.

Lopes, R. (2000, February). *Community disaster education.* Proceedings of the Planning for Earthquakes in New Zealand Conference, IRL Conference Centre, Gracefield, Lower Hutt: Insitute of Geological and Nuclear Sciences.

McClure, J.L. (1985). The social parameter of "Learned" Helplessness: Its recognition and implications. *Journal of Personality and Social Psychology, 48,* 1534–1539.

McClure, J.L., Allen, M., & Walkey, F.H. (2001). Countering fatalism; Causal information in news reports affects judgments about earthquake damage. *Basic and Applied Social Psychology, 23,* 109–121.

McClure, J.L., Walkey, F.H. & Allen, M. (1999). When earthquake damage is seen as preventable: Attributions, locus of control, and attitudes to risk. *Applied Psychology: An International Review, 48,* 239–256.

McIvor, D. & Paton, D. (in prep). Intention to prepare for natural hazards: The role of attitudes and subjective norms. *Disaster Prevention and Management.*

Mileti, D.S. & Darlington, J.D. (1995). Societal response to revised earthquake probabilities in the San Francisco Bay area. *International Journal of Mass Emergencies and Disasters, 13,* 119–145.

Paton, D. (2000). Emergency Planning: Integrating community development, community resilience and hazard mitigation. *Journal of the American Society of Professional Emergency Managers, 7,* 109–118.

Paton, D., (2003). Disaster Preparedness: A social-cognitive perspective. *Disaster Prevention and Management, 12,* 210–216.

Paton & Burgelt (2005, October). Living with bushfire risk: Residents accounts of their bushfire preparedness behaviour. AFAC/Bushfire CRC Conference, Auckland, New Zealand.

Paton, D., & Johnston, D. (2001). Disasters and communities: Vulnerability, resilience, and preparedness. *Disaster Prevention and Management, 10,* 270–277.

Perry, R., Lindell, M., & Greene, M. (1981). *Evacuation planning in emergency management.* Lexington, MA: Heath-Lexington.

Paton, D. & Bishop B. (1996). Disasters and communities: Promoting psychosocial well-being. In D. Paton and N. Long (eds) *Psychological aspects of disaster: Impact, coping, and intervention.* Palmerston North, Dunmore Press.

Paton, D., Johnston, D., Bebbington, M., Lai, C-D, & Houghton, B. (2001). Direct and vicarious experience of volcanic hazards: Implications for risk perception and adjustment adoption. *Australian Journal of Emergency Management, 15,* 58–63.

Paton, Kelly, Bürgelt & Doherty (in press). Preparing for Bushfires: Understanding intentions. *Disaster Prevention and Management.*

Paton, D., Millar, M., & Johnston, D. (2001). Community Resilience to Volcanic Hazard Consequences. *Natural Hazards, 24,* 157–169.

Paton, D., Smith, L.M., & Johnston, D. (2005). When good intentions turn bad: Promoting natural hazard preparedness. *Australian Journal of Emergency Management, 20,* 25–30.

Simpson-Housley, P. & Bradshaw, P. (1978). Personality and the perception of earthquake hazard. *Australian Geographical Studies, 16,* 65–77.

Sims, J.H. & Baumann, D.D. (1972). The tornado threat: Coping styles of the North and South. *Science, 176,* 1386–1392.

Smith, K. (1993). *Environmental hazards: Assessing risk and reducing disaster.* London: Routledge.

Strickland, B.R. (1989). Internal-external control expectancies: From contingency to creativity. *American Psychologist, 44,* 1–12.

Syme, G. J., Bishop, B.J. & Milich, D. (1992). Public involvement and dam safety criteria: Towards a definition of informed consent. *ANCOLD Bulletin, 92,* 12–15.

Turner, R.H., Nigg, J.M., & Paz, D.H. (1986). *Waiting for disaster: Earthquake watch in California.* Los Angeles: University of California Press.

Chapter 8

WEATHERING THE STORM: WOMEN'S PREPAREDNESS AS A FORM OF RESILIENCE TO WEATHER-RELATED HAZARDS IN NORTHERN AUSTRALIA[1]

ALISON COTTRELL

INTRODUCTION

This chapter goes some way to meet the challenge issued by Weichselgartner and Obersteiner (2002) to resist seeing people as "passive victims" of hazards, to shift the focus from vulnerability to resilience, and to focus on adaptive capacities already evident in communities. The research was conducted on the assumption that there would be women who had adaptive strategies for dealing with wet season hazards in northern Australia. This is in accordance with the views of Morrow and Phillips (1999) and Fordham (1999) that women's experiences are in some ways unique and embedded with varying levels of vulnerability but also with differences in capacities to respond and be resilient. It was decided to specifically approach women with dependents because we assumed that their responsibilities would make them more aware of the types of strategies that were necessary to deal with the natural hazard. As well, we recognized that women are still those mainly responsible for caring for the young and the aged (Poole, 2005; Poole & Issacs, 1997). By identifying the different strate-

1. This research was largely funded by and reported to Emergency Management Australia as Project 13/2002.

gies that women used then this information could be passed on to other women, particularly newcomers to an area who may have little experience of the local hazards.

CONDUCTING THE RESEARCH

A grounded theory approach was taken to the research, using qualitative research methods (Berg, 2001; Ezzy, 2002; Rice & Ezzy, 1999; Strauss & Corbin, 1994). Grounded theory uses an inductive approach to research, developing concepts and themes from the research as it progresses rather than presupposing outcomes which might inhibit new findings.

Originally, it was proposed to use only focus group discussions as the means of obtaining data. This proved somewhat problematic, lack of interest being the main issue. In itself, this would seem to confirm views that people tend to view wet season hazards as not particularly important. The final data collection methods included focus group discussions, telephone surveys and individual interviews.

Sampling was opportunistic, depending on responses to advertisements and referrals from other people in the community concerned. The discussions focused on exploring whether women perceived the wet season to be a problem, how they prepared for it, what issues arose for caring for dependents and what advice they would recommend for newcomers to their region. Theme analysis was then undertaken to identify key issues arising from the material.

For the purposes of this discussion, three main integrative themes arise: cultural influences, social networks, and personal style. It is important to be mindful that these are somewhat arbitrary categories and the points at which each begins and ends are rather fuzzy. Most women were interviewed about their perspectives on their own experience, but there were several interviews with women who have responsibilities for others in formal settings outside the family who provided a broader perspective.

Culture

There is little doubt that location is an important part of the culture of dealing with natural hazards (Blaikie, Cannon, Davis, & Wisner,

1994; Fordham, 1999; Hewitt, 1997). Women living in Northern Australia are regularly confronted with the potential hazard of heavy rainfall, including cyclonic conditions, which may result in their families being isolated from basic services. Three different types of locations were surveyed. Differences between large metropolitan areas (Townsville and Thuringowa), regional towns (Broome and Port Hedland) and remote towns (Normanton, Kurumba and Giru) (see Figure 8.1) resulted in marked differences in how women needed to plan for the rainy season. Beyond that, differences that reflected more localized social or cultural views were also present.

In the large urban center of Townsville/Thuringowa the expectation of women was that services and supplies would be restored within about three days after a major weather event that led to cyclones or flooding. In the smaller centers there was the expectation that one could be without supplies for a little longer because they would need to come in from elsewhere. In the very small centers, the expectation was that the individual households needed to be well prepared for the wet season. In general, women in remoter areas prepared for the wet season by starting to stockpile essential items on a gradual basis from November or December. Some women in the larger metropolitan cen-

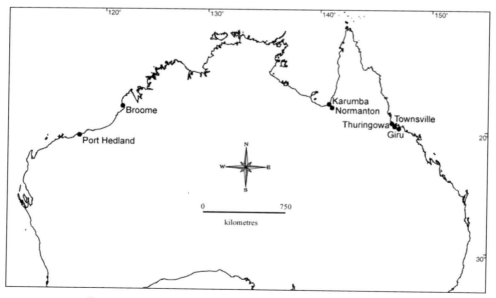

Figure 8.1. Map of Locations Surveyed in Northern Australia.

ters did so as well.

It is not surprising to find that women in the larger cities expect that power and water supplies will be resumed after approximately three days. This reflects messages received from emergency services advising them to have food, water and other necessities such as medicines, personal and children's needs to last for at least three days.

In remoter areas, people are reliant on supplies arriving by long-haul trucks or barges, both of which are vulnerable to flooding and/or high wind conditions. The size of the commercial enterprises supplying these localities also creates limitations because they can only afford, financially and in terms of space, to stock so much. Enarson and Morrow (1998) and Fordham (1999) remind us that localities and communities should not be viewed as homogenous and this is the case here. At remoter locations women with the capacity to do so would travel to the nearest major center to stock up on goods to last the three to five months of the wet season. This clearly required them to have the financial capacity to do so. The costs of grocery and pharmacy supplies could easily amount to two or three thousand dollars for that time frame. In addition, there is often a need for generators as back-up electricity supply, particularly for frozen goods.

Women without that economic capacity are reliant on what is available at the local store. The shopkeepers may or may not have strategies to prevent some customers overbuying to the detriment of others. In at least one small town, the shopkeeper kept aside supplies of milk and bread for women with children.

In remoter areas, women would not "dream" of getting into a car without drinking water, snacks for the children to eat, insect repellant and something for the children to keep them occupied should they get stuck between creeks or the vehicle breaks down. Other women mentioned that since the main highways have been much improved, they and/or others have become complacent about taking provisions when traveling.

In another town, there is evidence of the impact of structural inequality (Altman, 2004; Altman & Hunter, 2003; Altman & Sanders, 2002; Australian Bureau of Statistics, 2004) that impacts strongly on capacity for resilience—indigenous women living in what are described as Aboriginal towns, or town camps or Aboriginal communities (Monaghan) who also experience varied levels of vulnerability and capacities for resilience. In the case of town camps (sometimes referred to as fringe-dwellers) women are often in the situation of having to provide for their families in very difficult circumstances. They have insubstantial housing, have no access to electricity, and often limited access to reticulated water. Breakfast and school lunches are purchased in the morning before school, then afternoon teas and the evening meal are purchased after school. Their low incomes are exacerbated by the need to purchase food in small amounts which builds in a much higher unit cost for food for these women and their families. If the men of the household are paid, often their work will finish by early December before the Christmas holidays and will not resume until late January. This means they have a large payout which is not usually metered out over the time they are not working, it is usually spent in a short period of time. Women have to manage their households with this precarious financial situation. This is also the time of the wet season.

Another group of Aboriginal women living in a community on their traditional lands (country) at one time had to be evacuated because of a cyclone. They were evacuated to a tent city in the nearest large town where they stayed for six weeks. This situation was very distressing for them. The women had to take on the lifestyle of fringe-dwellers when they were used to having their own homes, they were off their country, their husbands and children were being blamed for every misdemeanor that happened in the town, and they just wanted to get home. This led to recommendations for cyclone resilient structures being built on the community lands so people would not have to leave again. There really is a need to better understand resilience in indigenous communities. As an outsider viewing the situation, the fact that people actually survive these situations indicates a startling level of vulnerability, but also of resilience (Fothergill, 1998).

Another example of the need for local sensitivity is from the same region but part of other research (Cottrell, Cunliffe, King, & Anderson-Berry, 2001). An indigenous woman who managed the Home and Community Care Program in a remote Aboriginal Community was charged with the task of, among other things, providing meals for the elderly in her area (indigenous and non-indigenous). Provisioning for this task faced her with two difficulties. The first was actually having the space to store food and the other was the issue of the pressure of social obligations, preventing relatives making culturally appropriate requests for food. The way she managed this was to only have two weeks supply of food available. On this basis she felt able to refuse requests by people other than the elderly and meet the requirements of the job. She clearly recognized that supplies would be vulnerable during the wet season, but relied on the fact that the Community Council would need to have food brought in by helicopter anyway because the region was very quickly isolated by rainfall. This was an eminently pragmatic way to operate under the circumstances.

The culture of communities also seemed to influence the receptiveness of newcomers to the area which had an impact on women's capacity to develop support networks. As Fordham (1999) suggests, the notion of community is problematic and this research reinforces the danger of assuming homogeneity and inclusiveness at the local level. In addition to these more pragmatic issues, capacity to adapt was also found to be influenced by social factors.

Social Networks

Family support was important for many women. For women without family where they lived, friends, especially women friends, were very important. For new arrivals, people at work or other parents of children at the local school were important sources of information. Over time friends could be relied upon to help. For example, in Port Hedland, many of the women were married to men who worked away from the home town in mines or out on fishing or pearling boats. As well, where some of the women lived could easily be separated by flood waters from the school which their children attended, or similarly, the children's school could be cut off from where they work. Friends, especially mothers of other children at the school were very important in making arrangements to have children picked up and housed should they be separated by flood waters. Having clear arrangements in place and good telephone communication was important. In Normanton, a woman with a child at boarding school had arrangements with friends in the city to pick up and care for the child during holiday times if weather conditions prevented her from picking up the child herself. Another woman in Broome who often worked away herself, and had recently divorced, had friends check on her home, especially if there was a power outage or heavy rain and organized for them to advise her of repairs or damage.

Women with certain work-related roles were also relied upon by others. Nurses often found themselves as support in emergency situations in their locality and most simply saw this as an extension of their work and their living in a community. Some women who worked as nurses also had to live with the possibility of being called into work or being isolated from their families at work if the need arose. This resulted in some of them feeling very uncomfortable about the vulnerability of their own families and very much needed to rely on family and friends to help care for their children.

For some women, their support networks included formal support agencies such as child care centers, a women's refuge, a community "drop-in" center, and a support group for people with disabilities. The types of support these people can provide are limited, but can be very useful. For example, the drop-in center also offers help sessions for young, inexperienced mothers on parenting, how to manage their finances, household strategies and so on and included in that is preparations for the wet season, based on guidelines from emergency services.

The people who organize the support group for a disabled group were unaware of the information available from government emergency services specific to their interest groups. However, they had taken it upon themselves to amass the information necessary to prompt women in particular to be mindful of their needs in the event of flooding, cyclones and other emergencies. In this case, the recommendations were eminently practical and broadly applicable. It was framed in terms of needing to be prepared for a number of eventualities such as having the flu or some other minor illness which prevented them from getting out of the house or apartment for a few days. It was also stressed that people with disabilities really did need to maintain contacts with their families and friends to reduce their vulnerability. For many people with disability, the physical is often linked with mental problems due to acquired brain injuries. The women themselves also stressed the importance of family support.

For women with roles in other support agencies such as childcare and women's refuges there were limitations to the support they could provide. For some women, the agency was their only link with information relevant to a hazard situation. Because of the trust relationships that develop over time, the agency manager is seen as a reliable source of information, but the agency cannot provide shelter or refuge in a hazard situation because they are required by law to close operations. This can cause levels of anxiety for the agency manager who is torn between providing support for clients, meeting employees' needs, meeting statutory obligations and meeting the needs of her own family.

In Kurumba, the local police had a system whereby those who were leaving town on holidays let the police know so that if any issues arose they would definitely know who may or may not be missing. Apart from the Police who are very much linked in with emergency service provision, the role of community support groups in assisting members of their communities could be better utilized (Fordham, 1999).

Women who were renting their homes indicated that they closely observed which houses were flooded in the area so that they knew not to rent them and to warn off friends from renting. Another type of network used by some women is the internet. The Australian Bureau of Meteorology (BoM) has a website that can be consulted for advice on river heights and weather forecasts. Women with access to the internet reported using the website regularly during the wet season. If they lived in remote areas, they would check whether the river heights were going up or down to make decisions on optional travel. If they had medical appointments which couldn't be changed they would plan the travel on the basis of needing to prepare for someone to care for the children for longer if they could not get home on time. At the town of Giru, the weather reports on the radio concentrate on coastal conditions whereas flood waters for their town primarily come from a catchment 100 kilometers to the west. They log in to the BoM website to check the weather details they need. Then they use local networks to pass on the information to other women. In the city, the women reported that reliance tended to be on radio and the men of the household tended to consult the internet once a cyclone warning had been issued.

It is circumstances such as these that highlight the importance of networks. A similar role for networks as a feature of resilience was identified by Fordham (1999). Fordham concluded that it is important not to generalize too far in assuming the availability of those networks, or the form they may take. It may well be that capacity to network is also linked to personal attributes.

Personal Attributes

Family influence also contributed to perceptions of the need for preparedness. Some women reported a family ethos of being prepared.
Irrespective of where women lived, personal experience was considered to be one of the most important aspects of being prepared for and
being able to deal with the wet season hazards. However, the general
view was that the longer the time since an event, the more complacent
people were becoming and the less prepared. A clear example of this
was one woman who had grown up in Townsville, married and moved
to a remote town where she managed a property and was the local
hairdresser. After divorce, she returned to Townsville and became a
teacher. Her experience of Cyclone Althea in 1971 in Townsville as a
young mother she considered was very instructive. The house she
lived in was not structurally sound so she moved in with her mother.
While growing up her mother had taught her to be prepared for the
wet season and cyclones, but she felt that living in a remote area made
her, by necessity, much more independent. On returning to live in
Townsville, now that she does not have children at home and now that
services are more readily restored and road infrastructure is better she
feels that she and others are becoming more complacent about preparing for wet season hazards.

Although living in remoter areas encourages women to stockpile the
necessities, it is also a matter of personal household management style.
In the larger urban areas, women reported a variety of strategies with
stockpiling. Some women like to have a highly organized pantry
where goods were rotated on a regular basis, others tended to have the
necessities on hand but not in one place. In some cases this tended to
be belief rather than practice, especially if it was a long time since a
cyclone warning. Other women preferred to maintain lean pantries to
avoid wastage, and viewed storage of many items as unwise, particularly if children were at an age that food preferences changed a lot.
Some women preferred to not keep much in the way of frozen goods
during this time while others would freeze plastic containers filled with
water to keep goods frozen over the couple of days they might be without electricity.

The women also indicated that there were items particular to the
ways of their household that they saw as essentials. For some it was felt
necessary to stockpile large amounts of toilet paper. For others it was

soap powder. Some women stressed the need to fill the bath with water on receiving a cyclone warning, while others purchased drinking water on a regular basis so didn't feel the need to do this. For a group of nurses, the need to keep a very well-equipped first aid kit was essential, because they knew the neighbors would be relying on them for those kinds of needs. One nurse who had been through a cyclone indicated the need for a stock of condoms because women would run out of contraceptives if supplies were unable to get through.

Women who camped as part of family activities tended to be well-stocked with the necessary items and were also better able to deal with the vagaries of being without modern conveniences. However, several women in all locations stressed the problems of being overprepared. In the climates of northern Australia, batteries do not store well because of the heat and humidity. Even dried, tinned and aseptic packaged foods can be difficult to store in these conditions. Therefore, if women stock up too much on goods there may be wastage, which they really cannot afford. One woman laughingly said that when she first arrived in Broome she stockpiled enough goods for four camping trips, but at least it didn't go to waste.

Apart from provisioning the household, one of the most common comments by the women interviewed was the need to have things to keep the children occupied, be it for traveling, while they are rushing around after a cyclone alert has been broadcast to get better organized, or when sitting through the storm itself, or afterwards when there is no electricity and the children cannot be outside. The 'things to do' need to be independent of an electricity supply. Another issue raised in the context of the storm itself was, no matter how frightened they felt themselves, to endeavor to keep the children calm and not transmit concern.

There were also quite different approaches to the timing of starting to make preparations. Some women were very organized on a routine basis and then made checks as the wet season approaches and then more detailed checks when a cyclone alert was announced. Around early November some women started to gather together the sorts of items they felt they needed. Each time they went shopping they would include extra items that would carry them over the season. For some women, leaving things to the last minute is still a strategy, and they will wait until they believe a cyclone is imminent before taking much action.

In general, women are not waiting around for a hazard to happen, they are busy with their lives and fit in preparations for hazards when they feel the need to act. These decisions are based on prior experience, but personal attributes also seem to be important.

The case of one woman, Susan, serves to provide an example of how the three levels interlink. Susan is a nurse specializing in critical care anaesthetics. She has 3 children - 13, 10 and 4. Susan starts to shop in the first week of December, at which time she starts to add items for Christmas and the cyclone season. She gets candles early because if you leave it too late there are none left, and buys a bit more tinned food than they would usually use. In terms of personal style:

> *"Two weeks before Christmas I fill up the gas cylinders and Martin makes sure the gas light works. We get batteries for toys and emergencies. Martin watches the weather closely. When there is a potential cyclone he goes into a bit of a panic and checks stuff. We never tape the windows because you can't get it off. I seem to not worry so much. I get the photos and put them in a plastic bag, and organize my jewellery.*

> *"We ate well for the first few days getting rid of stuff. By the end we were down to 3 minute noodles. We coped though, there was enough to eat and we played games, cards. You do and eat things you don't normally. It was actually a good time, a bit like camping aside from the uncertainty of when the power is coming back on.*

> *"The power was off for a week for Cyclone Tessi, so by the end the food was getting a bit low, but we managed."*

Susan's family culture of preparedness came from her mother:

> *"My mum taught us really well. Mum would clean out the bath on a cyclone warning and then fill it up with water. As little kids we were traveling to Brisbane and were caught at Connor's Creek for a week, but Mum had brought enough in the car to see us through."*

And her father:

> *"Dad worked for NORQEB (electricity authority) so he knew that the power could be off."*

Susan made it clear that weather reports of a low pressure system in the region make her start to be more conscious of weather issues. She consciously checks the weather reports for more information in order that she would consider changing her routines to take into account the possibility of bad weather. If she thinks its not going to happen she will continue as normal. However, if she thinks it really does look like bad weather then she changes her routine to accommodate. Susan also had to balance work and family:

> *"During Cyclone Tessi I had to go to work because of an emergency operation. Martin was really mad about it. I was stuck at work until the next afternoon. I was really worried about the children in the house on their own if Martin had to go outside to check on anything. It's a big responsibility to place on young children to look after the little ones. (Her youngest was 1 at the time)."*

As her mother has aged, Susan is less able to rely on her for help and in fact needs to check on her mother to ensure she is safe. Because she lives in a city, Susan expects the electricity supply to be restored within a few days and her personal style of gradual accumulation is readily possible. It is all about minimizing disruption to daily routines (see also Finlay, 1992).

IMPLICATIONS FOR RISK MANAGEMENT

The use of qualitative methods in researching these issues has been particularly useful for highlighting the need for an integrated approach to the issue of hazards resilience. Although we do not have a clear picture of all the elements involved in resilience that contributes to sustainability of individuals their households and their communities, it is clear that disaster resilience is not a unidimensional construct. Further understanding of disaster resilience requires us to clarify how concepts such as hazards and resilience are socially constructed at various levels by communities, households and individuals. The results of this research indicate the need for risk management to approach to disaster reduction, readiness and recovery planning from a local perspective that takes into account the multifaceted nature of communities and the people within them and interaction between culture, social networks and personal attributes (Figure 8.2). This may actually involve working with a variety of people living in communities to develop a variety of strategies for risk management at the community, household and individual levels. There is a need to reinforce the real need for people to risk manage for themselves while at the same time recognizing that in the main people do have strategies to cope and that by encouraging effective networks, these strategies might be transmitted more easily.

In conclusion, the women interviewed here proved to be a rich source of information about resilience in the context of wet weather natural hazards. Risk management approaches to wet season hazards need to:

- Go beyond the generic and be tailored to suit different communities and different sub-sections of communities.
- Emphasize reference to family, friends and neighbors as support before, during and after hazardous weather events,
- Acknowledge that people may have different styles of preparation

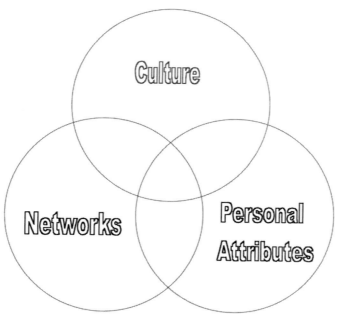

Figure 8.2. Key themes arising from the interviews with women in northern Australia.

while emphasizing the essentials,
*   Rank the resources that are recommended to people for accumulation and suggest accumulation over time so as to reduce the financial impost on households and to prevent panic buying,
*   Emphasize the need for activities to keep children occupied,
*   Discourage travel, but emphasize the need for water, food, insect repellent, and activities to keep children occupied,
* Tap into existing community organizations.

REFERENCES

Altman, J. (2004). *Economic development and indigenous Australia: Contestations over property, institutions and ideology?* Retrieved June 30, 2004 from http://www.anu.edu.au/caepr/Publications/topical/Altman_Economic_Development_2004.pdf

Altman, J. C., & Hunter, P. H. (2003). *Monitoring 'practical' reconciliation: Evidence from the reconciliation decade, 1991–2001.* Retrieved November 25, 2004 from http://www.anu.edu.au/caepr/Publications/DP/2003_DP254.pdf

Altman, J., & Sanders, W. (2002). *Submission to the house of representatives standing committee on Aboriginal and Torres Strait Islander affairs Inquiry into capacity building in indigenous communties.* Retrieved October 23, 2003, from http://www.anu.edu.au/caepr/Publications/topical/CAEPRCapacityBuildingsub.pdf

Australian Bureau of Statistics. (2004). *National Aboriginal and Torres Strait Islander social survey.* Retrieved March 3, 2005, from http://www.abs.gov.au/Ausstats/abs@.nsf/0/9ad558b6d0aed752ca256c7600018788?OpenDocumentAustralian

Berg, B., (2001). *Qualitative research methods for the social sciences.* Boston: Allyn and Bacon.

Blaikie, P., Cannon, T., Davis, I., & Wisner, B. (1994). *At risk: Natural hazards, people's vulnerability, and disasters.* London: Routledge.

Cottrell, A., Cunliffe, S., King, D., & Anderson-Berry, L. (2001). *Awareness and preparedness for natural hazards in remote communities: Bloomfield River region and Rossville.* Rockhampton: James Cook University, Centre for Disaster Studies.

Enarson, E., & Morrow, B. H. (1998). *The gendered terrain of disaster.* Miami: Laboratory for Social and Behavioral Research.

Ezzy, D. (2002). *Qualitative analysis: Practice and innovation.* Crows Nest: Allen and Unwin.

Finlay, C. C. (1992). *'Floods, they're a damned nuisance': Women's experiences during flood time and meanings for 'disaster.'* Unpublished honour's thesis, James Cook University, Australia.

Fordham, M. (1999). The intersection of gender and social class in disaster: Balancing resilience and vulnerability. *International Journal of Mass Emergencies and Disasters, 17*(1) 15–37.

Fothergill, A. (1998). 'The neglect of gender in disaster work: An overview of the literature.' In E. Enarson and B. H. Morrow (eds) Miami: Laboratory for Social and

Behavioral Research Florida International University. pp. 11–26.

Glaser, B. A., & Strauss, A. (1968). *The discovery of grounded theory.* Chicago: Aldine.

Hewitt, K. (Ed.). (1997). *Regions of risk: A geographical introduction to disasters.* Harlow: Addison Wesley Longman.

Morrow, B. H., & Phillips, B. (1999). What's gender "got to do with it"? International *Journal of Mass Emergencies and Disasters, 17*(1)5–13.

Poole, M. (Ed.). (2005). *Family: Changing families, changing Times.* Crows Nest: Allen and Unwin.

Poole, M., & Issacs, D. (1997). Caring: A gendered concept. *Womens Studies International Forum, 20*(4)529–536.

Rice, P. L., & Ezzy, D. (1999). *Qualitative research methods.* Melbourne: Oxford University Press.

Strauss, A., & Corbin, J. (1994). Grounded theory methodology: An overview. In N. K. Denzin & Y. S. Lincoln (Eds.), *Handbook of Qualitative Research* (pp. 273–285). Thousand Oaks: Sage.

Weichselgartner, J., & Obersteiner, M. (2002). Knowing sufficient and applying more: Challenges in hazards management. *Environmental Hazards, 4,* 73–77.

Chapter 9

ENCOURAGING PROTECTIVE BEHAVIORS IN COMMUNITIES

Leigh Smith

INTRODUCTION

Disasters come and go and terms like "once-in-a-lifetime" and "a-one-hundred-year-event" are used, often hyperbolically, as socially motivated indices of their severity. But for most people the Boxing Day, 2004 tsunami that caused such devastation in Asia and the coast of East Africa was a "once-in-a-lifetime" event. The scale of human loss and property loss has yet to be fully reckoned. Statements like "the worst disaster in living memory" have appeared regularly in the press and other media. Whose memory? What type of disaster— "natural" or "manmade"? The 1976 earthquake in Tangshan according to official Chinese figures killed 240,000; however, the actual figure is likely to have been closer to 750,000. Famine and pogroms in Africa have led to far more deaths and displacement in the last decade than the tsunami. The Second World War is still in the memories of some people.

I wish to make two points in relation to this opening stanza on disasters—the causes are never simple and all disasters involving people have social components. The event that precipitated the tsunami disaster was geomorphic but its consequences were a function of many human decisions. The immediate effects were a mix of individual, political and social decisions and the longer-term responses—rescue and rebuilding infrastructure and social amenities—were more transparently affected by local and international political and humanitarian decisions. In Thailand and Malaysia the economics and politics of the tourism industry created working and social living conditions that directly contributed to the death toll and physical havoc while lifestyles for the affected peasant fishing communities were partly a consequence of economic underdevelopment and partly a reflection of traditional culture. The international response to the disaster emerged in the context of media saturation and the actions of Governments and humanitarian organizations. Government aid to Indonesia has occurred in the context of Real Politics in relation to the strategic use of aid—one has only to follow the discussions on debt suspension to see this. The Indonesian Government was in a clear quandary in relation to letting foreign (particularly Australian and American) troops operate in the territory of Aceh where they were attempting to suppress civil unrest. Similarly the tardiness of the distribution of aid among Tamils in the north of Sri Lanka has been attributed to the central government's involvement with the civil war and separatists. It is also worth recognizing that some companies and organizations will do very nicely out of the contracts that are let for reconstruction. Every cloud has a silver lining!

In this chapter I argue that *disasters are social phenomena.* Consequently, protective behaviors are acquired and actualized in social contexts. From this point of departure I shall develop the argument that behaviors that are protective for a community are not necessarily those that maximize any given individual's protection. Furthermore, several distal factors that affect the development of appropriate protective behaviors at both the community level and the individual level are supra-individual. The term "supra-individual" carries the implication that the factors are not apprehended by those who actualize the behaviors. These conditions; namely, the possibility of conflict between optimizing collective protection and optimizing individual protection, and the opacity of some distal influences on protective behaviors, have methodological and ethical consequences. The methodological consequences relate to the question of how the processes generating, sustaining and changing the peoples' behaviors can be understood and ascertained. Those who seek to put programs intended to maximize community protection must grasp the nettle of ethical decisions. From the viewpoint of the analysis presented here in order to be optimally effective such programs must involve a degree of coercion and manipulation. In what follows I outline a case for this conclusion.

HAZARD PERCEPTION

When experts and members of the general public discuss hazards and risks in the context of disasters they often talk at cross-purposes. For experts (actuaries, insurance brokers, epidemiologists, and the like) assessments are made from a technical/instrumental perspective, while for the rest of us affective and personal issues imbedded in a social context of mores and values influence our judgments. Of course, the adoption of an expert perspective is not value-free. A great deal has been written about how people (lay and expert) form their judgments and how these judgments relate to actions in the face of perceived risks. In this chapter I shall be concerned with how people's judgments are influenced by community factors and how these processes might be understood in ways that will better inform strategies to get people to adopt protective lifestyles where they are at risk of disasters precipitated by events such as earthquakes, volcanic eruptions, bushfires and epidemics.

In studying human behavior researchers are typically interested in the internal and intentional psychological causes (traits, beliefs, attitudes, moods, motives, intentions) of the actors' behaviors and the effects of past behaviors on present behaviors. In the field of Disaster Research the behaviors that are the focus include: current reactions to disaster situations (past and/or present), and the way in which previous behavior and experience affect adaptation and reaction to disasters. This includes such reactions as those classified as *protective behaviors* (van der Plight, 1996; Weinstein, 1989; Weinstein, Lyon, Rothman, & Cuite, 2000; Windle, 1999). A problem for the researcher is how to assess behaviors in a manner that facilitates modeling their role in the adaptation/reaction process (Smith, 2004). The problem for those who want to change behavior is twofold: how to identify the precursors of change and how to effect changes in them.

RISK ASSESSMENT

In the technical literature a "hazard" is the precondition for a "risk," which is the consequence (e.g., cost) of an event weighted by the probability of its occurrence. While not all outcomes of hazards are negative, "cost" is generally the focus of experts and is usually reckoned in deaths and dollars. However, for members of the lay public costs and benefits are more broadly reckoned: including–psychological, economic, and social effects on themselves and other members of their community. This broader perspective of community members partially accounts for differences in lay and expert judgments about risks. Rushefsky (1982) has also argued that even among experts different perspectives lead to disagreements over risks. While establishing objective indices of risk in terms of economic and environmental damage are necessary and valuable for planning responses to potential disasters, the emphasis in this chapter is on understanding and modeling the psychological and behavioral responses of people and communities to perceived danger and their risk in order to effect lifestyle changes. The broader construal of costs and benefits outside expert circles is a central factor in the dissonance between the goal of risk-reduction strategies and the individual and collective actions of community members.

Single-Level Component Models

Elsewhere (Smith, 2004) I described how the assessment of behavioral responses to risks construed as traits fails to capture the transpersonal influences. In that analysis I argued that behavioral responses to perceived risks cannot be modeled as internal traits and that the use of factor analysis for this purpose was based on an inappropriate metaphor. The emphasis of that chapter was on measurement and I recommended an alternative approach to measurement of inventories of response behaviors. In this chapter I intend to show how the behaviors of people can be understood as arising from the interaction of their perceptions of risks and their perceptions of the efficacy and cost of protective behaviors and how the formation of these perceptions and beliefs are contextually influenced by community and larger social factors. Without an appreciation of such contextual influences the success of change strategies will be very limited.

The concern of professionals who have to deal directly (emergency services, police, fire brigades, local government etc.), or indirectly (insurance companies, planners, etc.) with disasters is the reduction of risk. This concern has motivated the development of public safety and information programs and strategies designed to promote protective behaviors among members of the at-risk communities. Much of the information presented in these programs is actuarial estimates of the possible hazards and their consequences. However, the contention that people will change their behavior if they "know the facts" ignores the role of other personal and social factors in formation of action strategies (Paton, Smith & Johnston, 2005). Too often this misplaced faith in the efficacy of "facts" in behavioral change has formed the basis of unsuccessful attempts to have communities and individuals adopt protective behaviors and strategies against the potential negative outcomes of hazards. Facts outside their interpretive context may mean very little to the nonexpert. Fluctuations in subterranean activity that might be alarming to a seismologist may be of no consequence to the general public. Subtle technical nuances do not make grist for the mills of public decision-making and action: When well-founded probabilistic predictions do not obtain, or do so only infrequently, the advice of experts tends to be ignored or discounted (crying wolf).

The manner in which professionals disseminate information about risk can also affect how the advice is perceived and reacted to by the public. In April, 1978 Cyclone Alby came further down the coast of Western Australia than predicted and caused major damage in the capital city. The Bureau of Meteorology had not issued appropriate warnings. There followed a period of heightened warnings for what turned out to be winds of only moderate intensity. The failure of the predicted storms to eventuate led to a loss of credibility by the public in the Bureau of Meteorology. In this chapter the emphasis is on the relation among perceived risks associated with hazards, the protective behaviors people adopt, and attempts to persuade people to adopt protective behaviors

The Individual and the Community

Dake (1992) has argued that risk is socially constructed and is influenced by cultural biases and worldviews. The question we need to answer is how these influences affect the development of risk perception and interacts with other social factors and individual factors to affect protective behaviors. Joffe (2003) has questioned the theoretical adequacy of the asocial approach to an understanding of how people assess risks. For Joffe the problems lie in the metaphor of the person as an information processing machine where inputs in the form of perceptions are weighted and concatenated to form a judgment. Joffe sees two problems with this approach. First, it does not explain how and why people make the judgments they make. Second, it is based on the assumption that all or most of what is relevant to the manner people act in the face of a potential hazard is determined in their individual consciousnesses. It follows from this that attempts to change people's behaviors need to proceed from an understanding of how they come to adopt beliefs and behaviors. Knowing the relation between these states may assist to some extent in predicting what will happen in a given situation but be of little value in establishing effective protective behaviors.

It is Joffe's (2003) view that "[. . .] individuals faced with potential danger operate from a position of anxiety that motivates them to represent the danger in a specific way" (p. 62). Social Representation Theory (Flick, 1998; Moscovici, 1998; Moscovici & Duveen, 2001) provides a framework for describing the process whereby a person anchors and objectifies common sense (including the lay apprehension of risk). Anchoring involves the use of familiar symbols and metaphors to make sense of the potential risk. The repertoire of metaphors, which Joffe describes as the "trove of familiarity" (p. 64), is both constructed and employed in the public domain by such processes as the transformation of scientific discourse into media reportage. Objectification works in conjunction with anchoring by aligning the particularities of the current risk with the metaphorical attributes of the past event to which it is being linked. Therefore the messages that are used to convey dangers gain their meaning and impact through their connection with the history and collective experiences of the community. The things people have experienced in common with other members of their community form the trove of familiarity that can be called upon to effect changes in protective behaviors.[1] For example, the SARS outbreak of 2003 was limited in scope and resulted in relatively few casualties. Nonetheless, it was often portrayed in the media as directly

---

1. Not all changes will be necessary, be appropriate, or protective.

comparable with the flu pandemic of the 1920s which resulted in millions of deaths. This alignment with the effects of the pandemic affected the way SARS was perceived and the way people acted. Such connections through metaphors can profoundly affect the way we think about things. Susan Sontag (1977) in her book *Illness as metaphor* describes the consequences for cancer sufferers of the use of this disease to carry negative connotations about the subject of the metaphor. The use of "cancer" to convey the notion of insidiousness tinged with malevolence places an extra burden on people who actually have the disease. Both the subject and the object of the metaphoric comparison can be transformed.

THE SUPRA-INDIVIDUAL CONTEXT

Shinn and Toohey (2003) have identified a failure in conceptualization among those who have attempted to theorize and model behaviors in the domain of human welfare they call the *context minimization error*. This error consists in not taking account of the community context in which a person makes decisions about social change. The studies they review provide evidence for community-level factors, which are not apprehended consciously, that affect peoples' judgments and behaviors. Shinn and Toohey show how such factors can moderate the relations among individual-level factors. It follows that in attempting to change peoples' protective behaviors those responsible need to bring about a social change as well as individual changes. This is because the meaning of the behaviors has to become embedded at the community level.

In discussing the relationship between "sense of community" and "social capital," Perkins and Long (2002) have presented evidence that reveals the role of supra-individual components of these constructs in formation of social behaviors. The strong inference of their analysis of the formation of cognitions and actions is that they are subject to supra-individual influences. Many of these influences are generally not directly apprehended in individual awareness and so are not open to measurement through self-report, however, their influence can be estimated through the use of multilevel analysis when appropriate measures can be found.

The existence of supra-individual influences on individual decision making in respect of hazards suggests that any attempt to model the processes that influence the adoption of protective behaviors will fail to the extent that supra-individual processes are relevant and uncaptured in individual ratings. Attempting to cope with the poor performance of prediction models by the segmentation of the analysis of risks through a typology of hazards cannot adequately cope with the problem as it fails to capture the community, social and cultural influences that drive respondents' judgments. Elsewhere (Smith & Violanti, 2003), we have recommended the use of multilevel models for unravelling the relation between risk perceptions, the mediators of the effects, and the outcomes of being exposed to hazards. A schematic multilevel model for the adoption of protective behaviors is shown in Figure 9.1. The components of the categories of influence are not detailed, however, a description and rationale for individual-level and community-level influences is given in Smith and Violanti (2003).

A central feature of the generic model shown in Figure 9.1 is the inclusion of influences that are features of the community in which an

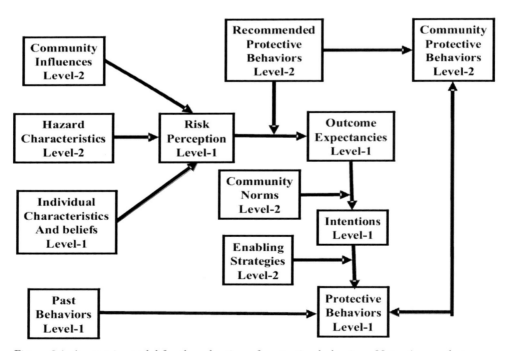

Figure 9.1. A generic model for the adoption of protective behaviors. Note: Arrows between boxes imply direct effects and arrows to arrows imply mediators.

individual operates. These influences may have direct effects on the individual's perceptions, beliefs and behaviors or may mediate the relation between them. In this context Joffe's (2003) notion of a *trove* of shared metaphors for interpreting new events is a set of level-2 influences giving meaning to events and an interpretive framework within which perceptions and intentions are formed. Thus, the trove is an indispensable resource for interpreting events while the action repertoire provides the means-end linkage. In a similar manner communities support *action repertoires* that encourage and sanction ways of behaving and these affect the development of an individual's own action repertoire. An action repertoire consists of behaviors, which may or may not have been actualized, and facilitators of behaviors. In the latter case these consist of past actions that set the conditions such that another behavior can be performed in the future. For example, it is unlikely that an individual could administer CPR to a person in an emergency unless she had untaken a course in CPR. This more than the mere banality that you need to know how to do something in order to do it. The reasons why a person would undertake a CPR course are embedded in motivation systems that derive from the community trove.

Action repertoires are in effect inventories of behaviors and their potentiators which can be hierarchically ordered in relation to their perceived appropriateness in any given situation. This hierarchical evaluation is determined by two considerations: The likelihood of success as a means-end linkage regardless of the cost (psychological and economic) of implementation and the likelihood of being deployed given the personal cost of the action. An action with a high probability of success may be too costly to deploy. For example, running from a burning house to save oneself while leaving one's pre-school children in the house to fend for themselves. In the face of disasters people will draw behaviors from the repertoire according to their locus in the cost/benefit hierarchy, subject to disruption by panic and injury. Knowing what to do in a wide range of circumstances can reduce the likelihood of panic and training can also expand the repertoire to include the contingency of injury.

There are three forms of potentiation for behavioral responses to perceived risk—*transparent, translucent* and *decoupled.* These three terms are borrowed here from evolutionary biology (Sterelny, 2003) and connote; a fixed response to a fixed cue, a set of responses to a particular cue, and a flexible repertoire of behaviors that is available to be deployed in any circumstance that is evaluated as a risk.[2] Automatic transparent responses have a very steep cost-benefit function. They can be disastrous if inappropriate: a possibility that is ever present in a rapidly changing, complex and dangerous environment. Human behavior is not by-and-large characterized by transparent responses though they may be the fall-back option where the immediacy of danger evokes an evolutionarily primitive fright-flight reaction. Since translucent and decoupled responses involve evaluative processes their use invokes an epistemic process of evaluation. Here is the link to what I have described as an hierarchical action repertoire.

Translucent behaviors have a greater cognitive component as the relation of cue to response is one to many. However, they are still bounded by a necessitarian relation of the form—if this, then this, or this or this etc. The problem for any program designed for encouraging people to adopt protective behaviors is that an analysis of potential hazards and their associated risks will likely lead to a very long list of cues and their response sets in order to adequately cover the range of potential danger situations that an individual might find themselves in. In addition, most hazards generate some idiosyncratic properties. The epistemic character of decoupled relations provides much greater flexibility since it involves problem analysis and then response selection or generation; that is, the response may be novel and not present in any current response repertoire of the individual. I suspect most protection programs opt for engendering translucent response repertoires for the general public through advertising and pamphlets. These programs are also predicated on the assumption that the content of individuals' awareness drives their behavior.

Here, however, I have argued that supra-individual influences, some of which are not apprehended consciously, influence the way people react to disasters. Of course, intentional behaviors are always the results of conscious proximal causes. The problem is how to increase the likelihood of appropriate protective behaviors when the source of intentions lies partly or wholly beyond the scope of introspection. Information about beliefs and intentions can be ascertained

---

2. Sterelny has used these concepts to account for the emergence of reflective and reflexive cognition, specifically Theory of Mind, in phylogenetic elaboration. The use of the terms here is not strictly in his sense, but rather as a useful analytic parallel.

Figure 9.2. The individual in context.

by asking people (self-report questionnaires) or through indirect means (abduced from responses to issues and events known to relate to specific attitudes, beliefs and intentions). Similarly, psychologists have developed a range of instruments to measure personality traits and other dispositions. I shall now turn to the role played by community influences and how they might be accounted for in the development of a comprehensive approach to understanding and facilitating the development of protective behaviors.

This conception of the individual embedded in a nested set of social contexts is both informative and problematic (Figure 9.2). I have dealt with how this conceptual framework brings into focus the relation between individuals' assessments of situations and the behaviors they resort to. However, community influences and those of the wider social context can generate two kinds of problems: theoretical and practical. The theoretical problems relate in turn to causation and the question of what constitutes an empirically sufficient explanation[3] of the behaviors of interest. The danger exists that we can be drawn into a situation that is akin to Laplace's Nightmare of Determinism—in order to know anything you need to know everything. While this is

---

3. One that is better than guessing tested against a specified set of outcome measures. How much better is a judgment call (statistical, economic and ethical).

avoidable[4] the problem of what factors need to be included at each level for an empirically efficient explanation remains. The practical problem follows in the wake of this. A satisfactory theoretical explanation of why people adopt protective behaviors may contain factors that are of no immediate practical application. There are person-characteristics that cannot be changed and other factors that are either unchangeable or can only be changed at unjustifiable expense or through unacceptable social manipulation. A program intended to increase readiness and resilience within an at-risk community has to be based on influences that can be used to bring about behavioral changes.

It is not my intention to go into detail about specific influences at any level. I have described how these may be measured in two other papers (Smith, 2004; Smith & Violanti, 2003). However, I do wish to consider some issues that affect the use of characteristics of communities in modeling the process of generating protective behaviors. Supraindividual influences on behavior can be structural (economic, physical, social relations) or ideological (values, mores, social relations) and these will differ in the degree to which they are apprehended in awareness or accessible through introspection. These influences operate to generate and shape beliefs, intentions and behaviors. Incorporating manipulations of those community influences of which people are generally unaware in a program to bring about change raises ethical questions. Those who are responsible for initiating such programs will need to address how transparent their actions are in relation to the public good. Social programs always raise issues of interests. Whether the decisions are based on Utilitarian principles or Communitarian principles may lead to different outcomes in relation to the way a program is structured and administered. The participation of community members in the design and running of the program has generally proved helpful in ensuring acceptance by other community members.

When diasters occur they unfold as series of events in a cascade. As a consequence different protective behaviors become important. The generic sequence of events includes indications that the precipitating

---

4. I do not wish to be diverted into a discussion of causation here. I have argued (Gare & Smith, 1984) that a Theoretical Realist account of causation in principle avoids explanatory inflation of the sort feared by Laplace.

event (earthquake, tsunami, flood, bushfire, epidemic, etc.)[5] will occur; the precipitating event and the flow-on consequences of this event. Taking a tsunami as an example, we have the indications immediately preceding the arrival of the wave, the inundation resulting from the wave, the destruction of infrastructure, the breakdown of civil structures, the emergence and spread of disease, and the political and social wrangling over reconstruction. Other kinds of disaster unfold in an analogous fashion. Social, legal and psychological consequences may continue for a very long time after the precipitating event. So "events" need to be seen as loose and permeable categories.

It is not necessarily the case that if each individual acts to maximize their own short-term benefit it will maximize the benefit of the community. The example of the parent fleeing the fire to save himself and leaving the children to save themselves does not maximize the survival of the group as whole. The drive for self-preservation is very strong and behavioral management may well be necessary to drive protective behaviors that maximize the best outcomes for a community. For example, where a bushfire is sweeping down on a community that needs to be evacuated, traffic anarchy cannot be allowed if the majority of people are to be evacuated efficiently. The two-level explanation of the development of protective behaviors that has been described in this chapter underwrites the development of programs that balance community behaviors and individual behaviors.

The diagram shown in Figure 9.3 indicates how a Precipitating Event is interpreted and the Action Repertoire of an individual is brought into play to determine what response they will make. The depiction of the process is sufficiently generic to cover action that is immediate and direct in relation to a threat or for the preparation for action with respect to a perceived future threat. Those involved in the process of developing programs aimed at increasing the repertoire of protective behaviors among community members need to align expert evaluations with community perceptions and their priorities with those of the community.

Disasters by their nature unfold in ways that are not entirely predictable. Responses need to be flexible. An appreciation of the

---

5. This is partly in the eye of the beholder. For a geomorphologist the precipitating even may be the movement of tectonic plates. I mean, loosely, when it becomes an immediate danger and concern for community members. A case when overprecision is not helpful.

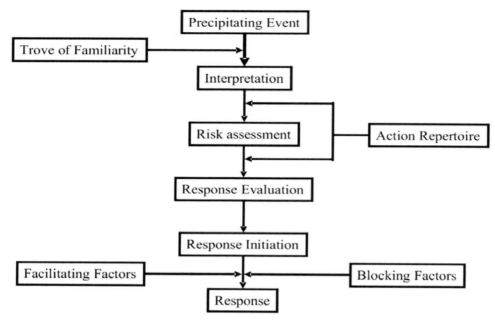

Figure 9.3. The process of response generation.

processes depicted in Figures 9.1 and 9.3 suggest that the targets of any intervention for change should be the Trove of Familiarity and increasing Facilitating Factors.[6] The Trove of Familiarity can be targeted in two ways: by employing it to provide an interpretative context for the messages promoting the protective behaviors or by modifying the Trove to this end. As already suggested the Trove is in part promulgated by the media.

   To some extent a successful program will have to include some elements of manipulation. The use of the Trove to change an individual's and a community's perceptions of risk, to change the evaluation of potential protective behaviors and to change protective behaviors is a case in point. As previously pointed out, traffic anarchy does not facilitate efficient evacuation of a community faced with a bushfire. There is an analogy here between immunization and the building of a protective action repertoire; namely, second order protection. The effects of a disaster will be mitigated to the degree that is a function of the pro-

---

6. This also involves eliminating Blocking Factors where possible, or providing strategies (including more protective behaviors) to deal with them.

portion of a community who are able to respond with appropriate protective behaviors. This is analogous to the situation where the likelihood of contracting a contagious disease for an unimmunized person is a function of the percentage of the population who are immunized. At the community level this relates to the rate and to the extent of spread of the disease and this in turn affects the demands on the community's resources to deal with the situation. The protection of a majority of a community indirectly protects *all* its members. In a disaster this means less chaos and the better deployment of community resources. Once again there is a need to balance public good and individual choice.

I have contended that disasters are not unitary events; they cascade into many effects that can then develop a life of their own. Just as all disasters do not develop along the same lines (even within types—earthquakes, bushfires, etc.) so they do not eventuate in the same manner. Both the etiology and the degree of risk to individuals and communities vary. The etiology covers the lag between the first indication of the precipitating event and the reliability of the indication that it will occur. For this reason the chart shown in Table 9.1 might be useful in classifying possible precipitating events for risk analysis.

When these factors—risk, event likelihood and lag are treated as continuous variables they can be represented as three-dimensional action-potential surface (Figure 9.4). Other things being equal it will be most difficult to generate protective behaviors for events located in the lower left corner of the plot. The compensation is that there will be

TABLE 9.1. TYPOLOGY OF PRECIPITATING EVENTS.

RISK	**INDICATORS**		**LAG**		
	High reliability	Low-moderate reliability	Short term	Intermediate	Long term
Imminent					
Acute					
Chronic					
Remote					

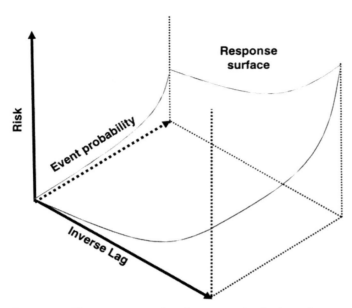

Figure 9.4. The response surface for potential risks from disasters.

more time to achieve the desired take-up of recommended protective behaviors.

The complexity of public responses to public safety campaigns is illustrated by public reaction to the situation at Lake Taupo in New Zealand. The build-up of volcanic pressure under Lake Taupo has been going on since solidification after the last major eruption some 1,800 years ago. Although according to vulcanologists a catastrophic eruption is virtually inevitable the present indicators are in the low probability range on a daily basis and the time scale is very long (perhaps another millennium!) It has proved very difficult to generate public enthusiasm given their perception of the risk. There has been a tendency for people to displace the responsibility for their own safety to others–local government and the Earthquake Commission. Several perspectives could be responsible for this: "not in my lifetime" (and therefore of no concern); "too big for me to cope with" (lack of perceived resources); or, a devaluing by the community of the expertise underwriting the indicators (values imbedded in the Trove). Each of these possible explanations is best understood by expanding the explanatory framework for the adoption, maintenance and use individual protective behaviors to incorporate the community level.

In this chapter I have argued that disasters are complex cascades of events that have manifold consequences for individuals and their communities. In order to capture peoples' responses to this complexity and show how planners and communities at risk can develop better protective behaviors I have recommended that a two-level (individual in the community) conceptual model be employed to research the influences that affect the uptake of protective behaviors. I have also suggested that it is not possible to capture all the influences by merely asking people of what they are aware. Furthermore, the conflict between the individual's benefit and the goal of community benefit, together with the necessity to use factors outside awareness in some form of behavior management raises important ethical, social and legal issues that need to be considered by those who plan programs to increase protective behaviors. In this sense, the term "protective behavior" raises the question—"whose behavior, whose protection"?

REFERENCES

Dake, K. (1992). Myths of nature and the public. *Journal of Social Issues, 48*(4), 21–38.

Flick, U. (Ed.). (1998). *The psychology of the social.* Cambridge: Cambridge University Press.

Gare, A., & Smith, L. M. (1984). The philosophical foundations of humanistic psychology: A reply to McMullan. *Australian Journal of Psychology, 36*, 103–108.

Joffe, H. (2003). Risk: From perception to social representation. *British Journal of Social Psychology, 42*, 55–73.

Moscovici, S. (1998). The history and actuality of social representation. In U. Flick (Ed.), *The psychology of the social* (pp. 209–247). Cambridge: Cambridge University Press.

Moscovici, S., & Duveen, G. (Eds.). (2001). *Social representations: Explorations in social psychology.* Cambridge: Polity Press.

Paton, D., Smith, L.M., & Johnston, D. (2005). When good intentions turn bad: Promoting natural hazard preparedness. *Australian Journal of Emergency Management, 20*, 25–30.

Perkins, D. D., & Long, D. A. (2002). Neighbourhood sense of community and social capital. In A. T. Fisher, C. S. Sonn, & B. J. Bishop (Eds.), *Psychological sense of community: Research, applications, and implications* (pp. 291–318). New York, NY: Kluwer Academic/Plenum.

Rushefsky, M. (1982). Technical disputes: Why experts disagree. *Policy Studies Review, 1*(4), 676–685.

Shinn, M., & Toohey, S. M. (2003). Community contexts of human welfare. *Annual Review of Psychology, 54*, 427–459.

Smith, L. M. (2004). Measuring protective behaviors for perceived risks of hazards. In D. Paton, J. M. Violanti, C. Dunning, & L. M. Smith (Eds.), *Managing traumatic stress risk: A proactive approach* (pp. 49–67). Springfield, IL: Charles C Thomas.

Smith, L. M., & Violanti, J. M. (2003). Risk response model. In D. Paton, J. M. Violanti, & L. M. Smith (Eds.), *Promoting capabilities to manage posttraumatic stress: Perspectives on resilience* (pp. 186–203). Springfield, IL: Charles C Thomas.

Sontag, S. (1977). *Illness as metaphor.* New York, NY: Farrar, Straus and Giroux.

Sterelny, K. (2003). *Thought in a hostile world: The evolution of human cognition.* Malden, MA: Blackwell Publishing Ltd.

van der Plight, J. (1996). Risk perception and self-protective behavior. *European Psychologist, 1*(1), 34–43.

Weinstein, N. (1989). Effects of personal experience on self-protective behavior. *Psychological Bulletin, 105*(1), 31–50.

Weinstein, N., Lyon, J. E., Rothman, A. J., & Cuite, C. L. (2000). Preoccupation and affect as predictors of protective action following natural disaster. *British Journal of Health Psychology, 5*(4), 351–363.

Windle, M. (1999). Critical conceptual and measurement issues in the study of resilience. In M. D. Glantz & J. L. Johnson (Eds.), *Resilience and development: Positive life adaptations. Longitudinal research in the social and behavioral sciences* (pp. 161–176). New York, NY: Kluwer Academic/Plenum Publishers.

Chapter 10

LINKS BETWEEN COMMUNITY AND INDIVIDUAL RESILIENCE: EVIDENCE FROM CYCLONE AFFECTED COMMUNITIES IN NORTH WEST AUSTRALIA

JULIE ANN POOLEY, LYNNE COHEN, AND MOIRA O'CONNOR

INTRODUCTION

Ensuring that communities can respond and recover from disasters requires organization and preparation prior to their occurrence (Quarantelli, 1985). This chapter considers how the goals of organization and preparedness can be pursued from two perspectives. First, it briefly considers how individual and community characteristics influence vulnerability. Then discussion turns to the role of resilience factors and how interactions between individual- and community-level factors influence post-disaster outcomes. This process is illustrated with a case study of the impact of cyclones on communities in Northwest Australia.

DISASTER VULNERABILITY

Vulnerability describes those characteristics of a person or group in terms of their capacity to anticipate, cope with, resist, and recover from the impact of a natural hazard (Blaikie, Cannon, Davis & Wisner,

1994). Vulnerability research has focused on social and/or economic disadvantage or marginalization that limits the capacity to cope with disasters (Blaikie et al., 1994; Bolin & Stanford, 1998; Buckland & Rahman, 1999; Morrow, 1999). The identification of vulnerabilities in, for example, residents, structures, eco-systems and economies has played an important role in mitigating natural hazard risk (Blaikie et al. 1994). The identification of vulnerabilities has challenged emergency managers and researchers to look more systemically as disasters strike whole communities as well as the individuals within them (Boyce, 2000).

Analysis of the distribution of structural (e.g., housing, building construction), social (e.g., community isolation, cultural insensitivities) and psychological (e.g., language, avoidance coping) factors (Bachrach & Zautra, 1985; Bishop, Paton, Syme & Nancarrow, 2000; Fothergill, Maestas, & Darlington, 1999; Millar, Paton & Johnston, 1999) has informed the development of community vulnerability maps. These maps aid emergency managers in decision making for disaster responses and disaster planning for community needs (Morrow, 1999; Sullivan, 2003). The maps integrate geographical, social and political patterns using geographical information systems (GIS) to assist planning and preparation and identify response needs in the event of a disaster (Morrow, 1999).

Despite the value of this approach, it would, however, be erroneous to apply this construct in an unqualified way. In Australia, in 1998, the state of Victoria's gas supply was severely reduced when it was shut down by an explosion, with full capacity not being restored for many months. Buckle (2001–2002) reports that one of the lessons learned from the gas crisis was its differential impact on segments of the population, but in ways inconsistent with predictions derived on the basis of traditional vulnerability indicators. Traditionally, the elderly have been seen as more vulnerable. Buckle, however, found that during the crisis the elderly coped better with the stress associated with having no gas than younger people, even though the elderly required gas for heating. The elderly generally had more capacity in terms of past experience of dealing with different resource needs and supplies, and had different expectations about the aid they would receive. The nature of these differences poses a challenge to traditional ways of conceptualizing natural hazard risk. To develop a positive, strength-based, capacity building approach, the focus needs to move beyond the identification of vulnerabilities to understanding resilience (Handmer, 2003; Paton, Johnston, Smith & Millar, 2001).

COMMUNITY RESILIENCE:
BEYOND DISASTER VULNERABILITY

Kulig (1999) defined community resilience as "the ability of a community to not only deal with adversity but in doing so reach a higher level of functioning" (p. 2). Resilience has been used interchangeably with other terms, for example, thriving (Massey, Cameron, Ouellette, & Fine, 1998), invulnerability (Anthony & Cohler, 1987), stress resistant (Garmezy, 1993), hardiness (Kobasa, 1979; Tarter & Vanyukov, 1999), and toughening (Dienstbier, 1989). Resilience is seen as important in the area of prevention as it could provide salient information and direct programs to reduce the effects of negative experiences of disaster impacts by focusing on the strengths and capacities of individuals and communities (Kumpfer, 1999).

The term community resilience has been identified as important to understanding such diverse issues as oppression (Sonn & Fisher, 1998), risk management (Paton et al., 2001), and hazard planning (Tobin & Whiteford, 2002). Several researchers (e.g., Brodsky, 1997; Sonn & Fisher, 1998; Tolan, 1996) have argued that to further our understanding of resilience there is a need to consider the wider context and our connection to it. Brown and Kulig (1996–1997) argued that community resilience is "grounded in the notion of human agency" (p. 41) where the community engages in intentional meaningful action. That is, it does not just bounce back from adverse situations; the community actively chooses change, despite any limitations the community may possess. Factors contributing to community resilience include community capacity (e.g., the assets and skills of community members), community sustainability (e.g., meeting individual needs within a culture that harmonizes with nature), and community competence (e.g., processes by which community members work together to identify needs and determine ways to meet those needs) (Brown & Kulig, 1996–1997). These factors represent the dynamic enabling qualities of a community. To this end, at any point in time, understanding the dynamics of any given community is essential to moving a community toward being more resilient (Brown & Kulig, 1996–1997).

Within the community psychology literature, the concepts Brown and Kulig (1996–1997) describe are not new. One of the cornerstone concepts for community psychology is that of sense of community. Recently, researchers have identified that an individual's sense of belonging and attachment to their community is important to every age group within a community. It has been implicated in predicting psychological well-being, workplace satisfaction, political participation, crime prevention, community resilience, community participation, and community development (Chavis & Wandersman, 1990; Davidson & Cotter, 1989; Perkins, Florin, Rich, Wandersman, & Chavis, 1990; Pooley, Pike, Drew, & Breen, 2002; Sonn & Fisher, 1998). The operationalization of the attachment and belonging to community has been through the development of the concept of psychological sense of community (SoC).

Sarason (1974) argued that individuals who have an emotional interconnectedness to the collective created healthy communities. To understand this we needed to define and measure a person's SoC. One of the most developed and researched models of SoC, by McMillan and Chavis (1986) argues that there are four components of SoC: namely membership; influence; integration and fulfillment of needs; and a shared emotional connection.

Membership encompasses shared history, emotional safety, common symbols and personal investment. **Influence** accounts for the two-way process where an individual has influence within the collective and the collective has influence over the individual. **Integration and fulfillment** of needs reflects that an individual's needs and community needs can both be met at the same time thus the fulfillment of belonging to the collective is realized. Finally, **shared emotional connection** characterizes the bond that develops between members of the collective through important, salient events (McMillan & Chavis, 1986).

The utility of SoC has been tested in various settings including small neighborhoods, midsize communities, large cities, organizations and schools (Brodsky, 1996; Pooley et al., 2002; Pretty, Andrews, & Collett, 1994; Pretty, Conroy, Dugay, Fowler, & Williams, 1996). It has also been implicated in predicting community involvement in the placement of a hazardous waste facility (Bachrach & Zautra, 1985), farming communities involvement in managing salinity hazards (Bishop et al., 2000), and in assessing the long-term impact of disasters on mental health (Paton, 1994). The concept of sense of community has greatly increased our understanding of what community means to people and how it becomes a resource for people, particularly in times of stress. People's attachment to community may also influence the capacity for action; its competence.

In endeavoring to understand community resilience, Sonn and Fisher (1998) drew upon the concept of community competence. A competent community is one that utilizes, develops or otherwise obtains resources, including human resources in the community (Iscoe, 1974). Therefore, Goeppinger, Lassiter, and Wilcox (1982) argue that community competence can be regarded as an indicator of the health of a community. In terms of its constituent components, Cottrell (1976) argued that a competent community:

- is able to collaborate effectively in identifying needs and issues;
- can achieve a working consensus;
- can agree on ways to implement agreed-upon goals; and
- can carry this out collaboratively and effectively (p. 197).

A competent community comprises a constituency that has a commitment to the community; is aware of their own and others' identities and positions; can clearly articulate views on community matters; can hear what others are saying; can accommodate to differing views; has a willingness to be involved; can manage community relations; and, has interaction and decision-making processes (Armour, 1993).

Sonn and Fisher (1998), in their exploration of oppressed or non-dominant communities, argued that communities that are able to provide resources, both social and psychological, and that are organized are competent communities. This enhances their capacity to cope with adversity. Cook (1983) also argued that communities with a higher level of competence can respond better to environmental threats. Cook found that residents that felt threatened by a proposed hazardous waste treatment plant, and were more attached to their community, and utilized processes in their community (attendance at community meetings, rallies, and petitions) to harness support against the plant being established. Similarly, Buckland and Rahman (1999) argued that high social capital (similar to sense of community, see Pooley, Cohen, & Pike, in press) underscores a community that is soundly structured and able to respond to a disaster more effectively.

In their study of the aftermath of Red River flood in Canada in 1997, Buckland and Rahman (1999) found that, of the three communities studied, the community that was better resourced and organized and had greater internal capacity (community competence), was better placed to cope with the flood. Recently, Kulig (2000) refined and clarified her model of community resilience which is comprised of three components: {1} interactions that are experienced as a collective, {2} the expression of sense of community, and {3} community action. It could be argued that Kulig has centralized the concepts of community competence, through looking at collective interactions (component one) and community action (component three), and sense of community (component two) in measuring community resilience.

Other components of resilience have emerged from the hazard planning (Tobin, 1999) and risk management (Paton & Johnston, 2001; Paton, Smith, & Violanti, 2000; Paton et al., 2001) literature. Utilizing an ecological approach, Tobin (1999) developed a conceptual framework for understanding how sustainable and resilient communities may be created. He describes these communities as those that are low risk, low vulnerability, have ongoing planning initiatives, a high level of political support, have partnerships between government and private sectors, have independent and interdependent social networks and appropriate planning taking into account local and national stability.

Tobin's (1999) conceptual framework combines three theoretical models. The first is a mitigation model which involves reducing risk in the community through the use of design standards and policies. The second is a recovery model which involves governmental policies to aid relief and recovery with a view to reaccumulating capital and distributing resources. The third is a structural-cognitive model which incorporates issues to do with structural (societal) changes, situational factors (sociodemographic and community characteristics) and cognitive (psychological/attitudinal) variables.

Paton et al. (2001) evaluated the structural-cognitive element of Tobin's (1999) model in relation adapting to volcanic hazard effects resulting from the 1995–1996 eruption of Ruapehu volcano, New Zealand. The three factors (self-efficacy, problem-focused coping and sense of community) previously identified by Bachrach and Zautra (1985) and Bishop et al. (2000) were used as predictors. The results reiterated the role of self-efficacy and problem-focused coping as indicators of psychological resilience. In contrast to the findings of others, sense of community did not predict resilience. Paton et al. (2001) proposed that this could have reflected social fragmentation between two groups (one of whom, ski-field employees, was seasonal) in the community. The ski-field employees were the only group significantly affected by the eruption. The seasonal nature of their employment means that SoC was either less salient to them or they had had insufficient time to forge this belief. The context in which they experienced the disaster meant that SoC was not a salient characteristic of their hazard experience. The role of context was recognized by Tobin (1999) when considering the difficult transition of this framework from theory to practice. He argued that a way forward would be to understand the social, economic and political nature of hazard planning in context.

Following the eruption of Tungurahua, in Ecuador in 1999, Tobin and Whiteford (2002) utilized Tobin's (1999) conceptual framework of community resilience, to understand the response and recovery effort of officials and residents of three small communities. Government officials, relief workers, leaders and community people were interviewed and surveyed at three and eight months after the initial eruption. The most salient finding was that the official response and recovery efforts exacerbated existing health issues and created social and economic issues for some community members. The authors suggest that identifying health problems early and evacuating families together to similar environments would increase the capacity of community members to participate in their own recovery process. By increasing the resilience of each community member an effective community recovery is more likely to follow.

Tobin and Whiteford's (2002) study is one of the first attempts to understand the sociopolitical nature of a disaster community and its relation to community resilience. Through qualitative interviews at various levels of the community (resident through to government level) information from the disaster impact across three different communities provides an understanding of the contextual nature of disaster recovery and response. Importantly, it also provides a comprehensive framework for the empirical analysis of community resilience in disaster studies. Taken together, Tobin and Whiteford's (2002) and Paton et al.'s (2001) work indicate the importance of the context in disaster studies and the potential of individual- and community-level fac-

tors to predict a capacity for those impacted by natural hazard consequences to adapt to these consequences. Given that individuals and
communities co-exist in a state of dynamic equilibrium, understanding
resilience requires that the nature of this interaction be taken into
account. How this interaction might influence the experience of disaster is illustrated by a case study of community members' response to
cyclone impacts in several communities in Northwest Australia.

CASE STUDY

Context: Cyclone Communities in Northwest Australia

Four communities (Kununurra, Broome, Exmouth, and Carnarvon)
in the Northwest of Australia were chosen to participate in this study
as they fulfilled certain criteria. They had experienced disaster-related
losses in excess of A$10 million, they had had varying cyclone expe-
riences, and they had had at least one significant threat within the
three-year time period previous to data collection. Full details of the
study can be found in Pooley (2005). In total 512 residents participated in the study. The sample comprised 329 females and 169 males,
with a mean age of 35 years who had lived in their respective communities for an average of four years.

A comprehensive postal survey that assessed salient individual and
community variables was conducted. The individual level factors were
Mastery (self-efficacy) (Pearlin & Schooler, 1978), Coping Style
(Carver, Scheier & Weintraub, 1989), and social networks (Social
Embeddedness Scale (Kaniasty, Norris, & Murrell, 1990). The community level factors were sense of community (Sense of Community
Index (Perkins et al., 1990) and community competence (Eng &
Parker, 1994). The disaster experience was assessed using the Impact
of Events Scale-Revised (Horowitz, Wilner, & Alvarez, 1979) and the
Posttraumatic Growth Inventory (Tedeschi & Calhoun, 1996). Data
were analyzed using path analysis (Klem, 1995). To obtain the path
coefficients for the disaster experience model a number of multiple
regressions were performed. The model was trimmed according to
Klem (1995) and path co-efficients were reestimated with the redun-
dant paths excluded (Figure 10.1).

Overall, the findings provide some insights into the relationship

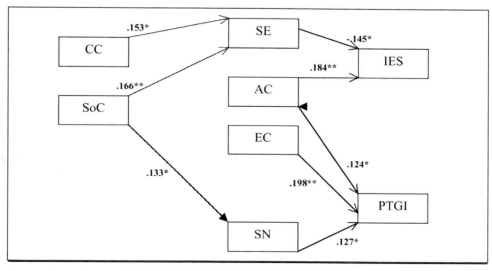

Figure 10.1. Observed Associations Between Community Resilience Variables, Individual Resilience Variables and Disaster Experience Variables.

between individual and community factors and adaptive response to hazard consequences. The data supported the argument that the influence of community factors on posttraumatic growth is mediated by the individual factor, social networks (Figure 10.1). A role for avoidant coping and emotion-focused coping as predictors of posttraumatic growth was also found (Figure 10.1). While the role of the latter is consistent with some work on adversarial growth (Linly & Joseph, 2004), the influence of avoidant coping is inconsistent with previous work. These data results indicate that growth outcomes emerge from increased use of emotion focused coping and the quality of social network.

This study reiterates the findings of Bachrach and Zautra (1985), Paton et al. (2001) and Kulig (2000), but suggests that it is essential to view resilience in terms of the interaction between the individual resilience and community resilience factors in the context of community members' disaster experience. The factors which underpin community resilience (sense of community and community competence) are important precursors to individual resilience variables, in particular social networks. Therefore, in order to understand and promote adaptive capacity one needs to understand the relationship between community variables (e.g., sense of community and community competence) and individual variables (e.g., self-efficacy, coping styles, social networks). Both the individual and community variables may provide avenues for intervention. This case study suggests that attention to community resilience variables will enable residents to develop some of the protective factors at the individual level. Interventions aimed at increasing attachment to the community or at increasing the competence of the community will indirectly reduce disaster stress and increase the potential for psychological growth following experience of disaster.

Importantly, this study supports the argument that measurable benefits from adverse events may emerge (Dunbar, Mueller, Medina, & Wolf, 1998). The current research supports posttraumatic growth as an outcome of a disaster event such as a cyclone. This implies that in order to fully understand the effect of an adverse experience such as the impact of cyclones, one must take into account the whole experience, which includes both deficit and growth perspectives.

CONCLUSION

To fully understand the disaster experience a systemic approach is needed. Factors operating at both the community and individual level, and how they interact, need to be recognized. A greater appreciation of these factors and their interrelationships will facilitate more focused and localized interventions for disaster communities to be developed. This will contribute developing empowered, disaster-resilient communities.

REFERENCES

Anthony, E. J., & Cohler, B. J. (Eds.). (1987). *The invulnerable child.* New York, NY: Guildford Press.

Armour, A.M. (1993). *Coping with Impacts: An approach to assessing community vitality.* Faculty of Environmental Studies, York University, North York, Ontario, Canada.

Bachrach, K. M., & Zautra, A. L. (1985). Coping with a community stressor: The threat of a hazardous waste facility. *Journal of Health and Social Behavior, 26,* 127–141.

Bishop, B., Paton, D., Syme, G., & Nancarrow, B. (2000). Coping with environment degradation: salination as a community stressor. *Network, 12*(1), 1–15.

Blaikie, P., Cannon, T., Davis, I., & Wisner, B. (1994). *Risk: Natural hazards, peoples vulnerability, and disasters.* London: Routledge.

Bolin, R., & Stanford, L. (1998). The Northbridge earthquake: Community-based approaches to unmet recovery needs. *Disasters, 22*(1), 21–38.

Boyce, J. K. (2000). Let them eat risk? Wealth rights and disaster vulnerability. *The Journal of Disaster Studies, Policy and Management, 24*(3), 254–261.

Brodsky, A.E. (1996). Resilient single mothers in risky neighborhoods: Negative psychological sense of community. *Journal of Community Psychology, 24,* 347–363.

Brodsky, A. E. (1997). Why the concept of resilience is resilient. *The Community Psychologist, 30,* 29–32.

Brown, D. D., & Kulig, J. C. (1996-1997). The concept of resiliency: Theoretical lessons from community research. *Health and Canadian Society, 4*(1), 29–50.

Buckland, J., & Rahman, M. (1999). Community-based disaster management during the 1997 red river flood in Canada. *Disasters, 23*(2), 174–191.

Buckle, P. (2001-2002). Managing community vulnerability in a wide area disaster. *Australian Journal of Emergency Management, 16,* 13–18.

Carver, C. S., Scheier, M. F., & Weintraub, J. K. (1989). Assessing coping strategies: A theoretically based approach. Journal of Personality & Social Psychology, *56 (2), 267–283.*

Chavis, D. M., & Wandersman, A. (1990). Sense of community in the urban environment: A catalyst for participation and community development. *American Journal of Community Psychology, 18*(1), 55–81.

Cook, J. R. (1983). Citizen response in a neighborhood under threat. *American Journal of Community Psychology, 11*(4), 459–471.

Cottrell, L. S. (1976). *The competent community.* In B.H. Kaplan, R.N. Wilson, & A.H. Leighton, (eds). *Further Explorations in Social Psychiatry,* New York: Basic Books. pp. 195–209.

Davidson, W. B., & Cotter, P. R. (1989, April). Sense of community and political participation. *Journal of Community Psychology, 17,* 119–124.

Dienstbier, R. A. (1989). Arousal and physiological toughness: Implications for mental and physical health. *Psychological Review, 96*(1), 84–100.

Dunbar, H. T., Mueller, C. W., Medina, C., & Wolf, T. (1998). Psychological and spiritual growth in women living with HIV. *Social Work, 43,* 144–154.

Eng, E., & Parker, E. (1994). Measuring community competence in the Mississippi Delta: The interface between program evaluation and empowerment. *Health Education Quarterly, 21,* 199–220.

Fothergill, A., Darlington, J. D., & Maestas, E.G.M. (1999). Race, ethnicity and disasters in the United States: A review of the literature. *Disasters, 23*(2), 156–173.

Garmezy, N. (1993). Children in poverty: Resilience despite risk. *Psychiatry: Interpersonal & Biological Processes, 56*(1), 127–136.

Gist, M. E., & Mitchell, T. R. (1992). Self-efficacy: A theoretical analysis of its determinants and malleability. *Academy of Management Review, 17*(2), 183–211.

Goeppinger, J., Lassiter, P. G., & Wilcox, B. (1982). Community health is community competence. *Nursing Outlook, 13,* 464–467.

Handmer, J. (2003). We are all vulnerable. *The Australian Journal of Emergency Management, 18*(3), 55–60.

Horowitz, M. J., Wilner, N., & Alvarez, W. (1979). Impact of event scale: A measure of subjective stress. *Psychosomatic Medicine, 41,* 209–218.

Iscoe, I. (1974, August). Community psychology and the competent community. *American Psychologist, 29,* 607–613.

Kaniasty, K. Z., Norris, F. H., & Murrell, S. A. (1990). Received and perceived social support following natural disaster. *Journal of Applied Social Psychology, 20,* 85–114.

Klem, L. (1995). Path analysis. In L. G. Grimm & P. R. Yarnold (Eds.), *Reading and understanding multivariate statistics* (pp. 65–98). Washington, DC: American Psychological Association.

Kobasa. (1979). Stressful life events, personality, and health: An inquiry into hardiness. *Journal of Personality and Social Psychology, 37,* 1–11.

Kulig, J. C. (1999). *Individual community resiliency among Mexican Mennonites: Final report.* Canada: University of Lethbridge.

Kulig, J. C. (2000). Community resiliency: The health potential for community health nursing theory development. *Public Health Nursing, 17*(5), 374–385.

Kumpfer, K. (1999). Factors and processes contributing to resilience: The resilience framework. In M. J. Glantz, J. (Ed.), *Resilience and development: Positive life adaptions* (pp. 179–224). New York: Plenum Press.

Linley, P.A. & Joseph, S. (2004). Positive change following trauma and adversity: A review. *Journal of Traumatic Stress, 17,* 11–21.

Massey, S., Cameron, A., Ouellette, S., & Fine, M. (1998). Qualitative approaches to the study of thriving: What can be learned? *Journal of Social Issues, 54*(2), 337–355.

McMillan, D. W., & Chavis, D. M. (1986). Sense of community: A definition and theory. *Journal of Community Psychology, 14*(January), 6–19.

Millar, M., Paton, D., & Johnston, D. (1999). Community vulnerability to volcanic hazard consequences. *Disaster Prevention and Management, 8*(4), 255–260.

Morrow, B. H. (1999). Identifying and mapping community vulnerability. *Disasters, 23*(1), 1–18.

Paton, D. (1994). Disasters, communities and mental health: Psychological influences on long-term impact. *Community Mental Health in New Zealand, 9*(2), 3–14.

Paton, D., & Johnston, D. (2001). Disasters and communities: Vulnerability, resilience and preparedness. *Disaster Prevention and Management, 10*(4), 270–277.

Paton, D., Johnston, D., Smith, L., & Millar, M. (2001). Responding to hazard effects: Promoting resilience and adjustment option. *Australian Journal of Emergency Management, 16,* 47–52.

Paton, D., Smith, L., & Violanti, J. (2000). Disaster response: Risk, vulnerability and resilience. *Disaster Prevention and Management, 9*(3), 173–179.

Pearlin, L. I., & Schooler, C. (1978). The structure of coping. *Journal of Health and Social Behavior, 19,* 2–21.

Perkins, D. D., Florin, P., Rich, R. C., Wandersman, A., & & Chavis, D. M. (1990). Participation and the social and physical environment of residential blocks: Crime and community context. *American Journal of Community Psychology, 18*(1), 83–115.

Pooley, J. A. (2005). *Indicators of community resilience: A study of communities facing impending natural disasters.* Unpublished manuscript, Edith Cowan University,

Perth, Australia.

Pooley, J. A., Cohen, L., & Pike, L. T. (in press). Can sense of community inform social capital. *The Social Science Journal, 42*(2).

Pooley, J. A., Pike, L. T., Drew, N. M., & Breen, L. (2002). Inferring Australian children's sense of community: A critical exploration. *Community, Work and Family, 5*(1), 5–21.

Pretty, G. M. H., Andrews, L., & Collett, S. (1994). Exploring adolescents' sense of community and its relationship to loneliness. *Journal of Community Psychology, 22*(October), 346–358.

Pretty, G. M. H., Conroy, C., Dugay, J., Fowler, K., & Williams, D. (1996). Sense of community and its relevance to adolescents of all ages. *Journal of Community Psychology, 24*(4), 365–379.

Quarantelli, E. L. (1985). An assessment of conflicting views on mental health: The consequences of traumatic events. In C. Figley (Ed.), *Trauma and its wake* (pp. 173–215). New York: Brunner/Mazel.

Sarason, S.B. (1974). *The psychological sense of community: Prospects for a community psychology.* Jossey-Bass, San Francisco

Sonn, C. C., & Fisher, A. T. (1998). Sense of community: Community resilient responses to oppression and change. *Journal of Community Psychology, 26*, 457–472.

Sullivan, M. (2003). Integrated recovery management: A new way of looking at a delicate process. *Australian Journal of Emergency Management, 18*(2), 4–27.

Tarter, R., & Vanyukov, M. (1999). Revisiting the validity of the construct of resilience. In M. J. Glantz, J (Ed.), *Resilience and development: Positive life adaptions* (pp. 85–100). New York: Plenum Press.

Tedeschi, R. G., & Calhoun, L. G. (1996). The posttraumatic growth inventory: Measuring the positive legacy of trauma. *Journal of Traumatic Stress, 9*(3), 455–471.

Tobin, G. A. (1999). Sustainability and community resilience: The holy grail of hazards planning? *Environmental Hazards, 1*, 13–25.

Tobin, G. A., & Whiteford, L. M. (2002). Community resilience and volcanic hazard: The eruption of Tungurahua and evacuation of the Faldas in Ecuador. *Disasters, 26*, 28–48.

Tolan, P. H. (1996). How resilient is the concept of resilience? *The Community Psychologist, 29*, 21–24.

Chapter 11

THE HAKKA SPIRIT AS A PREDICTOR OF RESILIENCE

LI-JU JANG AND WALTER LAMENDOLA

INTRODUCTION

This chapter is part of a larger study that retrospectively examined the effects of social support networks and spirituality on the resilience and consequent posttraumatic growth of people in a collectivist culture who experience natural disasters (Jang, 2005). In that study, the Taiwanese township of Tung Shih was exposed to an almost continuous series of natural disasters. This included a major earthquake, the 921 Earthquake, on which this study focused. This chapter discusses the emergence of the *Hakka spirit* as a significant cultural influence on how people respond to disaster.

Generally speaking, people in Taiwan consider natural disasters the will of gods. They do not try to control nature, but strive to live with it in a harmonious way (Davison & Reed, 1998; Jordan, 1999). At the same time, a key emerging facet of contemporary risk management is one of encouraging resilience through creating a capacity for co-existence within the environment (Paton, in press). In Taiwan, co-existence with nature is incorporated into a unique set of cultural beliefs that are supportive during a crisis and that mutually align the will of gods and natural events. The argument in this chapter is that the *Hakka spirit* can be understood, in this respect, as an example of a set of social practices that (a) are performed in a manner that encourages resilience and growth, and (b) increase the capacity of human agents to thrive in adversarial situations.

THE TAIWAN CONTEXT

Taiwan is located between the Philippines and Japan. It is an island that covers "approximately 14,000 square miles, lying some 100 miles east of Mainland China" (Goltz, 1999, p. 1). Geographically, Taiwan is extremely mountainous. The central portion of Taiwan, from north tip to south tip, is the Central Range. Some people recognize Taiwan as "Formosa," which means beautiful island in Portuguese (Taiwan: Culture, 2001). Most of the population live in cities along the western coast of Taiwan.

Taiwan has a long history of battling natural disasters, including typhoons, floods, earthquakes, and mudslides. Lin (2002) has claimed that there has been a tendency for natural disasters to become more severe and occur more frequently because people are increasingly excessive in their natural resource use. Because Taiwan is located at the corner of the Manila Trench and Ryukyu Trench (Chichi, n.d.), earthquakes are a common phenomenon on the island. Two destructive earthquakes, the 921 Earthquake (September 21) and the 1022 Earthquake (October 22), occurred in 1999 (Brief analysis of natural disasters in Taiwan, 2002). According to Lin (2002), of all the deaths and injuries caused by natural disasters, about 15,000 or 47.8 percent have been victims of earthquakes.

THE 921 EARTHQUAKE

On September 21, 1999, a devastating earthquake, which Taiwanese people refer to as the 921 Earthquake, with a magnitude of 7.6 on the Richter scale, struck central Taiwan. It was a shallow, inland earthquake caused by the collision between the Philippine Sea and Eurasian plates (Shaw, 2000). The 921 Earthquake produced a linear zone of surface ruptures extending about 105 km long from north to south. A massive seismic force lifted Feng Shih Road several meters into the air in the Shih Kang section. It created a huge crack that split open roads and flattened buildings along the Road. The Taichung

County's main water supply source, Shih Kang Dam, was breached and displaced up to 7.5 meters vertically by fault rupture through the dam. It caused forest, fishery, and livestock losses of about 5.6 billion, as well as the destruction of 91 factories. It also caused a water supply problem for the two million citizens living in the Taichung area. In addition, 11 bridges were broken and several overpasses were laid flat on highways due to strong ground shaking, fault rupture, or both. Conversely, the land sank about 3 meters all along the fault line in eastern Taichung County (Anderson, 2000; Lee & Loh, 1999; Shaw, 2000). A fault study reported that a middle school was completely destroyed, 22 schools were seriously damaged, and 44 others became dangerous sites in the catastrophe ("School safety," 1999).

Experts in the Central Weather Bureau have indicated, "The magnitude of the 921 Earthquake might have broken all past earthquake records, including biggest shift in moving fault, longest fault length, highest horizontal surface acceleration, and shift direction change" (as cited in Pai, 1999, p. 10). The catastrophe was responsible for approximately 2,423 deaths, 11,305 injuries, and making more than 100,000 people homeless. The damage was estimated at US$ 20 to 30 billion (Comfort, 2000; Shaw, 2000). At the township level, Tung Shih suffered the highest death toll with 358 (or 29.98%) ("Social aid," n.d.; Liao, 1999).

RESILIENCE IN DISASTER

Despite the widely accepted assumption of the theoretical linkage between disasters and mental health concerns, it is becoming increasingly apparent that people frequently demonstrate a capacity to adapt to adverse circumstances and may even experience a sense of psychological and social growth (Echterling, 2001; Greene, 2002; Joseph, Williams & Yule, 1993; Paton & Johnston, 2001). Echterling found that positive meaning in the disaster helped survivors to cope better, and a natural helping network was evolved among the survivors to promote recovery process by offering practical assistance as well as emotional support such as sharing stories. Joseph et al. found that survivors often reported positive changes in appreciation of and valuing life, self and relationships as a result of their disaster experience. Furthermore, disasters are often followed by a period of heightened altruism and helping behavior (Bolin & Stanford, 1998; Fischer, 1998).

Several studies have indicated that culture has a role to play in this context (Doherty, 1999; Norris, Byrne, & Diaz, 2001). Webster, McDonald, Lewin, and Carr (1995) suggested that culture offered the survivors meanings of disaster, and contributed to their psychological well-being. Al-Naser and Sandman (2000) found that cultural factors, by virtue of their influence on the healing process and ameliorating emotional distress, positively affected the nature and quality of recovery from disasters.

Qualitative Study Description

The criteria for participant selection was that they must be: (a) 18 years or older, and (b) survivors of the 921 Earthquake, or (c) service providers to survivors in Tung Shih, or (e) volunteers who involved in relief efforts and/or reconstruction projects in Tung Shih. Data collection methods included in-depth interviews and direct observation. Direct observation was used to collect information about activities, behaviors, actions, and interactions among the survivors in Tung Shih (Patton, 1990). The most important element of the research was to give participants the opportunities to share their unique perspective and ways of thriving in the face of adversity. A total of 28 individuals including 16 survivors, six service providers, and six volunteers were interviewed. Most of them were female, Hakka, and married. Twenty-five participants reported experiencing loss of loved ones or houses, or suffering from property damage. Fifteen participants believed in folk religion. Sixteen participants played at least two major roles in the process of recovery. For instance, Chen was a survivor and volunteer, Chiu was a survivor, cultural preserver, and community developer. Most participants from the service provider and volunteer groups were professionals (e.g., clinical psychologist and teacher), associate professionals (e.g., government employee and social worker), or skilled workers (e.g., cook). On the other hand, participants from the survivor group were more likely to be skilled workers (e.g., accountant and hairdresser) or individuals with no income (e.g., retiree and housewife).

Here the term *survivor* refers to people who (a) were injured, (b) whose family members or relatives were severely injured or killed, (c) whose houses were severely damaged, or (d) who witnessed massive destruction in their community. *Service providers* included clinical psychologists, social workers, teachers, and outreach service workers. Teachers were considered service providers because of the roles they played during and after the disaster. They were expected to provide crisis counseling services for their students. Also, they were assigned to be in charge of the information booths to help the survivors with available community resources. *Volunteers* referred to people from religious groups or nonprofit organizations that participated and/or continue participating in relief efforts or reconstruction projects. Because most rescue and relief efforts as well as reconstruction projects of the 921 Earthquake were accomplished by volunteers, their inputs were important to this study. (Note: Participants' names have been replaced with common Chinese family names.)

THE HAKKA SPIRIT AS A THEME

Several themes emerged on the subject of cultural attributes influencing survivors' resilience. Most of the participants—regardless of their roles as survivors, service providers, or volunteers—reported that the *Hakka spirit* played a key role in the resilience of Tung Shih residents.

Although the *Hakka spirit* has been assimilated in one form or another across everyone now living in Tung Shih, it is originally derived from a cultural contribution of the Hakka, who were Chinese peasants from Northern China (Copper, 1993, 1999; Davison & Reed, 1998; Kaulbach & Proksch, 1984). Ren literally means guest or nonnative. Some 12–15 percent of people in Taiwan are descendents of Hakka immigrants and speak the Hakka language ("Taiwan," 1995). They are best known as frugal, hardworking, and family-oriented people.

Because Tung Shih was a mountainous township, the forestry industry was quite prosperous there. In the *Tourist Guide,* the Hakka are described primarily as carpenters who immigrated into Tung Shih. However, the indigenous people did not like the Hakka. Those new immigrants were often attacked by the natives. At one point, the Hakka reportedly sent messengers back to mainland China to plead with Lu Ban, a god who is the master of carpenters, craftsmen, and all other construction-related fields, to come to Taiwan with them and protect them from harm. The Hakka built a temple in Tung Shih to welcome him and serve as his home–the Chyao Sheng Cian Shr Temple. After the temple was built in 1775, the Hakka enjoyed peace and were prosperous in Tung Shih (Tourist guide for mountainous township, 2004). Obviously, this temple is a significant cultural symbol for the Hakka in Tung Shih. It was the first temple to be built in Tung Shih. Unfortunately, it collapsed in the 921 Earthquake. A rebuilding effort was soon underway based on its original design and the reconstruction was completed in early 2004 (Tourist guide for mountainous township, 2004). The reconstructed temple brought hope to survivors of the 921 Earthquake in Tung Shih. To them, it meant, "My gods are here with me. My family and I can be protected and prosperous again."

Hakka spirit was defined by some participants (e.g., Yeh, Chian, Wang, and Yu) as "The *spirit of sturdy neck* which means to hold on firmly despite extreme adversity, or to keep on doing something without regard to one's own strength." Others described traits such as frugality, diligence, self-reliance, responsibilities, and persistence as part of Hakka spirit. A junior high school principal in Tung Shih said that a Hakka folk song, *Hakka Spirit,* provided perfect explanation for the term. The lyrics follow:

Hakka Spirit
Migrated from China to Taiwan without a penny
Worked hard tilling the fields and mountains
Lived frugally for decades without complaint
The tradition of frugality and diligence passed on from generation to generation without change in three hundred years
Never, never, never abandon the Hakka spirit
Living standards are improving, society is changing
Traditional morals and values are facing challenges
Advice to all the Hakka is to seek perfection in conscience
Be a righteous and kindhearted person just like our ancestors
Never, never, never forget the teaching of our ancestors

Here *Hakka spirit* is not reserved for the Hakka people only. It is presented as the spirit shared by all residents of Tung Shih regardless of their ethnicity. Indeed, all participants had lived in Tung Shih for at least five years by the time of interview, excluding three service providers. People reported constant adjustments to their behaviors and values, based on the norms set by the majority. Even non-Hakka participants could be said to have adapted *Hakka spirit*. A case-oriented cross-case analysis (Miles & Huberman, 1994) was employed to continue to "deepen understanding and explanation" (p. 173). The cross-case comparison was started by forming three groups: (a) survivors, (b) service providers, and (c) volunteers. The following sections are organized by the three-group cross-case analysis.

Survivors

Almost all participants from the survivors group believed that *Hakka spirit* was the key to quick recovery in Tung Shih. Yu stressed that the traditional Hakka were very determined and persistent. Yeh commented that a main reason for survivors in Tung Shih to recover so fast was because of their unique traits. She said:

> The Hakka are very frugal and diligent. They are hardworking people. They are prepared for rainy days. They always have savings for emergency funds. They firmly believe that they can do something to support their families. They want to prove that they are capable of being self-reliant. They are survivors.

Both Yeh and Yu confirmed that growing up, they were trained to save at least 50 percent of their incomes for times of need.

Some participants thought that their responsibilities to their family members as well as community helped them move forward with their lives. For instance, Li felt that she had to move forward because of her responsibilities to her two sons. Wu attended vocational training and worked outside of her home for the first time in 22 years because of her responsibilities to her three children. Yu affirmed "In times of crisis, their focus is on life goals and responsibilities, but not emotions or losses. Family is their first priority. Providing a home for their elderly, children, and ancestral tablet is a major responsibility of all Hakkas."

Yu rejected her son's invitation to move to Taichung because she believed that it was her social responsibility to preserve Hakka culture and to reconstruct her hometown. She wanted to stay in Tung Shih to help her people recover from the disaster.

Other participants stressed the importance of self-reliance. Li said that being self-reliant gave her a sense of satisfaction. Ju thought that it was her responsibility to find ways to be self-reliant. Lu wanted to be self-reliant. He did not want to rely on people's mercy. Lin and Liu were amazed that a majority of collapsed houses were rebuilt within two years.

Li said, "Potential surfaces after great challenges." She likened challenges to the darkness before dawn. As soon as the sun rose, the darkness was gone in no time. Li asserted that she chose to have a happy life, and her focus was on the positive side of life. Lin said, "I am doing ok. I am willing to let go of many things. I don't dwell on that traumatic event." Lin believed that all people had the required potential to survive through hardships.

Hu reminded herself by saying "The sun will still rise tomorrow morning. Even though my life will not be the same, life goes on. My loss will not cause any changes to the world. The earth continues its regular motion regardless of my agony." With such a realization, she moved forward with her life. Hu stressed "Life is full of challenges. We need to have a positive thinking pattern. We need to focus on the positive side of all happenings. Normalize the challenges. Don't ever give up." Liu found that the residents of Tung Shih were more grateful for what they had.

They cherished everything they could put their hands on. She commented that by the summer of 2001, Tung Shih had been transformed. Liu said that she had learned to not blame Heaven or people for what happened. She continued, "When you blame Heaven or people, you relive the traumatic experience." Liu believed that crisis and opportunity were two sides of the same coin of disaster. She asserted that the Hakka were determined and hardworking people. They endured all hardships. She concluded, "Survivors in Tung Shih are doing well."

Hsiao declared that she enjoyed talking about her experience related to the 921 Earthquake. Because of the disaster, she got to know many wonderful people. She confirmed that the 921 Earthquake created many new possibilities for her and her family. Because of the disaster, it opened her eyes to see the real world, to know how wonderful people were, and more. Hsiao said that her life was quite simple before the disaster. The disaster enriched her life. She claimed that the 921 Earthquake was a crisis to her family, yet, it was a turning point for her family as well.

Hsiao and Chen expressed their appreciation for new possibilities resulted from the 921 Earthquake. They attended vocational trainings for disaster survivors; they attended the seeding support group; and they even tried out the free counseling services that were offered by pro bono clinical psychologists at the Health Center of Dongshih Township. Hsiao said, "I am more open-minded in terms of meeting new people and trying new things. Before, I didn't like counseling. I thought that it meant that I was sick. Now, I think counseling can be helpful. It's good to have an active listener or emotional trash can."

Service Providers

Jau noticed that some clients were well-organized and self-reliant even in times of crisis. They accepted what happened to them, and coped with it without any complaint. Jau affirmed that most of the survivors were ready to move forward with their lives. Hou found that many survivors discovered strengths from within. They cultivated ways to help themselves. He believed that those inner strengths helped survivors cope with the disaster, and moved forward with their lives. Hou affirmed, "Without such a great challenge, people would not have realized how resourceful they can be." Hou indicated the importance of acceptance in resilience. After survivors accepted the fact, they started coping with the problems that followed the disaster. Hou said that survivors accepted the 921 Earthquake as a natural disaster. They realized that they had no power to change the fact, but were capable of coping with its effects. Also, survivors in Tung Shih valued family and responsibilities. They often felt that it was their responsibility to provide daily necessities and a safe home for their family. Hence, they wanted to rebuild a house as soon as possible. Many survivors believed that after their houses were rebuilt and family incomes were stabilized, their lives could go back to the routines. Hou added, "They are self-reliant."

Su confirmed that the survivors of Tung Shih possessed many qualities that helped them move faster than survivors in other affected areas. He felt that people in Tung Shih had a strong support system within the township. Most of them were financially secure.

While many participants considered Hakka spirit *a strong positive cultural attribute influencing resilience* of survivors in Tung Shih, Chian pointed out that it sometimes caused stress. Her example was that the Hakka loved "face." For instance, a survivor lost his house to the disaster. He was not a rich man and had no resources to build a new house. But, he looked around his neighborhood and found that many of them had already started constructing new houses. He took the interest-free loans from the government, and borrowed some more money from relatives or friends to build a new house. The upside of this story was that he worked harder than usual to replace his house. The downside of this story was that he eventually lost his new house because he could not afford the mortgage.

Worst of all, it was difficult to sell these new houses because people knew many victims were crushed to death in those houses. Local people did not feel comfortable about living at a place where people died in the disaster. Outsiders had no interest in settling down in Tung Shih because of the fault lines. Jan stressed that most of her clients were low-income families and they moved forward with great difficulties.

Jau stated that working with survivors broadened his perspective. Wang affirmed that she was more willing to expression her emotions, had more compassion for others, learned to let go of many things, and learned to see things from different angles. In addition, she changed her priorities of important things in life. Before the disaster, work was her first priority. Afterwards, health was more important than anything else. Jan said that she learned to appreciate each day, and to focus on the here-and-now. She stressed, "Life is very precious, and don't procrastinate."

Hou enjoyed working with survivors in Tung Shih. He said that it was a very rewarding project for him. He considered it a great learning opportunity. Hou stated "Working with survivors of the 921 Earthquake fosters my personal growth. It has strengthened my ability to cope with challenges. Those survivors taught me great lessons in holding on firmly despite extreme adversity, and keeping on pursuing my goals."

Su considered working with survivors of the 921 Earthquake in Tung Shih a turning point in his life. Su stressed that he was there to learn life lessons from those survivors. Su affirmed "Working with survivors in Tung Shih has changed my attitude towards life. I am better able to accept the way things work out, and appreciate every day. This experience also helps me cope better with a severe car accident I experienced."

While helping others, our needs are met. Actually, I think survivors are more considerate than we service providers. When we home-visit survivors, they often respond with smiles. They do it even when they don't feel like to, because they don't want us to feel disappointed.

When we see smiles on their faces, we feel good about what we have done. We think we have done something good for others. Yet, it is the other way around. The survivors help us to feel good about ourselves by smiling at us. Su stressed that he had been going to Tung Shih for five years because that experience enriched his life.

Volunteers

Chiu and Fu said that the Hakka were resilient and flexible. They thought the Hakka were capable of surviving any kind of hardship. Although many of them were quite wealthy, there were no beautiful mansions in Tung Shih. Most of them had emergency funds handy that accelerated the process of recovery. Although some survivors became unemployed after the disaster, many of them had their orchards to fall back on. In addition, their relatives, friends, and neighbors were very supportive of them. In line with Chiu and Fu, Sun added, "The Hakka are very persistent, they don't give up easily." Further, the Hakka were self-reliant. They started cleanup and reconstruction projects right after the aftershocks diminished. They didn't wait for the government, religious groups, or NPOs to help them. Sun and Huang said that they hardly heard any Hakka sit there and wait for assistance from outsiders.

All six volunteers commented that their priorities of important things in life were changed. Sun said that the disaster helped her realize that life was ever-changing and life was too fragile. Shu changed his value system and ways of dealing with people. He said, "Life is too short and too fragile. There is no time for procrastination." Huang confessed that before the disaster, he had a lot of bad habits such as drinking, smoking, and gambling. After the disaster, he quit those habits and conducted a simpler lifestyle that consisted of home, work, and volunteer work.

Fu learned to cherish her life and appreciate each day. Fu said that before the disaster, she was hungry for wealth. She always wanted to make more money. After the disaster, wealth did not mean much to her anymore. Jeng learned to focus on the here-and-now. She was more active after the disaster. She said that interacting with people helped her move on with her life.

Chian commented that about 80 percent of the survivors were emotionally ready to move forward with their lives. Hou affirmed that he was in awe of how resilient the people of Tung Shih were. Those people experienced such a great shock, suffered from deaths of family members, relatives, friends, neighbors and/or severe property damages, yet they kept moving forward. Hou admired the people of Tung Shih. He was deeply touched by the resilience of people in Tung Shih and their positive attitudes. They were not defeated by the devastating earthquake. They faced the challenges and moved forward with their lives. Hou emphasized that even though he was an outsider, he noticed the growth of many people in Tung Shih.

Su was aware of positive changes in the survivors of Tung Shih through their conversations and interactions. Their attitudes toward the 921 Earthquake changed. Right after the disaster, survivors' conversations often conveyed a message of hopelessness and helplessness to some extent. After for a while, they seemed to be proud of themselves because of the reconstruction. According to Su, all survivors experienced posttraumatic growth. Their abilities of coping with natural disasters or crisis were strengthened. Su stated

> I don't have any research result to show you that survivors in Tung Shih have experienced posttraumatic growth. It is difficult to measure people's growth in thoughts or emotions. However, I am aware of survivors' changes through the way they converse with my team members and other people. Their economic conditions or living arrangements may not have changed. But, their attitudes toward those challenges have changed. I am not saying that all people in Tung Shih have experienced such a change; but at least, a majority of them have.

Based on those people whom Su associated with, he estimated that about 25 percent of them already reached the highest level of posttraumatic growth. Those survivors were able to enjoy their lives again. The remaining 75 percent also experienced positive changes in perceptions and attitudes. They moved forward with their lives to some extent. Survivors were resilient and definitely experienced posttraumatic growth.

CONCLUSION

This study indicates that disaster survivors' resilience can result from its cultural underpinnings. According to the official reports from the Taiwanese government, people in Taichung County, where Tung

Shih is located, experienced 13 natural disasters that caused life loss and/or property damage to that area from 1999 to 2001. In addition, a destructive earthquake, the 921, that devastated the entire town occurred five years prior to this study. Its ratio of death to population was 0.61 percent ("Social aid," n.d.). Yet, people in Tung Shih have a very different opinion about natural disaster. Many of them do not even think that they have experienced multiple natural disasters. Likewise, (Mead, 1934) has indicated that meaning is the construction of social reality. People learn to interact with others within a specific cultural context as they learn to share symbols. Sharing symbols means sharing expected action patterns. Symbolic interactionists point out that meanings vary between cultures and contexts, and change over time. In this case, the theory can provide a rationale that supports the manner in which the 921 disaster survivors in this study define their reality and meaning of the disaster.

Service providers and volunteers testify that people in Tung Shih are resilient survivors. Chian comments that about 80 percent of the survivors are emotionally ready to move forward with their lives. Hou affirms that survivors are brave in facing tremendous challenges. They face the challenges and move forward with their lives. Su finds that after survivors are strengthened, they reach out to people in need. Their roles change from a service receiver to a helper. Su claims that survivors' growth is obvious to him. Many survivors are better able to accept the way things work out. Survivors in Tung Shih not only accept the event, but also effectively cope with the challenges that follow. Su estimates that about one-quarter of the survivors in Tung Shih already reach the highest level of posttraumatic growth. Those survivors are able to enjoy their lives again. The rest of three-quarters also experience positive changes in perceptions and attitudes. However, they are not yet to the point that they can reenjoy their lives.

The most important lesson learned from this study is that culture plays a key role in terms of survivors' recovery, both emotional and physical. Almost all participants from the survivors, service providers, and volunteer groups identify *Hakka spirit* as a key cultural attribute influencing survivors' resilience. *Hakka spirit* is defined as "The *spirit of sturdy neck* which means to hold on firmly despite extreme adversity, or to keep on doing something without regard to one's own strength." It consists of qualities such as frugality, diligence, self-reliance, responsibilities, persistence and more. It is a lifestyle, a belief, a history of their ancestors, and the essence of their unique culture that has been developed over time.

It could also be pointed out that the *Hakka spirit* may have added to the stress of some survivors due to face-saving issues. Many survivors reconstructed their houses soon after aftershocks diminished because they had emergency funds available. But other survivors simply followed the trend regardless of financial strain. This is consistent to some extent with Cooley (1983), who claimed that people have a tendency to perceive of the self through the eyes of the other—the famed *looking glass self.* Because people are conscious about how they appear to others and how others judge them based on that appearance, they learn to adjust their responses to comply with the norms or the standards set by the majority and behave accordingly.

Many participants stress that *Hakka spirit* is a major cultural set of beliefs and behaviors that influenced resilience. This report was repeated by participants in each of the three groups in cross-case analysis. It is also important to note that the *Hakka spirit* was *pre-existing,* and that without the qualitative analysis, it may have gone unidentified. In summary, the *Hakka spirit* can be understood in this study as an example of a set of social practices that (a) were performed in a manner that encouraged resilience and growth, and (b) increased the capacity of human agents to thrive in adversarial situations. Further research can explore more directly the predictive qualities and specific contributions of *Hakka spirit* to the development of resilience.

REFERENCES

Al-Naser, F., & Sandman, M. (2000). Evaluating resilience factors in the face of traumatic events in Kuwait. *SQU Journal for Scientific Research, 2,* 111–116.

Anderson, R. (2000). *Earthquake disaster recovery.* Paper presented at the LEA conference.

Bolin, R., & Stanford, L. (1998). The Northridge earthquake: Community-based approaches to unmet recovery needs. *Disasters, 22*(1), 21–38.

Brief analysis of natural disasters in Taiwan. (2002). Taipei, Taiwan: Ministry of Interior Statistical Information Service, Taiwan.

Chichi (Taiwan) earthquake: Report of a quick investigation. (n.d.). Retrieved August 27, 2002 from http://www2.rcep.dpri.kyotou.ac.jp/~sato/taiwan/index.html

Comfort, L. K. (2000). Response operations following the Chichi, Taiwan earthquake: Mobilizing a rapidly evolving, interorganizational system. *Journal of Chinese Industrial Engineering.*

Cooley, C. H. (1983). *Human nature and the social order.* New York: Charles Scribner's & Sons.

Copper, J. F. (1993). *Historical dictionary of Taiwan.* Metuchen, NJ: The Scarecrow Press.

Davison, G. M., & Reed, B. E. (1998). *Culture and customs of Taiwan.* Westport, CT: Greenwood Publishing Group.

Doherty, G. W. (1999). Cross-cultural counseling in disaster settings. *The Australasian Journal of Disaster and Trauma Studies.*

Echterling, L. G. (2001). Hidden wounds, hidden healing of disaster. *Services to Disaster Responders.* Retrieved January 6, 2003 from http://cep.jmu.edu/vadisaster/hidden.htm

Fischer, H. W. (1998). *Response to disaster: Fact versus fiction & its perpetuation* (2nd ed.). New York: University Press of America.

Goltz, J. D. (1999). The "921" Chi-Chi, Taiwan Earthquake of September 21, 1999: Societal impacts and emergency response. Retrieved April 8, 2001 from http://www.eeri.org

Greene, R. R. (2002). *Resiliency: An integrated approach to practice, policy, and research.* Washington DC: NASW Press.

Jang, L. J. (2005). *The 9/21 Earthquake: A study of the effects of Taiwanese cultural factors on resilience.* Unpublished doctoral dissertation, University of Denver, Denver.

Jordan, D. K. (1999). *Gods, ghosts, & ancestors: Folk religion in a Taiwanese village* (3rd ed.). San Diego, CA: Department of Anthropology, UCSD.

Joseph, S., Williams, R., & Yule, W. (1993). Changes in outlook following disaster: The preliminary development of a measure to assess positive and negative responses. *Journal of Traumatic Stress, 6*(2), 271–279.

Kaulbach, B., & Proksch, B. (1984). *Arts and culture in Taiwan.* Taipei, Taiwan: Southern Materials Center.

Lee, G. C., & Loh, C.-H. (1999). Human and institutional perspectives of the 921 Earthquake in Taiwan: Lessons learned. Retrieved May 19, 2005 from http://mceer.buffalo.edu/research/taiwaneq9_99/docs/lessons.asp

Liao, Y. L. (Ed.). (1999). *Trauma of century.* Feng Yuan, Taiwan: Taichung County Government.

Lin, L. (2002). *Analysis of natural disasters in Taiwan.* Taipei, Taiwan: Ministry of Interior Statistical Information Service, Taiwan.

Mead, G. H. (1934). *Mind, self & society: From the standpoint of a social behaviorist.* Chicago: The University of Chicago Press.

Miles, M. B., & Huberman, A. M. (1994). *Qualitative data analysis: An expanded sourcebook* (2nd ed.). Thousand Oaks, CA: Sage.

Norris, F. H., Byrne, C. M., & Diaz, E. (2001). *50,000 disaster victims speak: An empirical review of the empirical literature, 1981–2001.* The National Center for PTSD and the Center for Mental Health Services (SAMHSA).

Pai, R. Y.] (1999). *9/21.* Taichung, Taiwan: The Vitalon Welfare Association.

Paton, D. (2006). Posttraumatic growth in disaster and emergency work. In L. G. Calhoun & R. G. Tedeschi (Eds.), *Handbook of posttraumatic growth: Research and practice.* Mahwah, NJ: Lawrence Erlbaum Association.

Paton, D., & Johnston, D. (2001). Disasters and communities: Vulnerability, resilience and preparedness. *Disaster Prevention and Management, 10*(4), 270–277.

Patton, M. Q. (1990). *Qualitative evaluation and research methods* (2nd ed.). Newbury Park, CA: Sage.

School safety questioned after the fault study. (1999). *9/21 Earthquake Special Report* Retrieved September 12, 2001, from http://www.yam.com/921e/after100703.html

Shaw, D. (2000, July 6–9). *Emergency relief measures and rehabilitation policies in the aftermath of the 9/21 Chi-Chi (Taiwan) Earthquake.* Paper presented at the EuroConference on Global Change and Catastrophe Risk Management: Earthquake Risks in Europe, IIASA, Laxenburg, Austria.

The social aid to and placement of refugees in 9/21 big quake analysis. (n.d.). Taipei, Taiwan: Department of Statistics, Ministry of Interior, Taiwan. Retrieved May 26, 2005 from http://www.moi.gov.tw/stat/english/index.asp

Taiwan. (1995). Retrieved November 5, 2003 from http://www.taiwandc.org/folk.htm

Taiwan: Culture. (2001). *Taiwan.* Retrieved March 31, 2001 from http://web.lexis-nexis.com/universe/docu.zV&_md5=d7fcb2f8005d378474de8b024fae12f7

Tourist guide for mountainous township. (2004). Tung Shih, Taiwan: Dungshr Township Administration, TCG.

Webster, R. A., McDonald, R., Lewin, T. J., & Carr, V. J. (1995). Effects of a natural disaster on immigrants and host population. *The Journal of Nervous and Mental Disease, 183*(6), 390–397.

Chapter 12

EXPLORING THE COMPLEXITY OF SOCIAL AND ECOLOGICAL RESILIENCE TO HAZARDS

DOUGLAS PATON, GAIL KELLY, AND MICHAEL DOHERTY

INTRODUCTION

The relationship between people and environment has long been recognized as an important context for the study of natural hazards (Mileti, 1999). Indeed, interaction between established human settlement (e.g., urban development, agriculture) and enduring natural systems (e.g., river systems, flood plains, forests) is fundamental to the study of relationships between natural processes, hazards, and disaster. The factors that influence whether or not the relationship between human and natural systems is sustainable, and how each responds to perturbations that impact on this interaction, is the subject of this chapter. Conceptualizations of this relationship have focused predominantly on two issues. One concerns how human settlement and behavior constitutes an adaptive demand for the environment. The second considers how people and communities cope with and adapt to environmental hazard consequences. It is, however, possible to add to another dimension to the way in which social-ecological interaction is conceptualized.

This chapter views social-ecological resilience from three perspectives. The first relates to the capacity of an ecological system to adapt to demands made upon it that are independent of human involvement. The second discusses how human action can constitute a demand on the adaptive capacity of ecological systems and its implications for understanding the social determinants of ecological sustainability. The third considers how social-ecological interaction can constitute a source of adaptive capacity for people and communities. While discussion focuses primarily on the second and third perspectives, it commences with a brief overview of the first.

RESILIENCE OF ECOLOGICAL SYSTEMS

In discussing ecological systems, Holling (1973) defined resilience as "the capacity of a system to absorb and utilize or even benefit from perturbations and changes that attain it, and so persist without a qualitative change in the system's structure" (p. 9). More recently, the concept has been defined as "the potential of a system to remain in a particular configuration and to maintain its feedbacks and functions, and involves the ability of the system to reorganize following disturbance-driven change" (Walker et al. 2002, p. 14).

The adaptation of the Australian flora to fire provides a good illustration of ecological resilience. While wildfire in Australia is rightly regarded as a hazard to human life and property, Australian ecosystems, which share these properties with others elsewhere in the world, have evolved over many millions of years to cope with fire and drought and have a high level of resilience to these forms of disturbance.

To appreciate the adaptive capacity of ecological systems it is necessary to consider the relationship with the characteristics or regime of the demands made upon a system. The particular fire regime—the combination in a given area of intensity, frequency and seasonality—influences the composition and structure of the vegetation and so while the responses of many plant species make them resilient to an individual fire, local populations and hence composition and structure may change in the long-term if the fire regime changes. Fire frequency is of particular significance to those species that are reliant on seed germination for reestablishment as there is a window of vulnerability between fires where the adults have been killed and the seedlings have not yet set new seed to reestablish a seed bank. Too frequent fire will lead to local extinction of such species.

Many Australian plant species are resilient to even intense fires. Fire *per se* (i.e., fire as a hazard event) cannot thus be regarded as being immediately detrimental to these species for any individual fire. Such species have evolved mechanisms that facilitate a capacity for co-existence with these environmental perturbations. These disturbance regimes are, however, the aspects of the system most likely to be defined as hazards by humans.

For example, the 2003 wildfires in the Brindabella Ranges west of Canberra (Australia) burnt large tracts of bushland but within 12 months of the fire 80 percent of all the plant species burnt had responded by resprouting. Of the other 20 percent of species that are reliant on seed germination after a fire, the majority had reestablished from seed within 12 months of the fire (Doherty, 2004). However, despite the vigorous ecological recovery after the wildfire, social recovery is less clear-cut—of the 491 homes destroyed during by the fire, only 33 percent have been rebuilt some two years after the fire (Hull, 2005). Only a proportion of residents have stayed to rebuild in the fire affected areas and there are still many vacant blocks pending a decision to rebuild from the owners. Although planning issues and underinsurance have contributed to the slow rebuilding process, there is also a strong residual effect relating to social resilience and how people have coped with the trauma of losing their homes.

Increasingly, people are an active component of the disturbance regime and, as such, represent an adaptive demand on ecological systems. For example, agricultural practices, economic and lifestyle choices and arson influence the demands faced by an ecological system and the rate of change of these demands and their sustainability. Understanding sustainability is thus best considered within the context of social-ecological interaction.

Human Demands on the Ecological System

While the Australian environment has produced ecological systems that are resilient to drastic change from hazard events, the same cannot be said of the human population, or at least the more recent arrivals. It could be argued that Aboriginal occupation was actually buffered against drastic change from hazard events due to the ability of people to move either seasonally or episodically as resources became locally diminished. This is evidenced by the long-term

(60,000 years plus) occupation of the Australian continent through not only individual fire and other hazard events, but also through major evolutionary forcing periods such as ice ages and the climatic and sea level changes associated with them. This illustrates the importance of adaptive strategies that reflect social-cultural acceptance and assimilation of the consequences of disturbance regimes, or hazards, which are intrinsic elements of the environments within which humans have elected to live. Contemporary human populations cannot, however, adopt adaptive strategies based on, for example, seasonal mobility. This begins to identify the factors that influence successful co-existence with disturbance regimes (hazards) in ways that facilitate sustained, long-term social-ecological integrity.

Historically, major international and national economic pressures have forced natural resource users to become more efficient in an effort to increase productivity (Kelly, 2000), placing greater stress upon ecological systems. Disturbance can also be traced to the fact that, within contemporary societies, economic and lifestyle choices make demands on ecosystems and typically take precedence over ecological sustainability, with any coincidence between them resulting more by chance than by sound judgment and planning (Berkes et al., 2003).

In their exploration of the reflexive relationship between the environment and human society, Fraser, Mabee and Slaymaker (2003) pointed out that while people impact on their environment, they are in turn vulnerable to environmental change. Declining economic viability due to the loss of productive farming land to salinity provides a good example of this. Fraser et al. (2003) highlighted three key complexities in the social-ecological system relationship: the response from the ecological system could take years to be seen (time lag between cause and effect); the population that impacts the ecological system and the population who experience the impact are often different (and sometimes different in terms of solution implementation and outcomes); and different communities respond differently to the hazard. That is, they vary in their adaptive capacity. Understanding reasons for the variance in the adaptive capacity of communities remains a vital area of research.

Klein, Nicholls and Thomalla (2003) concluded that resilience relates to those properties of the system that influences adaptive capacity (preparing for, planning for and managing hazards) and highlight-

ed a need to differentiate between reactive and proactive resilience
(Dovers & Handmer, 1992). Reactive resilience is associated with
adaptive capacity; the ability to prepare and plan for hazards, and to
implement strategies to manage hazards prior to, during and after the
event. Proactive resilience on the other hand, denotes the capacity of
humans to anticipate and learn. The latter construct embraces the concept of sustainability, and describes what Walker, Holling, Carpenter
and King (2004) refer to as transformative capital. This is defined as
the system's capacity to create a new system when changes to social,
economic and environmental conditions render previous systems
untenable. The significance of proactive resilience is heightened by
the recognized need to include intergenerational issues when considering chronic environmental hazards (Mileti, 1999; Paton, 1994).

SOCIAL-ECOLOGICAL INTERACTION
AND HUMAN ADAPTIVE CAPACITY

For Berkes et al. (2003) resilience of social-ecological systems is
related to sustainability. They define sustainability as an adaptive
capacity to deal with change and the maintenance of the capacity of
ecological systems to support social and economic systems in the context of the dynamic relationship between ecological systems and social
systems. It is when faced with crises such as environmental change
(e.g., to amenity, land use policy, climate etc.), environmental degradation, and natural hazard impacts that the dynamic nature of social-
ecological interaction becomes particularly salient (Gunderson, 2003).
Such crises also represent contexts within which adaptive capacity and
societal growth can occur (Berkes et al., 2003).

In areas susceptible to experiencing environmental hazards, a substantial portion of the attendant risk arises as a consequence of personal (e.g., living in peri-urban environment makes natural wildfire
activity a hazard for those making this choice) and societal choices
regarding economic activities (e.g., clear felling and farming practices
can influence the water table and hasten soil degradation, ground pollution from waste disposal, industrial production and fertilizer run-off).
Within this conceptualization, risk can be defined in terms of choices
which reflect a relatively enduring imbalance in the social-ecological
equation in the direction of the social side of the equation (Folke et al.,

2003). For example, clear felling may be regarded as an essential element in social (economic) resilience, but represent an activity that undermines long-term environmental biodiversity and sustainability.

The reciprocal nature of social-ecological resilience requires that, in order to effectively manage this risk, the level of coherence or balance between them be taken into account (Berkes et al., 2003). This is particularly so with regard to choices concerning agriculture, economic growth, industrial pollution and lifestyle choices that contribute to the social construction, in both a physical and a social-psychological sense, of hazards. Given that it is on the social side of the equation that these choices are made, a key issue concerns understanding the factors that influence social choices in ways that contribute to sustainability.

Social resilience has been described as the peoples' capacity to successfully adapt, and function positively, or competently regardless of chronic stress, severe trauma or their vulnerability to risk (Egeland, Carlson & Stroufe, 1993). It includes a capacity to withstand adversity and maintain adaptive behavior. It is important to note that being resilient does not imply invulnerability. Resilience is not absolute and will change over time and vary in different situations. The latter is particularly important when considering chronic environmental hazards (e.g., salinity, air and ground pollution) that impact social systems on several levels.

The individual has been the focus of much of the resilience research (Sonn and Fisher, 1998). However, Adger (2000) stated that social resilience has economic, spatial and social dimensions. Consequently, it must be defined at the community, and not individual, level. He defined resilience as "the ability of communities to withstand external shocks to their social infrastructure" (p. 349). This definition is closely related to the community competence construct (Iscoe, 1974; Eng & Parker, 1994). Iscoe summarized community competence as including: ". . . the provision and utilization of resources in a geographical or psychological community so that the members of the community may make reasoned decisions about issues confronting them, leading to the most competent coping with these problems" (p. 608).

Competent communities, like resilient individuals, develop effective ways of coping with the challenges of adversity, including the ability to respond to hazards and manage their impacts. This does not mean that the role of the individual is neglected. Rather it calls for the inclusion of both individual and community perspectives. For example, salinity affects whole communities, but often in an inconsistent manner as a result of the uneven distribution of its consequence (Paton, 1994). Consequently, to understand adaptation to salinity, it is necessary to consider individual (e.g., to deal with patchy distribution that affects some properties but not others) and community (e.g., mitigation requires collective action within a catchment) capacity to adapt. A comprehensive conceptualization of social-ecological resilience thus requires an integration of individual and community perspectives.

The capacity of a social system to adapt and respond to a crisis is also influenced by the nature of the hazard (Cross, 2001; Kelly & Steed, 2004; Paton, 1994). For example, wildfires are sudden, abrupt and fast moving. Their occurrence can, in a given area, be unpredictable and they tend to be episodic (e.g., with regard to the event/recovery/event cycle) and unless deliberately lit during winter months, seasonal. There can be a time lag between perceived cause (fuel build-up in a forest or around a property) and hazard occurrence, and there is a relationship between frequency and the vulnerability of the landscape (climate, forest, wind direction). Depending on the extent of the fire, there is usually a collective social response, but over time, individuals can be left to draw on their personal coping resources in order to manage the effects of the hazard.

In contrast, environmental degradation hazards (e.g., salinity) are insidious, incremental, possibly irreversible, have a diffusion pattern across the landscape, and possess a long-life expectancy. The latter requires that adaptation is conceptualized in a way that accommodates their long duration, their intergenerational implications, and a need to consider adaptation within a context of changing community membership. The impact of salinity initially draws on the coping capacity of individuals but eventually impacts at a collective level. The requirement to cope on a daily basis over a long period of time eventually erodes personal and collective coping resources. If this leads to depletion of resources, the effect is unidirectional leading to a permanent change of state in the local ecological system.

Chronic environmental hazards introduce another complication; their uneven distribution over time and within a community. For example, with these complex environmental hazards, there can be temporary relief (e.g., a wet season will flush the salt), a long time lag between the cause (tree clearing) and its effect (rising water table), and a time lag between the hazard and possible solution (revegetation).

These consequences can also change over time.

While salinity can affect whole catchments, the distribution of its consequences at any one time, and thus its social implications, are influenced by factors such as time since onset, the history of a property (e.g., regarding clear-felling and planting), topography, and so on. Uneven distribution of consequences can create a climate of dysfunctional community conflict. The fact that hazard characteristics and distribution can change over time adds an additional level of complexity to the management process. Consequently, it is necessary to consider the long-term issues that arise with regard to facilitating a capacity to co-exist with natural processes capable of becoming hazards and the need to integrate levels of analysis if a comprehensive understanding of social-ecological resilience is to be forthcoming. That is, it is important to understand the context of adaptation. This extends beyond the hazard per se to include the social dynamics of the community and how hazard characteristics interact with these social dynamics.

Hazard consequences that reflect social, political, or economic decisions (e.g., salinity resulting from social policy decisions supporting particular agricultural practices) can generate greater ambiguity and uncertainty regarding the nature and significance of their impact, disputes regarding their severity, disagreement regarding responsibility for causation and remedial work, and frequently require people to gather their own data in order to present a case as to their actual or potential effect (Hobfoll, Briggs & Wells, 1995; Jerusalem et al., 1995; Kelly, 2000; Paton, 1994).

Because they represent interaction between, for example, hazards, topography and meteorological conditions, consequences are often unevenly distributed over space and time. Uneven distribution can create social contexts characterized by feelings of unfairness, anger, mistrust, and alienation. The resultant social fragmentation can erode collective adaptive capacity (Paton, 1994; Solomon, 1986). Depletion of coping resources can reach a point where the social system is unable to cope with the situation (Hobfoll, et al., 1995). Crossing this threshold can lead to the deterioration of social ties and the breakdown of the social fabric that binds community members together, contributing to yet further erosion of collective adaptive capacity. The cumulative impacts of managing chronic or successive abrupt hazards can result in the loss of community coping resources that may take several generations to reverse, and in fact, may never actually be reversed

(Hobfoll, et al., 1995).

The complex relationship that can exist between personal and collective goals, hazard mitigation and environmental protection represents another source of conflict. For example, when dealing with chronic environmental hazards such as salinity, the goals of environmental protection and personal protection can overlap. That is, lifestyle and environmental sustainability, and thus, hazard reduction and environmental protection, are closely aligned as the economic viability of farming systems are usually reliant on environmental conditions. In contrast, with wildfire hazards, an environmental management strategy (e.g., controlled burning) may conflict with expectations derived from lifestyle choices (desire to live in close proximity to natural habitats such as forests). Resilience to wildfire hazards will be determined by individuals' and communities' success in reconciling the competing demands of environmental sustainability (e.g., land use, forest management), risk reduction (e.g., clearing or controlled burning), and personal lifestyle goals.

Given the diversity, and often conflicting nature of the interests within a community, conflict between citizens and land managers regarding hazard management are likely. This is particularly the case with activities such as hazard reduction burning where local opinion on the impacts of such activities and their desirability may conflict with the objectives of land managers. There is a clear need to link ecological understanding, education and community values in order to resolve these management issues. In many cases, there may be no need for a trade-off in values between managers and the community but where this is necessary, facts, opinions and values must all be explicitly taken into account if effective hazard management is to ensue.

Conflict should not, however, be automatically dismissed as a bad thing. Indeed, if well-managed it can play a significant role in facilitating community resilience (Berkes et al., 2003; Mileti, 1999; Paton & Bishop, 1996). In this respect, understanding the factors that influence these choices, and particularly those made in a context defined by competing needs, expectations and interests, becomes important.

A community that possesses the mechanisms for articulating issues and reconciling the diverse needs of its members is well-placed to use these conditions in beneficial ways. It provides a foundation for the development of a competent community with the social and psychological resources required to support future adaptive capacity (Bishop, Paton, Syme & Nancarrow, 2000; Eng & Parker, 1994; Kelly & Steed, 2004; Paton & Johnston, 2001). The benefits that accrue, however, depend on the degree to which these mechanisms and supporting norms and beliefs are integrated into the fabric and culture of the community. Furthermore, they must be managed in ways that sustain their existence over time, and within a context of changing community membership and interests (Paton & Bishop, 1996).

If they are to utilize these mechanisms to make decisions, communities need the data and information required to make informed choices regarding how they will manage their relationship with the environment and the hazards it could present. These issues are discussed next.

Social and Psychological Influences on Social-Ecological Interaction

To make decisions, people need information. The content and method of presentation of information influence perception of environmental risk and the degree of risk acceptance (Morgan & Lave, 1990; Nordlund & Garvill, 2002). Decision making is influenced by the level and depth of information provided, the level of trust in its source, its complexity, its consistency with salient expectations, and the extent to which environmental issues are believed to be personally threatening (Folke et al., 2003; Frewer, 2001; Lubell, 2002; Seguin, Pelletier & Hunsley, 1999). For example, people are more likely to adopt behavior that sustains social-ecological balance if they perceive information on the causes of environmental threats as personally relevant (Lubell, 2002). This indicates how, when people and communities are faced with competing choices about issues that affect their relationship with the environment, they strive to render it coherent within prevailing world views (Spash, 2002). A significant component of these world views are attitudes.

Environmental attitudes can be differentiated with regard to whether they are symbolic in nature or represent more fundamental or more salient beliefs. Symbolic environmental attitudes, such as those that reflect short-term fads or compliance with social norms or social desirability, rarely lead to more than token action (Jurin & Fortner, 2002; Lubell, 2002). In contrast, situation specific cognitions (e.g., a strong negative attitude to clear-felling) represent more reliable predictors of support for sustainable outcomes (Bamberg, 2003; Nordlund & Garvill, 2002; Steinheder et al. 1999). The influence of these attitudes is heightened if they are developed and sustained through social interaction within relational communities whose members endorse similar environmental attitudes (Eigner, 2001; McFarlane & Boxall, 2003). However, even amongst those who hold positive environmental attitudes, their influence on the interpretation of information presented and the behavior that ensues is a function of their relative importance rather than their existence per se.

While people hold attitudes to all facets of their life, they tend to organize them hierarchically according to their perceived salience or personal importance (Bagozzi & Dabholar, 2000; Bixler et al. 2002; Dietz Kalof & Stern, 2002; Hardin & Higgins, 1996; Nicholson, 2002). Dietz et al. (2002) discussed how value priorities, rather than values per se, differentiated peoples' choices regarding the balance between social and ecological objectives. In other words, support for sustainable action is more likely amongst those whose environmental beliefs are prioritized over those for other social issues (e.g., health care, crime, employment).

Maiteny (2002) concluded that support for environmental sustainability was a function of the degree of consistency between environmental attitudes and peoples' wider beliefs (e.g., social justice and equity in regard to the costs and benefits of environmental activities and their distribution throughout society). Lubell (2002) found that support for sustainable actions was predicted by beliefs that environmental protection did not threaten jobs, limit personal freedom or harm the economy. Here it can be inferred that environmental attitudes are less salient than those for employment and economic well-being and would, consequently, only be acted upon if other conditions (economic/employment) were satisfied. This discussion highlights one condition that influences whether attitudes predict action. How effectively this conversion is accomplished is a function of another set of factors.

Drori and Yuchtman-Yaar (2002) concluded that attitudes derived from specific hazard knowledge, particularly those with the potential to adversely affect people, increased the likelihood of attitudes predicting behavior. While attitudes increase intention to act, pro-environmental competence (a capacity to respond to the [specific] demands posed by conservation requirements), is essential for action to occur (Spash, 2002; Corral-Verdugo, 2002). This competence becomes increasingly important as the level of difficulty (e.g., curbside recycling versus lifestyle change to reduce resource use in the first place) in the behaviors required increases (Corral-Verdugo, 2002). Similarly, Pelletier (2002) argued that perceived competence predicts self-determination and intrinsic motivation which, in turn, predicts the search for information about environmental risk and actions required to mitigate this risk. While this competence influences individual behavior, additional issues affect collective action.

A belief in the power of collective action to result in sustainable outcomes is an important predictor of support for action (Montada & Kals, 2000; Nordlund & Garvill, 2002), as is a sense of responsibility to others (as opposed to personal responsibility to act) and concern for social justice (Kals & Russell, 2001; McMakin, Malone, & Lundgren, 2002; Montada & Kals, 2000; Syme, Kals, Nancarrow, & Montada, 2000). Strategies based on procedural justice principles are the preferred basis for arbitrating community environmental conflicts (Kals & Russell, 2001). Perceptions of justice do not appear to be based solely on equity regarding contemporary outcomes. Intergenerational equity judgments that extend the need for decisions to benefit present and future generations are also important (Mileti, 1999; Syme et al., 2000). That is, they include a need for sustainability and a capacity to engage in decisions that are beneficial to present and future generations.

Decisions regarding whether or not to support sustainable outcomes may be moderated by personal and community cost-benefit analysis (Mileti, 1999; O'Connor, Bord, Yarnal, & Wiefek, 2002). Perceived injustice in the distribution of costs and benefits of polluting activities may act in this capacity (Montada & Kals, 2000), as can community members' beliefs about the costs, benefits and achievability of collective environmental action (Lubell, 2002). While generally endorsed as important influences on choice (Lubell, 2002), the role of economic factors is influenced by the level of analysis adopted (Kemmelmeier, Krol, & Young, 2002). Kemmelmeier and colleagues found that economic factors predicted collective support for sustainable action, but were less influential as predictors of individual decisions. This difference reiterates the importance of integrating individual and community perspectives (Nonami, Kato, Ikeuchi, & Kosugi, 2002).

Nonami et al. (2002) concluded that while individual behavior was influenced by personal attitudes to environmental problems, collective behavior was affected by the level of attachment to specific environmental features. That is, behavior may be influenced by a sense of attachment to place. Hummon (1992) and Low and Altman (1992) described how place attachment, which reflects the degree of embeddedness of individuals within their social-ecological environments, results in people having an emotional investment in their community. This, in turn, increased motivation to protect salient facets of the environment.

The factors discussed here influence the likelihood of people and communities making choices that promote social-ecological balance. This increases their capacity to co-exist with natural processes and facilitates adaptive capacity through more effective management of environmental risk. While this social-ecological relationship has typically been interpreted with regard to understanding people as an adaptive pressure on ecological systems, and in regard to its consequences for their capacity to adapt to environmental perturbations, there is another way in which social-ecological interaction can be conceptualized. In the final section of this chapter, discussion focuses on social-ecological interaction as a source of peoples' adaptive capacity.

NATURAL ENVIRONMENT AS A SOURCE OF ADAPTIVE CAPACITY

There is growing evidence that direct and indirect experience of and engagement with the natural environment can promote, protect and restore subjective well-being following adverse experiences that disrupt a sense of psychological integrity (Conn, 1998; Day, 1998; Eigner, 2001; Kaplan, 1984, Kellert, 1997; Knapp & Poff, 2001). It has been linked to enhancing peoples' belief in their capacity to deal with challenging experiences (efficacy) and with enhancing social support quality.

The relationship between environmental experience and well-being may reflect a direct, restorative capacity of natural environment to reduce stress, anxiety and aggression, and to restore energy and health (Hartig, Mang & Evans, 1991; Hartig, Kaiser & Bowler, 2001). Exposure to natural environment, even if only indirectly in the form of watching videos, can enhance positive affect and reduce physiological arousal (e.g., lower blood pressure, muscle tension) (Parsons, Tassinary, Ulrich, Hebl, & Grossman-Alexander, 1998; Ulrich et al., 1991). Nature can compensate for the fatigue and exhaustion associated with dealing with adverse experiences through the sense of fascination it evokes and the opportunities it provides for personal reflection (Kaplan, 1995). Importantly, these researchers also concluded that environmental participation could act as a catalyst for developing and maintaining the competencies that predict adaptive capacity.

Self-efficacy, sense of community and problem-focused coping have been identified as predictors of people's capacity to adapt to environmental threat (toxic waste) and environmental degradation (salinity) (Bachrach & Zautra, 1985; Bishop et al., 2000). Kelly (2000) found that perceived control and past response to change at the community level (e.g., collective efficacy) was a significant factor in the adaptive capacity of communities. Thus, experiences that influence the development and maintenance of perceived control (e.g., self-efficacy) and a sense of belonging or community can contribute to the adaptive capacity of individuals.

What evidence exists to support the contention that environmental experience contributes to the development of these adaptive competencies? If this link exists, it would justify the inclusion of social-ecological interaction within hazard reduction, readiness and response planning, and support arguments for integrating hazard and environmental management (Mileti, 1999; Paton & Johnston, 2001).

Eigner (2001) linked well-being with the degree of life meaning derived from environmental activities. Deriving a sense of meaning in one's life from participating in the natural environment was also discussed by Conn (1998) and Feral (1998). Feral concluded that meaningful experience promoted personal development in the form of enhanced self-esteem, perceptual skills and self-efficacy. Other researchers have also posited a link between environmental experience and the development of self-efficacy and control beliefs (Eigner, 2001; Hwang, Kim & Jeng, 2000; Propst & Koesler, 1998; Riechard & Peterson, 1998). These are important individual-level competencies capable of enhancing capacity to deal with adverse experience. As noted by Paton (2003), the importance of self-efficacy lies with its role in facilitating confidence in dealing with new situations, expanding the number of action plans developed to deal with environmental problems and encouraging persistence in applying them. The latter is par-

ticularly important in the context of dealing with chronic environmental hazards such as salinity.

Meaningful experiences in natural environment can result in strong
environmental preferences being incorporated within the sense of self
(Bixler et al., 2002). This outcome can also be influenced by developmental experiences. Engagement in environmental activities during
childhood and adolescence, and growing up in family contexts characterized by positive attitudes towards environment, increase the likelihood of environmental experience enhancing subjective well-being
(Chawla, 1999; Legault & Pelletier, 2000; Maiteny, 2002). Attitudes
developed in this way may even fuel decisions to migrate to satisfy
personal needs to live in places that afford high quality environmental
experiences (Buergelt, 2003).

A capacity to adapt to environmental perturbations may also be
influenced by place attachment and sense of community (Harvey,
1996; Roberts, 1998; Vaske & Kobrin, 2001; Vorkin & Riese, 2001). As
outlined earlier, sense of community and place attachment represent
resources capable of contributing to the capacity of individuals and
communities to cope with or adapt to environmental hazard impacts
(Bachrach & Zautra, 1985; Bishop et al., 2000; Kelly & Doherty, 2004;
Paton & Bishop, 1996). How might this relationship be fostered?

Roberts (1998) argued that acceptance of the importance of a reciprocal relationship between self and environment contributes to the
development and maintenance of sense of place. That is, sense of
place is influenced by the perception of the interdependence between
personal benefits (e.g., satisfaction of personal needs) and the environment within which they are satisfied.

Vaske and Kobrin (2001) demonstrated an empirical relationship
between place attachment and support for ecological sustainability,
with place identity (e.g., the relationship between lifestyle preferences
and the environment within which one lives) mediating this relationship. Of interest was the finding that talking with others about environmental issues was an important indicator of place attachment.
From a risk management perspective, this is significant. Talking about
community issues is a significant predictor of hazard preparedness
(Paton et al., 2005), increasing the potential for place attachment to
constitute a predictor of adaptive capacity.

There is a clear interaction between where people live, their exposure to the environment in that area and their attachment to place.

That is, there is evidence that exposure can engender a positive and protective attitude to the local environment (e.g., Park Care, Bush Care, and Land Care groups). This exposure may come from passive or active participation in natural settings or from living in or near peri-urban areas.

Understanding people's attachment to place is necessary when considering the development and maintenance of personal and collective capacity to adapt to adverse hazard effects. Hummon (1992) and Low and Altman (1992) argued that people form emotional bonds to places as well as to other people, thus place attachments reflects the embeddedness of individuals within their social-ecological environments. Importantly, research suggests that people's perceptions of their physical environment most strongly influences their feelings toward their community (Campbell, Converse & Rodgers, 1976; La Gory, Ward & Sherman, 1985).

One construct to emerge from the place attachment research is community attachment; the emotional investment that people have in their community. Researchers (e.g., Goudy, 1982; Sampson, 1988) argued that community attachment is a process with bonds evolving over time through the day-to-day involvement in a residential setting. The subtle establishment of attachment causes many people to believe that these elements are unchanging (Brown & Perkins, 1992) and if changes in this relationship are severe (e.g., a natural hazard) the security of place attachment can be disrupted (Low & Altman, 1992). The disruption inevitably creates a period of stress, followed by a phase of coping and adaptation. Research involving disruption to place attachment, suggests that collective social attachments to places are particularly strong during times of relocation, upheaval and environmental disasters. In this way, community attachment could contribute to the capacity of a community to bounce back from disturbance or the motivation to adapt to new circumstances.

This relationship was explored by Kelly and Doherty (2004) in relation to place attachment, condition of the natural environment, and peoples' willingness to participate in the maintenance and planning of estuaries in their local urban area. They found significant correlations between attachment, perceived condition of the estuaries and willingness to contribute time to maintenance and planning. The role that the estuaries played in maintaining the social cohesion of the area was evident. For example, participants stated that the benefits of volunteering

through local bush care groups looking after the environment sur-
rounding the estuaries improved social networking and strengthened
people's attachment to, and pride in, the area.

The potential diversity that exists with regard to the social and economic uses of natural resources and patterns of recreational interaction with nature reiterates the importance of considering community
adaptative capacity as arising from how conflict over resources and
issues regarding equity are dealt with (Gunderson, 2003; Mileti, 1999;
Paton & Bishop, 1996). Equity and fairness in environmental consultation influence community risk acceptance (Syme, Bishop & Milich,
1992), an important precursor of intrinsically motivated action.
Community engagement based on social justice principles increases
community awareness of the trade-offs involved in environmental
management decisions and in creating safer environments. That is,
environments better equipped to deal with disturbance.

It is evident from the above discussion that interaction with the
environment can perform a restorative function and contribute to
well-being. It can also act as a protective factor in regard to mitigating
present and future stress, act as a catalyst for meaningful interaction
that facilitates the development and/or maintenance of adaptive competencies (e.g., self and collective efficacy), and contribute to the
development and maintenance of attachment and commitment to
place/community.

Additional work is required to identify how much environmental
experience is sufficient, what qualities it should contain and whether
different kinds of environmental engagement can be differentiated in
regard to their restorative and protective capacity (Bell et al., 2001).
For example, to what extent is its restorative and adaptive capacity
linked to passive (e.g., visiting a natural environment) versus active
participation (e.g., ornithology, volunteering for land care projects).
While passive interaction may still convey restorative benefits, it may
lack the quality of meaningful interaction that underpins the development and maintenance of adaptive capacity (i.e., that facilitate the
sense of challenge that contributes to environmental experience
enhancing self-efficacy) or that contribute to a sense of place attachment. In the absence of the latter, the quality of adaptive capacity may
be diminished. Furthermore, challenging activities can be differentiated in regard to their consistency with the goal of promoting ecological
sustainability (e.g., four-wheel driving versus estuary planning and

maintenance). Managing environment to facilitate hazard resilience thus adds a new dimension to an already complex management context. The issue of causality deserves additional attention. That is, to what extent does environmental experience elicit adaptive capacity or does the prior existence of these capacities increase the likelihood of engaging in environmental activities?

CONCLUSION

This chapter presented three perspectives on social-ecological resilience that have implications for natural hazard reduction, readiness and recovery planning. The reciprocal relationship between ecological resilience and social resilience is important at several interdependent levels. Ecological sustainability is vital. But it is important to encourage social-ecological interaction in ways that reconcile sustainability, the promotion of well-being and adaptive capacity, and the attainment of social goals. By identifying the factors and processes that facilitate this, it is possible to use this knowledge to provide a framework for intervention to facilitate community resilience to natural hazards. This will be particularly important for communities that must contend with the complex demands associated with chronic environmental hazards (e.g., salinity, air pollution).

The link between social-ecological reciprocity and hazard resilience means that it should play a more prominent role in emergency management planning than has hitherto been the case. Planning should include environmental and social-ecological strategies to mitigate hazard effects and to increase human adaptive capacity. Consequently, emergency management agencies, environmental management agencies and communities must work together to develop strategies to promote ecological sustainability in ways that reconcile environmental protection, reduction of natural hazard risk to people and society, and increasing resilience through social-ecological mechanisms.

REFERENCES

Adger, W. N. (2000). Social and ecological resilience: Are they related? *Progress in Human Geography 24*(3):347–364.

Bachrach, K. M., & Zautra, A. J. (1985). Coping with a community stressor: The threat of a hazardous waste facility. *Journal of Health and Social Behaviour, 26,* 127–141.

Bagozzi, R.P., & Dabholar, P.A. (2000). Discursive psychology: An alternative conceptual foundation to Means-End Chain Theory. *Psychology & Marketing, 17,* 535–586.

Bamberg, S. (2003). How does environmental concern influence specific environmentally related behaviours? A new answer to an old question. *Journal of Environmental Psychology, 23,* 21–32.

Bell, P.A., Greene, T.C., Fisher, J.D., & Baum, A. (2001). *Environmental Psychology* (5th Ed). Belmont, CA.: Wadsworth.

Berkes, F., Colding, J., & Folke, C. (2003). *Navigating social-ecological systems: Building resilience for complexity an change.* Cambridge: Cambridge University Press.

Bishop, B., Paton, D., Syme, G., & Nancarrow, B. (2000). Coping with environmental degradation: Salination as a community stressor. *Network, 12,* 1–15.

Bixler, R.D., Floyd, M.F., & Hammitt, W.E. (2002). Environmental socialization: Quantitative tests of the childhood play hypothesis. *Environment & Behavior, 34,* 795–818.

Brown, B. B., & Perkins, D. D. (1992). Disruptions in place attachment. In I. Altman & S. M. Low (Eds.), *Place attachment* (pp. 279–305). New York: Plenum Press.

Bürgelt, P.T. (2003). *Is New Zealand the right choice? The psychological and social factors influencing the decision for German immigrants to New Zealand to stay in New Zealand or to return to Germany.* Unpublished Masters thesis, Massey University, Palmerston North, New Zealand

Campbell, A., Converse, P., & Rodgers, W. (1976). *The quality of American life.* New York: Russell Sage.

Chawla, L. (1999) Life paths in effective environmental action. *Journal of Environmental Education, 31,* 15–26.

Conn, S.A. (1998). Living in the earth: Ecopsychology, health and psychotherapy. *Humanistic Psychologist, 26,* 179–198.

Corral-Verdugo, V. (2002). A structural model of proenvironmental competency. *Environment & Behavior, 34,* 531–549.

Cross, J. A. (2001). Megacities and small towns: Different perspectives on hazard vulnerability. *Environmental Hazards, 3,* 63–80.

Day, M.D. (1998). Ecopsychology and the restoration of home. *Humanistic Psychologist, 26,* 51–67.

Dietz, T., Kalof, L., & Stern, P.C. (2002). Gender, values, and environmentalism. *Social Science Quarterly, 83,* 353–364.

Doherty, M.D. (2004). *Post Fire Recovery after the 2003 Canberra Fires–Bouncing Back in Bimberi, Brindabella and Burrinjuck.* Paper delivered to the Bush fire 2004, Conference, Adelaide, 25–28 May 2004.

Dovers, S.R., Handmer, J.W. (1992). Uncertainty, sustainability and change. *Global Environmental Change, 2*(4), 262–276.

Drori, I., & Yuchtman-Yaar, E. (2002). Environmental vulnerability in public perceptions and attitudes: The case if Israel's urban centers. *Social Science Quarterly, 83,* 53–63.

Egeland, B.R., Carlson, E., & Sroufe, L.A. (1993). Resilience as process. *Development & Psychopathology. Special Milestones in the development of resilience. 5,* 517–528

Eigner, S. (2001). The relationship between "protecting the environment" as a dominant life goal and subjective well-being. In P. Schmuck and K.M. Sheldon (Eds.), *Life goals and well-being: Towards a positive psychology of human striving* (pp 182–201). Kirkland, WA: Hogrefe & Huber Publishers.

Eng, E., & Parker, E. P. (1994). Measuring community competence in the Mississippi Delta: The interface between program evaluation and empowerment. *Health Education Quarterly, 21*(2), 199–220.

Feral, C-H. (1998). The connectedness model and optimal development: Is ecopsychology the answer to emotional well-being? *Humanistic Psychologist, 26,* 243–274.

Folke, C., Colding, J., & Berkes, F. (2003). Synthesis: Building resileince and adaptive capacity in social-ecological systems. In F. Berkes., J. Colding, & C. Folke (Eds.), *Navigating social-ecological systems: Building resilience for complexity and change.* Cambridge: Cambridge University Press.

Fraser, E.D., Mabee, W., & Slaymaker, O. (2003). Mutual vulnerability, mutual dependence. The reflexive relation between human society and the environment. *Global Environmental Change, 13,* 137–144.

Frewer, L.J. (2001). Environmental risk, public trust and perceived exclusion from risk management. (pp. 221–248). In G. Boehm & J. Nerb (Eds.), *Environmental risks: Perception, evaluation and management.* Ukraine: Elsevier Science/JAL Press.

Goudy, W. J. (1982). Further considerations of indicators of community attachment. *Social Indicators Research, 11,* 181–192.

Gunderson, L.H. (2003). Adaptive dancing: Interactions between social resilience and ecological crises. In F. Berkes., J. Colding, & C. Folke (Eds.), *Navigating social-ecological systems: Building resilience for complexity and change.* Cambridge: Cambridge University Press.

Hardin, C.D., & Higgins, E.T. (1996). Shared reality: How social verification makes the subjective objective. In R.M. Sorrentino & E.T. Higgins (Eds.), *Motivation & Cognition, Volume 3, The interpersonal context.* New York: The Guildford Press.

Hartig,T., Mang, M., & Evans, G.W. (1991). Restorative effects of natural environment experience. *Environment and Behavior, 23,* 3–26.

Hartig, T., Kaiser, F.G., & Bowler, P.A. (2001). *Further development of a measure of perceived environmental restorativeness* (Working Paper No. 5). Gavle, Sweden: Uppsala University, Institute for Housing Research.

Harvey, M.R. (1996). An ecological view of psychological trauma and trauma recovery. *Journal of Traumatic Stress, 9,* 3–23.

Hobfoll, S. E., Briggs, S., & Wells, J. (1995). Community stress and resources: Actions and reactions. In S. E. Hobfoll & M. W. de Vries (Eds.), *Extreme stress and communities: Impact and intervention* (pp. 137–158). Maastricht, The Netherlands: Kluweer Academic Publishers.

Holling, C.S. 1973. Resilience and stability of ecological systems. *Annual Review of Ecology and Systematics,* 4:1–24.

Hull, C. (2005). Article in *The Canberra Times,* 30th April 2005.

Hummon, D. M. (1992). Community attachment: Local sentiment and sense of place. In I. Altman & S. M. Low (Eds.), *Place attachment.* New York: Plenum Press.

Hwang, Y-H., Kim, S-I., & Jeng, J-M. (2000). Examining the causal relationships among selected antecedents of responsible environmental behaviour. *Journal of Environmental Education, 31,* 19–25.

Iscoe, I. (1974). Community psychology and the competent community. *American Psychologist, 29:*607–613.

Jerusalem, J., Kaniasty, K., Lehman, D., Ritter, C., & Turnbull, G. (1995). Individual and community stress: Integration of approaches at different levels. In S. E. Hobfoll & M. W. de Vries (Eds.), *Extreme stress and communities: Impact and intervention* (pp. 105–129). Maastricht, The Netherlands: Kluwer Academic Publishers.

Jurin, R.R., & Fortner, R.W. (2002). Symbolic beliefs as barriers to responsible environmental behaviour. *Environmental Education Research, 8,* 373–394.

Kals, E. & Russell, Y. (2001). Individual conceptions of justice and their potential for explaining proenvironmental decision making. *Social Justice Research, 14,* 367–403.

Kaplan, S. (1995). The restorative benefits of nature: Towards a integrated framework. *Journal of Environmental Psychology, 15,* 169–182.

Kaplan, S. (1984). Wilderness perception and psychological benefits: An analysis of a continuing program. *Leisure Sciences, 6,* 271–290.

Kellert, S.R. (1997). Kinship to Mastery: Biophilia in human evolution and development. Washington, DC.: Island Press.

Kelly, G. J. (2000). *Communities adapting to Change: Case Studies from South Western Australia.* Unpublished Doctoral Dissertation, Curtin University of Technology, Perth, Australia.

Kelly, G.J. ,& Doherty, M.D. (2004). *North Wollongong lagoons: Social values and issues in the Fairy, Towradgi and Hewitts/Tramway estuaries.* Study commissioned by the Wollongong City Council. CSIRO Sustainable Ecosystems, Canberra.

Kelly, G.J., & Steed, L.G. (2004). Communities adapting to change: A conceptual model. *Journal of Community Psychology, 32*(2), 201–216.

Kemmelmeier, M., Krol, G., & Young, H.K. (2002). Values, economic, and proenvironmental attitudes in 22 societies. *Cross Cultural Research: The Journal of Comparative Social Sciences, 36,* 256–285.

Klein, R.J.T., Nicholls, R.J., & Thomalla, F. (2003). Resilience to natural hazards: How useful is this concept? *Environmental Hazards, 5:*35–45.

Knapp, D., & Poff, R. (2001). A qualitative analysis of the immediate and short-term impact of an environmental interpretive program. *Environmental Education Research, 7,* 55–65.

La Gory, M., Ward, R., & Sherman, S. (1985). The ecology of aging: Neighborhood satisfaction in an older population. *Sociological Quarterly, 26,* 405–418.

Legault, L., & Pelletier, L.G. (2000). Impact of an environmental education program on students' and parents' attitudes, motivation, and behaviours. *Canadian Journal of Behavioral Sceince, 32,* 243–250.

Low, S. M., & Altman, I. (1992). Place attachment: A conceptual inquiry. In I. Altman & S. M. Low (Eds.), *Place attachment.* New York: Plenum Press.

Lubell, M. (2002). Environmental activism as collective action. *Environment & Behavior, 34,* 431–454.

Maiteny, P.T. (2002). Mind in the gap: Summary of research exploring "inner" influences on pro-sustainability learning and behaviour. *Environmental Education Research, 8,* 299–306.

McFarlane, B.L., & Boxall, P.C. (2003). The role of social psychological and social structural variables in environmental activism: An example of the forest sector. *Journal of Environmental Psychology, 23,* 79–87.

McMakin, A.H., Malone, E., & Lundgren, R.E. (2002). Motivating residents to conserve energy without financial incentives. *Environment & Behavior, 34,* 848–863.

Mileti, D. (1999). *Disasters by design.* Washington, DC.: Joseph Henry Press.

Montada, L., & Kals, E. (2000) Political implications of psychological research on ecological justice and proenvironmental behaviour. *International Journal of Psychology, 35,* 168–176.

Morgan, M. G., & Lave, L. B. (1990). Ethical considerations in risk communication practice and research. *Risk Analysis, 10,* 355–358.

Nicholson, S.W. (2002). *The love of nature and the end of the world: The unspoken dimensions of environmental concern.* Cambridge, MA.: The MIT Press.

Nonami, H. Kato, J., Ikeuchi, I.H., & Kosugi, K. (2002). Environmental volunteer and average resident collective action towards rivers as public goods: Determinants of personal and group behaviour. *Japanese Journal of Social Psychology, 17,* 123–135.

Nordlund, A.M. & Garvill, J. (2002). Value structures behind proenvironmental behaviour. *Environment & Behavior, 34,* 740–756.

O'Connor, R.E., Bord, R.J., Yarnal, B., & Wiefek, N. (2002). Who wants to reduce greenhouse gas emissions? *Social Science Quarterly, 83,* 1–17.

Parsons, R., Tassinary, L.G., Ulrich, R.S., Hebl, M.R., & Grossman-Alexander, M. (1998). The view from the road: Implications for stress recovery and immunization. *Journal of Environmental Psychology, 18,* 113–140.

Paton, D. (1994). The psychosocial aspects of managing chronic environmental disasters. *Disaster Management, 6,* 13–18.

Paton, D. (2003). Disaster Preparedness: A social-cognitive perspective. *Disaster Prevention and Management, 12,* 210–216.

Paton, D., & Johnston, D. (2001). Disasters and communities: Vulnerability, resilience and preparedness. *Disaster Prevention and Management, 10,* 270–277.

Paton, D., Smith, L.M., & Johnston, D. (2005). When good intentions turn bad: Promoting natural hazard preparedness. *Australian Journal of Emergency Management, 20,* 25–30.

Paton, D. and Bishop B. (1996). Disasters and communities: Promoting psychosocial well-being. In D. Paton and N. Long (Eds.), *Psychological aspects of disaster: Impact, coping, and intervention.* Palmerston North, Dunmore Press.

Pelletier, L.G. (2002). A motivational analysis of self-determination for pro-environmental behaviours. In E.L. Deci & R.M. Ryan (Eds.), *Handbook of self-determination research* (pp. 205-232). Rochester, NY.: University of Rochester Press.

Propst, D.B., & Koesler,R.A. (1998). Bandura goes outdoors: Role of self efficacy in the outdoor leadership development process. *Leisure Sciences, 20,* 319–344.

Riechard, D.E., & Peterson, S.J. (1998). Perception of environmental risk related to gender, community socioeconomic setting, age and locus on control. *Journal of Environmental Education, 30,* 11–19.

Roberts, E.J. (1998). Place and the human spirirt. *Humanistic Psychologist, 26,* 5–34.

Sampson, R. J. (1988). Local friendship ties and community attachment in mass society: A multilevel systemic model. *Amercian Sociological Review, 53,* 766–779.

Seguin, C., Pelletier, L.G., & Hunsley, J. (1999). Predicting environmental behaviours: The influence of self-determined motivation and information about perceived environmental health risk. *Journal of Applied Social Psychology, 29,* 1582–1604.

Solomon, S. D. (1986). Mobilizing social support networks in times of disaster. In C. R. Figley (Ed.), *Trauma and its wake: Vol. 2. Traumatic stress theory, research, and intervention* (pp. 232-263). New York: Brunner/Mazel.

Sonn, C. C., & Fisher, A.T. (1998). Sense of community: Community resilient responses to oppression and change. *Journal of Community Psychology* 26(5):457–472.

Spash, C.L. (2002). Informing and forming preferences in environmental valuation: Coral reef biodiversity. *Journal of Economic Psychology, 23,* 665–687.

Steinheder, B., Fay, D., Hilburger, T., Hust, I., Prinz, L., Vogelgesang, F., & Hormuth, S.E. (1999). Social norms as predictors of environmental behaviour. *Zeitschrift fuer Sozialpsychologie, 30,* 40–56.

Syme, G.J., Kals, E., Nancarrow, B.E., & Montada, L. (2000). Ecological risks and community perceptions of fairness and justice: A cross-cultural comparison. *Risk Analysis, 20,* 905–916.

Syme, G. J., Bishop, B. J., & Milich, D. (1992). Public involvement and dam safety criteria: Towards a definition of "informed consent." *ANCOLD Bulletin, 92,* 12–15.

Ulrich, R.S., Simons, R.F., Losito, B.D., Fiorito, E., Miles, M.A., & Zelson, M. (1991). Stress recovery during exposure to natural and urban environments. *Journal of Environmental Psychology, 11,* 201–230.

Vaske, J.J. & Kobrin, K.C. (2001). Place attachment and environmentally responsible behaviour. *Journal of Environmental Education, 32,* 16–21.

Vorkin, M., & Riese, H. (2001). Environmental concern in a local context: The significance of place attachment. *Environment & Behavior, 33,* 249–263.

Walker, B., C. S. Holling, S. R. Carpenter, & A. King. (2004). Resilience, Adaptability and Transformability in Social-ecological Systems. *Ecology and Society, 9*(2):5 [online] www.ecologyandsociety.org/vol9/iss2/art5

Walker, B., S. Carpenter, J. Anderies, N. Abel, G. S. Cumming, M. Janssen, L. Lebel, J. Norberg, G. D. Peterson, & R. Pritchard. (2002). Resilience management in social-ecological systems: A working hypothesis for a participatory approach. *Conservation Ecology 6*(1):14 [online] http://www.consecol.org/vol6/iss1/art14

Chapter 13

THE MEDIA, BUSHFIRES
AND COMMUNITY RESILIENCE[1]

W. Peter Hughes and Peter B. White

INTRODUCTION

The media plays a pivotal role in the development of resilience in the face of potential and actual risks associated with bushfires. For most people bushfires are experienced through the media. They rely on media reports for their understanding of bushfires. For those living or working in potential fire zones the media are used by emergency services to both warn and educate their constituents about the potential dangers of bushfires and the strategies that they should adopt to mitigate risk prior to, and in the event of a fire. For people directly exposed to bushfires, the emergency services and the media provide up-to-date information about the status of fires. And in the aftermath of fires, the media play an important role in the public debate about causes and effects of bushfires and the preventative strategies and policies which should be adopted to reduce potential hazards in the future.

This chapter considers resilience, bushfires and the media from three perspectives. They are media constructions of bushfires and bushfire risk; the role the media play in shaping community responses to bushfires; and strategies for building more productive relationships between the media and fire authorities.

1. The authors wish to thank the Bushfire Cooperative Research Centre for funding this project, and Dr Linda Anderson-Berry, Bureau of Meteorology, Melbourne for her encouragement. We would also like to thank Heidi Zogbaum and Dinah Partridge for their research assistance and the staff of Emergency Management Australia for their help with locating documentary materials.

MEDIA CONSTRUCTION OF
BUSHFIRES AND BUSHFIRE RISK

Media Reports Perpetuate Myths

A common theme in the treatment of media representations of bushfires is an ambivalence toward the media. On the one hand they are seen as important sources of information for the community, but on the other hand there is a concern with the potential for misinformation, the perpetuation of myths and "flawed" story structures, and the possibility of alarm (Esplin, 2003, p. 137).

Conrad Smith (1992b), writing in the United States, has been a major critic of media reporting of wildfires. His major work on media reporting of fires concerned a study of the media coverage of fires in the Yellowstone area of Montana. His criticisms of media coverage concluded that they tended to reinforce myths about fires, that journalists are more interested in the context in which facts are presented than in accuracy, and that they made the mistake of applying story models to wildfires which were more appropriate to urban fires (Smith, 1992b, p. 64). Concern about the lack of a longer-term perspective is evident in a number of sources. McKay (1983), for example, points to the need for the media to present information to help reduce the personal impact of fires but is concerned that "vital issues in land use management such as restricting development or imposing building regulation on housing in fire prone areas were not given prominence" (p. 289).

Another criticism of the media arises in McKay's (1983) discussion: the representation of those affected by fires as victims. She noted that:

> reports focused on descriptions of victims as helpless during and after the event and also proved a general description of the loss. Over this period, victim and non-victim members of the public were provided with very little information which would help them to mitigate the personal impact of a future fire. (p. 289)

Along with the presentation of residents as victims, and a lack of attention to long-term public policy debates about the role played by urban development, there is a third issue, scapegoating:

> Often newspaper reports can undermine bushfire information campaigns by being too fatalistic and thus not stimulating the individual to adopt self-protecting measures. The fatalistic reporting arises when causes of the bushfires are scapegoated to be either arsonists or poor management behavior in areas of natural bush. (McKay, 1999, p. 317)

The concern here is that rather than developing a sense of self-reliance, the causes of fires are being presented as out of the control of residents, thereby encouraging an attitude of fatalistic passivity (see Chapter 7).

One explanation for this approach to reporting is that in searching for a "hook" for stories about fires, especially in the days after the immediate event, the media tend to fall back on tried and tested story structures. One of the prominent structures on which reporters fall back is the blaming of scapegoats, particularly arsonists (and sometimes looters) and fire authorities. For McKay (1999) the problem with scapegoating is it precludes deeper analysis of causes:

> It is a pity that in all that prominent news space coverage of the event there were no reports looking at the broader view about the multiple causes of the event and land-use policies. This is in keeping with the research on scapegoating. Once a scapegoat is found then any deeper underlying of causes are overlooked. Perhaps in the next major bushfire event the local papers will be able to reflect on the deeper issues and it will be possible to add a new category to the content themes in newspaper reporting that is, planning issues. (p. 318)

Another criticism of the media which arises is the role of the media in exacerbating stress, either for residents "because of their presentation and interpretation of events" or for fire authorities by their mere presence (Henderson & McKinney, 2003; Moran, 1995, p. 184). Linked to this is a concern of some authorities that reporting of fires will lead to alarm in the community. The coronial inquest into the Canberra bushfires was told that "firefighting authorities were wary of providing the media with information that might cause widespread alarm" (*ABC News* - Australia, 2004).

Initiatives designed to develop social capacity to adapt to hazard consequences and to continue to function in the face of disruption must acknowledge that the media are important sources of information for the community. However, the role of the media as vehicles for misinformation, perpetuating myths and reporting using story structures which search for scapegoats and generate both passivity and alarm must be acknowledged. Strategies that could be used by the media to complement the development of adaptive capacity are discussed in Chapter 7. With wildfire hazards, these strategies could be implemented annually as the season approaches. For hazards with more general prevalence, these strategies could be linked to mitigation actions conducted by emergency management agencies.

Differences Between the Media

Any attempt to understand how the media can be used to develop resilience needs to take into account the strengths and weaknesses of the different media, as well as any common patterns across them. Newspapers are seen by some commentators as being superior media for warnings and information. Speaking of the fires in the ACT, Sally Jackson (2002) quotes the editor of the *Canberra Times* claiming that "No one else could tell this story as well as we could," and

> that Saturday, and on following days, the paper completely remade itself, devoting up to 16 news pages to its fire coverage, with more space in its letters and opinion columns. The paper's print runs were substantially increased, but even so, two editions, on the Sunday and Monday, had to go to a second run after the first sold out.

Nevertheless, in the immediate crisis of a fire emergency radio is seen as the first place to go to for information. Writing about the Ash Wednesday fires of 1983 in South East South Australia, O'Connor and O'Connor (1993) comment "the radio stations . . . were, during the period of fire for people in endangered rural areas, often the only source of information" (p. 153). They go on to make the point that although relaying news reports was important the most effective function of local radio stations was to pass on important information to the public from police, the Community Fire Service and other authorities. Citing specific examples they point to the strength of radio in the presentation of continual reports, messages and information, including advice on where help was available and reassurance to parents of evacuated school children. In addition, authorities were able to use radio to request people not to use telephones needed for priority calls. Radio services attempted to alleviate the sense of disorientation and anxiety (O'Connor & O'Connor, 1993, p. 154).

An important point to note about this use of radio, as networking increases in Australian radio, is "how important it is for the regions to have their own media, which in times such as Ash Wednesday can be dedicated completely to meet the needs of their own community" (O'Connor & O'Connor, 1993, p. 155). The Esplin (2003) report into the 2003 Victorian fires noted a concern "that some rural radio stations have skeleton staff as they relay feed from another station–generally from a capital city that may be in another state. These stations are less able to respond to local emergency issues" (p. 137). The important role of local radio has been noted in relation to the fires in the ACT in 2003. The McLeod (2003) report comments that:

> Media coverage of the event varied. It was ABC Radio 666 that became the carrier of most information for the public in keeping with its service charter. The ABC had maintained close contact with ESB [Emergency Services Branch] as the fires were developing and had reporters available to deploy to ESB and the field as the emergency unfolded. (p. 46)

A number of sources have reported on the importance of radio in both providing information and a sense of connectedness in the Canberra fires (Worthington, 2004), The Canberra fires seem to be first for which the internet emerges as an important source of both information and personal stories about survival (Hughes, 2003).

In light of these findings strategies to enhance community resilience must take account of the strengths and weaknesses of potential media partners. Broad scale policy debates and campaigns designed to enhance preparedness for diasters which involve complexity and carefully reasoned argument will be best suited to newspapers. Localized responses to imminent or actual threats are best dealt with using the electronic media, particularly when specific local media are seen to be trustworthy and reliable in local communities. With regard to its role in facilitating adaptive capacity, the media can play other roles. Prominent here is their relationship with emergency agencies responsible for response management, particularly with regard to their role in providing accurate information on the event and the dissemination of information from emergency management agencies.

BUILDING MORE PRODUCTIVE MEDIA
RELATIONSHIPS WITH FIRE AUTHORITIES

Need for a Disaster Media Plan

A key focus on the preparation for disasters and the development of societal resilience should be on the development of media plans where emergency services can develop a mutually productive relationship with media workers and media organizations. It is only relatively recently that much attention has been paid to relations between the media and fire authorities. The Royal Commission into the Victorian fires of 1939 (Victoria State Government, 1939) made scant mention of the media. However, the need for a disaster media plan, to enable fire authorities better to manage the media in emergency situations, has been recognized for some time now: "During a large incident, such as a bushfire or a major urban fire, the media is a resource to be exploited by the fire service. It is the critical conduit for information to the general public in terms of warnings and other information (Schauble, 1998, p. 367)."

In 1982, bushfires devastated large tracts of land in Tasmania. In his analysis of the events Britton (1983) highlighted a need to attend to communication between the news media and firefighting bodies in a bushfire situation. He provided a short list of areas where an improvement in dialogue was called for. Britton began with the most basic: that there be a recognition that media and firefighters are partners in a civil emergency, rather than antagonists. There has to be a flow of relevant, accurate, up-to-date, unambiguous information. This requires one or several trained media liaison officers who act as spokespersons and are known to media personnel. However, journalists also need training in order to report responsibly and without exaggeration, misinformation or fanciful interpretations of events (Britton, 1983).

That little progress has been made in the intervening years was shown in 1998 by John Schauble. He gave good advice to fire services as well as media personnel on how to proceed when gathering information on a bushfire. He proposed that an understanding of the other party's needs and constraints was essential. Tight deadlines on the side of the press; an ongoing emergency on that of the firefighters. But, he urged, firefighters have to put up with the inconvenience of reporters at the moment when they have least time to do so. The most senior officer, or should he be unavailable, a designated contact person should be in charge of delivering the required information. Since journalists are going to obtain a story in any way they can, this is the most responsible arrangement that will benefit both sides by delivering accuracy and a considered, calm approach to the emergency situation. To the individual who might be approached by media personnel he advises: "If you can't say it on the record, then don't say it at all" to guard against outbursts of anger or ill-considered remarks about fellow officers or the perceived misjudgements by state government officials (Schauble, 1998, pp. 368-372).

However, the scenario which Schauble recorded in 1998 no longer exists. No firefighter in Victoria is allowed to speak to media, although they can be photographed and filmed on the job. Because of the problems of inappropriate remarks or misleading comments by firefighters outlined by Schauble, all information on bushfires in Victoria is now issued by the Department of Sustainability and Environment.

Recently, three major fire events in Australia (Ash Wednesday, and fires in the ACT and northern Victoria in 2003) focused attention on relations between fire authorities and the media. The approach to the handling of the media in an emergency situation by O'Neill (2003) demonstrates the sophistication of thinking that has developed in this area in recent times. He argues the preparation of a "Crisis Media Plan" before an emergency occurs will avoid blunders and unnecessary diversions of personnel, and that this should be part of the overall "business continuity plans" of any organization. Making full use of computer technology and its ability rapidly to generate, distribute and disseminate information, O'Neill's (2003) recommendations aim at rapid response and damage control by professional media personnel who understand how the different media operate and how to address the needs of different audiences (p. 54). Stressing the need for up-to-date and accurate information his paper gives advice on what to consider in a media interview, so that the organization appears to in a positive light. O'Neill (2003) argues that well-prepared media releases can be used both to appease the public and please the media. In a media conference, he recommends what has always been commonsense strategy and basic politeness: "Keep the statement brief, provide a copy of your statement, express sympathy first, do not lie, do not apportion blame" (p. 12).

Discussing why a media disaster plan is needed, O'Neill (2003 or 2004?) draws on the experience of the Canberra fires which involved "a community that on the whole, was not aware of the threat or prepared for such a large disaster. The Australian Capital Territory Emergency Services (ACTES) had one media officer and had not developed a crisis communication plan to manage the media during the disaster." As a result the coverage of the fires was uneven and the information sought by the media was not always available (pp. 3–4). For O'Neill (2003) one of the significant advantages of a proper media strategy is that senior staff can devote full energies to fighting fires: "A significant consequence of the heavy media demands of the ACTES was the diversion of senior management from operational matters to assist in the media response" (p. 4).

O'Neill's (2003) recommendations point to the need for future planning to better enable an appropriate response at the time of an emergency. There are at least three phases to media coverage of fires which need to be planned for. The shortest term deals with the immediate fire situation, while the fire is still raging, the medium-term deals with recovery from the fire, while the longest-term deals with the debates which surround bushfires generally: the debates about land-use planning, debates about control burn and alpine grazing policies. These longer-term issues can too easily descend into blaming at the time, but do raise crucial issues which need to be debated in the community so that in the immediate situation community confidence is maintained.

In the short term a well-prepared media plan enables fire agencies to be proactive and develop community resilience, rather than to be reactive. O'Neill (2003) argues that in Canberra the ACT Emergency Services missed valuable opportunities to gain community support and disseminate fire preparedness information. Conrad Smith (1992b) pointed to several lessons for journalists and journalism educators from his research. These were: the need to resist the temptation to apply to all stories with a similar subject matter the same treatment; to aim for literal accuracy at the expense of the essence of the story; and for journalists who are outside their normal beats to be sensitive to their own lack of expertise and learn to rely on others (p. 69). Smith's observation points to several issues: the first raises again the question of news values and the ways in which story models are used by the media–however one might decry this practice, it nevertheless occurs. Given the economics of news gathering, a media plan needs to be developed to provide material which will either fit the story models being used, or preclude the need for journalists to drop their coverage into a standard story model. One way of effectively managing the media has been through the establishment of a media information centre. Well organized and well-equipped centers can serve as the focus of attention:

> . . . minimizing the chances that that focus will stray to areas you'd prefer to leave unexamined. It also provides a place to concentrate your organization's media resources so that they communicate more effectively with each other and with management, have a clearer idea of both the overall media strategy and the day-to-day tactics of the operation's media aspects, and can more rapidly respond to any changes in the crisis situation. (O'Neill, 2003, p. 8)

Training Issues

A well-developed media strategy calls for improved training. On the one hand firefighters need training in how to deal with media; on the other hand media organizations need basic fire awareness training. Knowlton (1989) provides a basic set of instructions on how to be properly prepared when a crisis breaks out. His training booklet deals with the need to have a well-prepared, designated spokesperson to manage media interviews; the need for everyone in the organization to be aware of who the spokesperson is and their role; the preparation of an adequate statement prior to media conferences; how to end an interview; how to decline an interview; and secrets of success in media interviews (stay in command by presenting sound reasons for action, do not apportion blame, and correct inaccurate reporting).

On the other side of the relationship the media need fire awareness training. The Victorian Country Fire Authority (CFA) has recognized this and during 2002 provided training and accreditation for media personnel. The CFA media forum seeks to address two common concerns about media at fires. The first is the minimization of risks to media personnel, and the second is to encourage more accurate reporting by "dispelling myths about why houses burn and why people die in bushfires" (Country Fire Authority of Victoria, 2000, p. 1). Such training seeks to address criticisms of media presence at fires as stressors for firefighters and "ensured that media were aware of operational procedures and protocols, fire behavior and foreground safety, with only accredited and properly equipped media being allowed near the fireground" ("Biggest event," 2003). Riha and Handschuh (1995) see fire training of journalists as part of the role of the joint media information center, which has been touched on above, however a longer term training program would seem consistent with the argument advanced by several writers for well-developed prior preparation for emergencies.

A Phased Role for the Media

As we have already indicated it is possible to recognize a number of distinct roles for the media in the planning for, dealing with, and recovery from bushfires. A well-thought-out media strategy would need to recognize the potential roles of the media in each of these phases. A number of the sources referred to above clearly recognize the role of the media in the immediate emergency. However, the role of the media needs to be recognized in the recovery stage after the fire. During the recovery phase after a disaster or emergency in which the performance of the organization will be more critically analyzed, O'Neill (2003) advises to draw attention to what is being done to restore and clean up the disaster site (p. 12).

The important role of the media was central to the work of the Bushfire Recovery Taskforce in the ACT in 2003. While there was national and international interest, the Taskforce's main emphasis was on working with local media outlets, which had an ongoing part to play in the recovery process. Print (*The Canberra Times*) and radio (*ABC Canberra*) media provided the majority of the coverage. However, local television stations ABC and WIN and commercial radio have also continued to run a range of recovery stories. In addition, there were significant local and national documentary style programs, including a number of stories on the local ABC Stateline program, ongoing stories on the ABC Dimensions series and a story on the Catalyst science program. Media interest has increased at anniversary points such as 100 days and when relevant reports were released (Bushfire Recovery Taskforce ACT, 2003, p. 80).

The longest-term phase is the period between fire events during which it is more appropriate to have debates, perhaps even at a national level, over urban development policies, control burn policies and so on. During these debates many other groups will inevitably participate: ecologists, farmers organizations, local councils and so on. Media management is still an option here, however more "strategy" is needed to create events on which media can hang stories. The release of reports into previous fires is an example of the sort of event that can be used to promote important long-term debates, and to reduce the chance of them becoming distractions during emergency fire events.

CONCLUSION

This discussion of bushfires and the media provides a useful case study of the potential benefits and pitfalls of media coverage of potential and actual disasters. While the limitations of much media coverage of bushfires has been well-documented, the emerging literature on bushfires and the media sees an ongoing relationship between emergency organizations and the media as potentially fruitful. With the creation of appropriate relationships, the development of training and information strategies and a carefully considered strategy for interacting with media organization before, during and after a disaster, the media can be seen as important contributors to strategies designed to develop community resilience.

REFERENCES

ABC news - Australia. (2004). *Fire authority wary of media, inquest told* (media release).
"Biggest event." (2003). The biggest event in CFA's history. *Fire International,* http://www.fireinternational-mag.com/shownews.asp?secid=8&nav=1&newstype=&key=&page=&newsid=5285. Retrieved 30 April 2005
Brady, N. (2004). *Times of crisis. The age.* Retrieved month day, year, from http://www.theage.com.au/.
Britton, N. R. (1983). *The bushfires in Tasmania, February 1982.* Rockhampton: James Cook University, Townsville, Australia: Centre For Disaster Studies.
Bushfire Recovery Taskforce ACT. (2003). *The Report of the bushfire recovery taskforce* (Publication No 03/1350) . Canberra: A.C.T. (Report available on the web– http://www.bushfirerecovery.act.gov.au/inquiries/bushfire_report.htm)
Country Fire Authority of Victoria. (2000). *CFA media forum.* Unpublished report.
Esplin, B. (2003). *Report into the 2002–2003 Victorian Bushfires.* Melbourne: Victorian State Government.
Ewart, J. (2002). Prudence not prurience: A framework for journalists reporting disasters. In M. R. Power (Ed.), *Communication: Reconstructed for the 21 Century– Proceedings of the ANZCA 2002 Conference.* Coolangatta, Australia: Bond University.
Edwards, J. (2004). Southern Star John Edwards Production for ABC TV and Austar

(Producer: John Edwards). *Fireflies* [Television series]. Broadcast ABC TV. (Program website- http://www.abc.net.au/fireflies/rfs_home.htm)

Fiske, J. (1987). *Television culture: Popular pleasures and politics.* London: Methuen.

Galtung, J., & Ruge, M. (1965). The structure of foreign news: The presentation of the Congo, Cuba and Cyprus crises in four foreign newspapers. *Journal of International Peace Research, 1,* 64–90.

Henderson, B., & McKinney, P. (2003, February). Talk is cheap. *Fire Chief, 47*(9), 54–55 (http://firechief.com/awareness/firefighting_talk_cheap/)

Hughes, P. (2003). *Self revelation and surveillance: Public rehearsals of the self on the web.* Paper presented at Australian International Documentary Conference, Byron Bay, Australia.

Jackson, S. (2002, October 17). Reporters learn bushfire hazard reduction. *The Australian,* p. Bo3.

Jackson, S. (2003, January 30). Media draws fire for laying blame on Canberra. *The Australian,* p. B03.

Knowlton, R. A. (1989). *The uninvited guest: Dealing with the media during a crisis.* Houston, Texas, TX: Gulf Publishing.

McGregor, J. (2002). Restating news values: Contemporary criteria for selecting the news. In M. R. Power (Ed.), *Communication: Reconstructed for the 21 Century– Proceedings of the ANZCA 2002 Conference.* Coolangatta, Australia: Bond University.

McKay, J. M. (1999). Reflecting the hazard or restating old views: Newspapers and bushfires in Australia. *International Journal of Mass Emergencies and Disasters, 14*(3), 305–320.

McKay, J. M. (1983). Newspaper reporting of bushfire disaster in South Eastern Australia - Ash Wednesday. *Disasters, 7*(3), 283–91.

McLeod, R. (2003). *Inquiry into the operational response to the January 2003 bushfires in the ACT.* Canberra: ACT Government.

Moran, C. (1995). The 1994 New South Wales bushfires: Perception of the disaster response from a psychological perspective. *International Journal of Mass Emergencies and Disasters, 13*(2), 179–196.

Netterfield, S. (1998). The joint media information centre: Our joint responsibility during emergencies. In D. I. Smith (Ed.), *Public information, media and disaster mitigation* (pp. 18–23). Canberra: Australian National University, Centre for Resource and Environment Studies.

O'Connor, P., & O'Connor, B. (1993). *Out of the ashes : The Ash Wednesday bushfires in the South East of S.A., 16th February, 1983.* Mt. Gambier, South Australia: P. and B. O'Connor.

O'Neill, P. (2003). *Developing an effective communication plan to manage the media response to a crisis.* Unpublished paper.

Rees, R., & Morgan, G. (2003). *Media safety at wildfires in rural Victoria.* Retrieved June 9, 2004, from http://www.dpi.vic.gov.au/dse/nrenfoe.nsf

Riha, B., & Handschuh, D. (1995). *National media guide for emergency and disaster incidents.* Durham, NC: National Press Photographers Association Inc. and Police-Fire-Press Relations Committee.

Schauble, J. (1998). Who is in charge here? Working with the news media. *Proceedings of the Australasian Fire Authorities Council Conference,* Hobart, Australia, 359–372.

Smith, C. (1989a). Flames, firefighter, and moonscapes: Network television pictures of the Yellowstone forest fires. Paper presented at Third Annual Visual Communications Conference, Park City, Utah, June 26, 1989).

Smith, C. (1989b). Reporters, news accuracy, and the Yellowstone forest fires. Paper presented at the annual meeting of the International Communications Associationn, San Francisco, May 1989.

Smith, C. (1992a). How the news media cover disasters: The case of Yellowstone. In P. S. Cook, D. Gomery, & L. Lichty (Eds.), *The future of news: Television-newspapers-wire services-newsmagazines* (pp. 223–240). Washington, DC: Woodrow Wilson Center Press.

Smith, C. (1992b). *Media and apocalypse: News coverage of the Yellowstone forest fires, Exxon Valdez oil spill, and Loma Prieta earthquake.* London: Greenwood.

Smith, C. (1992c). "This is what's left of Yellowstone tonight": Urban Reporters and Wilderness Fire. In C. Smith (Ed.), *Media and apocalypse: News coverage of the Yellowstone forest fires, Exxon Valdez Oil Spill, and the Loma Prieta Earthquake* (pp. 38-75). London: Greenwood.

Tuchman, G. (1978). *Making news: A study in the construction of reality.* New York: Free Press.

Victoria. State Government. 1939. *Report of the Royal Commission to Enquire into the Causes of, and Measures Taken to Prevent the Bushfires of January 1939 and to Protect Life and Property in the Event of Future Bushfires.* Melbourne: Victorian Government Printer.

Worthington, T. (2004). Dealing with Disaster–Using New Networking Technology for Emergency Coordination: A Personal View. Retrieved June 5, 2006, from http://www.tomw.net.au/2004/enetp.html

Chapter 14

ECONOMIC RESILIENCE TO DISASTERS: TOWARD A CONSISTENT AND COMPREHENSIVE FORMULATION

ADAM ROSE[*]

INTRODUCTION

During the past five years, the world has witnessed some unprecedented disasters in terms of type and extent of devastation, including the World Trade Center attacks, Asian Tsunami, and Hurricane Katrina. Policymakers rushed to assure the citizenry of remedial actions to reduce the risk of future potential catastrophes. Where possible, such as terrorist attacks or levee failures, they have emphasized preventative measures. But the reality is that all future disasters cannot be prevented, in part because of the likelihood that these events will involve unexpected forms, magnitudes, or locations.

What is often overlooked is the fact that individuals, institutions, and communities have the ability to deflect and withstand serious shocks in terms of the course of their ordinary workings or through ingenuity and perseverance in the face of a crisis. Moreover, this "resilience" is often invoked in a relatively costless manner, such as

*The author is Professor of Energy, Environmental, and Regional Economics, Department of Geography, The Pennsylvania State University, University Park, PA. The research in this paper is supported by funding from the DHS Center for Risk and Economic Analysis of Terrorist Events (CREATE) and by a grant from the NSF-sponsored Multidisciplinary Center for Earthquake Engineering Research (MCEER). The views expressed in this paper, however, are solely those of the author and not necessarily those of the institutions with which he is affiliated nor of his funding sources. Also, the author is solely responsible for any errors or omissions.

conserving resources in short supply, recouping lost production at a later date, or reallocating resources in response to market signals.

The concept of resilience was first put forth by ecologists more than thirty years ago (see, e.g., Holling, 1973). It has been adapted or re-invented for the case of short-term disasters (see, e.g., Tierney, 1997; Bruneau et al., 2003; and Rose, 2004b) and long-term phenomena, such as climate change (see, e.g., Timmerman, 1981; Dovers & Handmer, 1992). Klein et al. (2003) have noted, and this author concurs, that some definitions of resilience are so broad as to render the term meaningless. At the same time, few analysts have delved deeply into the economic dimension. I emphasize, however, that the economic dimension is only one of many related to resilience, a point that is a major theme of this volume.

The purpose of this chapter is to provide conceptual and empirical advances toward a consistent and comprehensive formulation of *economic resilience.* This is accomplished by first examining various definitions of resilience in general and identifying aspects unique to the economic realm. Second, I attempt to reconcile several competing definitions of economic resilience. Third, I put forth an operational definition. Fourth, I discuss some estimates of the strength of this important feature of disaster response. Fifth, I identify tangible actions that lead to economic resilience and how they are affected by internal and external conditions.

The discussion is important because economic resilience does not appear to be adequately appreciated as a cost-effective tool to manage catastrophic risk. Examples include views that price increases in the aftermath of a disaster represent "gouging" rather than a useful signal of increased scarcity. Also underestimated is the effectiveness of common sense responses by individuals, as well as the professionalization of this strategy through the formation of the business continuity service industry.

Consideration of resilience is critical in assessing potential losses from disasters and evaluating the benefits of their mitigation. Disaster loss estimation is still less than fully developed, and many models in current use are limited by inherent linearities and rigid behavioral assumptions (if behavior is included at all). They often simply extrapolate business as usual, or at least conventional responses, in the aftermath of a disaster. Examples include the application of basic input-output models, standard econometric models, or even some computable general equilibrium models (Rose, 2004a).[1] The more rigid economic models will overstate losses and hence understate resilience (see the criticisms by Cochrane, 1997; Rose et al. 1997; Rose & Lim, 2002), while the more flexible models will understate losses and overstate resilience (cf., Rose & Guha, 2004; Rose & Liao, 2005).

Accurate estimates of disaster losses at both the level of the individual firm and the macroeconomy are critical to the evaluation of risk-management strategies. Underestimation of losses will result in too few resources applied to the problem, while overestimation of losses will lead to excess resources being applied.

Another motivation is the practical need to distinguish two key strategies in dealing with disasters: pre-event measures (primarily mitigation) and post-event measures (primarily matters of recovery). Resilience, as it is typically known, focuses on the post-event response. This time phase of the disaster management problem and the appropriate strategies to deal with it are the focus of this paper.

DEFINING ECONOMIC RESILIENCE

In general, I define *economic resilience* as the ability or capacity of a system to absorb or cushion itself against damage or loss (see also Rose, 2004b). A more general definition that incorporates dynamic considerations, including stability, is the ability of a system to recover from a severe shock to achieve a desired state. I also distinguish two types of resilience in each context:

> *Inherent*–ability under normal circumstances (e.g., the ability of individual firms to substitute other inputs for those curtailed by an external shock, or the ability of markets to reallocate resources in response to price signals).
> *Adaptive*–ability in crisis situations due to ingenuity or extra effort (e.g., increasing input substitution possibilities in individual business operations, or strengthening the market by providing information to match suppliers with customers).

Resilience emanates both from internal motivation and the stimulus of private or public policy decisions (Mileti, 1999). Also, resilience, as defined in this paper, refers to post-disaster conditions and response

(Comfort, 1994), which are distinguished from pre-disaster activities to reduce potential losses through mitigation (cf., Bruneau et al. 2003). In disaster research, resilience has been emphasized most by Tierney (1997) in terms of business coping behavior and community response, by Comfort (1999) in terms of nonlinear adaptive response of organizations (broadly defined to include both the public and private sectors), and by Petak (2002) in terms of system performance. These concepts have been extended to practice. Disaster recovery and business continuity industries have sprung up that offer specialized services to help firms during various aspects of disasters, especially power outages (see, e.g., Business Continuity Institute, 2002; Salerno, 2003). Key services include the opportunity to outsource communication and information aspects of the business at an alternative site. There is also a growing realization of the broader context of the economic impacts, especially with the new emphasis on supply chain management (Paton & Hill, Chapter 15). One company executive recently summarized the situation quite poignantly and in modern business terms: "In short, companies have started to realize that they participate in a greater ecosystem—and that their IT systems are only as resilient as the firms that they rely on to stay in business" (Corcoran, 2003; p. 28). Experience with Y2K, 9/11, natural disasters, and technological/regulatory failures, as well as simulated drills, have sharpened utility industry and business resilience (Eckles, 2003). Similar activities of public agencies have improved community disaster resilience. Resilience can take place at three levels:

Microeconomic—individual behavior of firms, households, or organizations.

Mesoeconomic—economic sector, individual market, or cooperative group.

Macroeconomic—all individual units and markets combined, though the whole is not simply the sum of its parts, due to interactive effects of an economy.

Examples of individual resilience are well-documented in the literature, as are examples of the operation of businesses and organizations. What is often less appreciated by disaster researchers outside economics and closely-related disciplines is the inherent resilience of markets. Prices act as the "invisible hand" that can guide resources to their best allocation even in the aftermath of a disaster. Some pricing mechanisms have been established expressly to deal with such a situation, as in the case of noninterruptible service premium that enable customers to estimate the value of a continuous supply of electricity and to pay in advance for receiving priority service during an outage (Chao & Wilson, 1987).

The price mechanism is a relatively costless way of redirecting goods and services. Price increases, though often viewed as gouging, serve a useful purpose of reflecting highest value use, even in the broader social setting (see also Schuler, 2005). Moreover, if the allocation does violate principles of equity (fairness), the market allocations can be adjusted by income or material transfers to the needy.

Of course, markets are likely to be shocked by a major disaster, in an analogous manner to buildings and humans. In this case, we have two alternatives for some or all of the economy: (1) substitute centralized decree or planning, though at a significantly higher cost of administration; (2) bolster the market, such as in improving information flows (e.g., the creation of an information clearinghouse to match customers without suppliers to suppliers without customers).

COMPARISON WITH RELATED CONCEPTS OF RESILIENCE

The purpose here is not demonstrate that the definitions of this author are correct and those of others are not. In fact, the intent is to focus on points of agreement and to incorporate the work of others into the formulation of economic resilience. Criteria for conceptual and operational definitions of resilience, inclusive of some of its various dimensions and at the exclusion of others, should be based on consistency with fundamental economic principles, the needs of potential users, and the practical matters of data availability and computational manageability. My formulation of resilience is dependent on precedents in the established literature in ecology, economics, and related fields over the past thirty years.

Ecological Origins

As in many other fields, some researchers on the subject of resilience have reinvented the wheel narrowly in their own discipline, rather than looking carefully for precedents or at the big picture. To begin, ecologists have pioneered a useful, broad definition of resilience relating to the survival of complex systems. Holling (1973, p.17) is typically cited as the first to have defined *resilience,* his definition being "the ability of systems to absorb changes and still persist." He sometimes refers to it as "buffer capacity."

Adger (2000) suggests there is no single definition of ecological resilience, and offers two definitions analogous to my static and dynamic economic definitions above. An important contrast in the static definitions exists, however. The ecological definition emphasizes the amount of disturbance the system can absorb without incurring a change in its state. In economics, only the most severe hazard (a catastrophe) results in such a change, and thus such a definition would be of very limited usefulness. Instead I use the term resilience here more in line with the buffer concept, as the ability to mute the influence of the external shock. It is not just the decrease in economic activity, but rather the actual decrease relative to the potential decrease (see also the mathematical definitions below). Perrings (2001, p. 322) also defines resilience in a relative manner: "As a first approximation, this may be measured by an index of the level of pollution or depletion relative to the assimilative or carrying capacity of the ecological system concerned." Subsequently Perrings (p. 323) defines it in terms of the "gap between current and critical loads" to the ecosystem and even the ecological economic system (though this would seem to have application to engineered systems as well).

Here and below it is important to distinguish the concept of resilience and related terms. For example, Holling (1973; p. 17) defines *stability* as "the ability of a system to return to equilibrium after a temporary disturbance." This definition is often put forth as the essence of resilience or at least a special dimension. However, it is clear that resilience and stability are distinct. As Handmer and Dovers (1996) point out, a stable system may not fluctuate significantly, but a resilient system may undergo significant fluctuation and return to a new (and, implicitly, an improved) equilibrium rather than the old one.

Several ecologists and ecological economists have linked resilience to the concept of *sustainability,* which refers to long-term survival and at a nondecreasing quality of life (see, e.g., Common, 1995; Perrings, 2001). Common (1995) suggests that resilience is the key to sustainability. A major feature of sustainability is that it is highly dependent on natural resources, including the environment. Destroying, damag-

ing, or depleting resources undercuts our longer-term economic viability, a lesson also applicable to hazard impacts where most analysts
have omitted ecological considerations. Klein et al. (2003) note that,
from an economic perspective, sustainability is a function of the
degree to which key hazard impacts are anticipated. However, I agree
with the position that it is also a function of a society's ability to react
effectively to a crisis (see Mileti, 1999).

In the context of longer-term disasters, such as climate change,
Timmerman (1981) defined resilience as the measure of a system's
capacity to absorb and recover from the occurrence of a hazardous
event. Dovers and Handmer (1992) note an important feature that dis-
tinguishes man from the rest of nature in this context—human capacity for anticipating and learning. They then bifurcate resilience into
reactive and proactive, where the latter is uniquely human. I maintain
that proactive efforts can enhance resilience by increasing its capacity,
but that resilience is operative only in the response/recovery/recon-
struction (often referred to as "post-disaster") stages.

Adger (2000) was one of the first to extend the ecological definition
of resilience to human communities as a whole. He measured *social
resilience* as related to social capital and in terms of economic factors
(e.g., resource dependence), institutions (e.g., property rights), and
demographics (e.g., migration). Mileti and collaborators (Mileti, 1999)
analyzed many aspects of resilience to hazards in the attainment of
sustainable communities. However, Mileti (1999; p. 5) went too far in
defining a resilient community as not only one that "can withstand an
extreme event with a tolerable level of losses" but also one that "takes
mitigation actions consistent with achieving that level of protection."
My comment is no way a criticism of mitigation, which has been found
to be cost-effective in countless applications and is still underutilized,
but rather that mitigation is distinct from resilience for several reasons
discussed in the following subsection.

The work of Timmerman and others relate resilience to *vulnerability*. Specifically, Pelling (2003) decomposes vulnerability to natural hazards into three parts: exposure, resistance, and resilience. As does
Blaikie et al. (1994), Pelling defines resilience to natural hazards as the
ability of an individual to cope with or adapt to hazard stress. My view
is that vulnerability is a pre-disaster condition and that resilience is the
outcome of a post-disaster response. Resilience is one of several ways
to reduce vulnerability, the others being other forms of adaptation and

the entirely separate strategy of mitigation.

Ecology provides lessons for the economic system, especially the concept of *diversity*. This applies to both economic structure (economies composed of several industries are more likely to withstand shocks than are monocultures) and to the tools to cope with shocks (including the number of resilience responses that may be operative in a given crisis). Diversification has long been appreciated as a major strategy to mitigate risk, but its usefulness in cases of decisions regarding economic resilience has not.

Engineering-Based Definitions

Bruneau et al. (2003) provide a comprehensive and sophisticated analysis of the many aspects of earthquake loss reduction all under the heading of resilience. The authors apply the concept at four levels: technical, organizational, social, and economic. They contend that resilience has four dimensions, which are listed below along with a definition applied to the economic level:

1. Robustness—avoidance of direct and indirect economic losses
2. Redundancy—untapped or excess economic capacity (e.g., inventories, suppliers)
3. Resourcefulness—stabilizing measures (e.g., capacity enhancement and demand modification, external assistance, optimizing recovery strategies)
4. Rapidity—optimizing time to return to pre-event functional levels

Bruneau et al. (2003) also stipulate that the resilience of a system has three aspects:

a. Reduced probability of failures
b. Reduced consequences from failures
c. Reduced time to recovery

The relationship between the dimensions and aspects of a resilient system differs from the definition of economic resilience in Rose (2004b) and Rose and Liao (2005) in the following ways:

- My definition excludes the dimension of reduced probabilities of failure because this is more pertinent to measures taken before an event, primarily for the purpose of mitigation.
- Reduced consequences from failure comes the closest to my static definition of resilience.
- Reduced time to recovery is the same as my definition of dynamic resilience, though the state of restoration is more general in my formulation.[2]
- Robustness is also similar to my definition of static resilience and is a commonly-used term in engineering to convey this more narrow definition of resilience.
- Redundancy examples are a subset of resilience responses in my formulation.
- Resourcefulness is a major feature affecting adaptive resilience as I have defined it.
- Rapidity is consistent with my definition of dynamic resilience, though the Bruneau et al. (2003) formulation requires the condition of optimization.

This discussion is not intended as a criticism of the excellent analytical framework developed by Bruneau et al. (2003) per se. Rather, it is a criticism of their choice of terminology, which includes all aspects of hazard loss reduction under the banner of resilience. The exposition by Klein et al. (2003) is consistent with my argument to keep the definition of resilience from becoming too broad. They propose the concept of "adaptive capacity" as the umbrella concept that covers many of the features identified by Bruneau et al. (2003). This is also more consistent with defining resilience as an outcome or system attribute rather than as a tactic like mitigation.[3] Adaptation is also the complement to mitigation. When negative forces (e.g., conventional hazards, climate change) cannot be mitigated, we can only resort to adaptation.

It would appear that some analysts, such as Mileti and Bruneau et al., have envisioned a goal of a community that is able to take many steps to minimize its vulnerability to hazards. Resilience has become a convenient term to characterize all of these possibilities. However, this broad usage is inconsistent with the etymology of the term in general (*resilio,* meaning rebounding), its use in ecology, and its use in other areas of hazards research. Ideally, another term can be found to modify this ideal community, so that the term "resilience" can be applied to the subset of characteristics to which it is well suited.

Organizational Behavior

Organizational (also institutional) behavior focuses on resilience as a process (Paton & Hill, Chapter 15). As such, it is a strategy in risk management under the subheading of crisis and continuity management. Paton et al. (2003) define resilience in this dimension as "a capacity of people and systems that facilitate organizational performance to maintain functional relationships in the presence of significant disturbances as a result of a capability to draw upon their resources and competencies to manage the demands, challenges and changes encountered." This viewpoint extends even more fundamentally to natural ecosystems, whereby The Resilience Alliance (2001) includes as one of its three dimensions of resilience "the degree to which the system is capable of reorganization."

Comfort (1994) was one of the first researchers to venture into this area. Her definition is more narrow than the generic one just presented, because she confines resilience to actions and processes after the event occurs, or, as noted in my critique of Bruneau et al. (2003), appropriately limits the definition to reducing the *consequences* of failure. This also relates to process-oriented counterparts of the concept of dynamic resilience, where the focus is not on attaining a target level of output but rather a target level of "functioning." However, the trajectory of this functioning is clear from the major themes of nonlinear and adaptive dynamics (Comfort, 1999). It also leaves no doubt that the dynamic version of resilience, the ability to bounce back (or the rapidity to do so) is uniquely applicable to the post-disaster stages. Moreover, the recovery process this characterizes is another way of reducing the consequences of the hazard ensuing from structural or system damage ("failure" in the Bruneau et al. (2003) terminology).

Klein et al. (2003) have taken this even further to suggest that resilience goes beyond the Holling definitions, and by implication those I propose, to include the functioning and interaction of inter-linked systems (see also UN/ISDR, 2002). Again, I note that this does not go as far as suggesting resilience includes all aspects of adaptation or mitigation.

In contrast to resilience activities I have previously modeled and discussed in this paper (e.g., conservation, import substitution, market strengthening), the focus of organizational theory is on "competencies and systems" (Paton & Hill, Chapter 15). The relationship between the two approaches can be viewed as follows: most standard treatments of resilience in economics identify a set of options and assume that managers can optimize among their choices (see, e.g., Rose and Liao, 2005). Organizational analysis identifies vulnerabilities and limitations in managerial abilities and how they can be overcome through resilience.[4] The economics approach to reconciling these two views would be to assume some form of "bounded rationality" (see, e.g., Gigerenzer & Selten, 2002) and to view managerial resilience as an improvement over the basic outcome. Paton and Hill (chapter 15) analyze several aspects of the theory and practice of business continuity management and how it relates to resilience. They emphasize that a major prerequisite of success in this area is the willingness of an organization to adapt to its new environment.[5]

QUANTIFYING RESILIENCE

In this section, I provide mathematical definitions of resilience at two levels. Direct economic resilience refers to the level of the individual firm or industry (micro and meso levels) and corresponds to what economists refer to as "partial equilibrium" analysis, or the operation of an entity itself. Total economic resilience refers to the economy as a whole (macro level) and corresponds to what is referred to as "general equilibrium" analysis, which includes all of the price and quantity interactions in the economy (Rose, 2004b).

In terms of actual measurement of resilience, input-output (I-O) models of disaster impacts capture only quantity interdependence, often referred to as indirect or multiplier effects. Computable general equilibrium (CGE) models capture both price and quantity interaction through the explicit inclusion of market forces (see Rose, 2005).

An operational measure of *direct economic resilience (DER)* is the extent to which the estimated direct output reduction deviates from the likely maximum potential reduction given an external shock, such as the curtailment of some or all of a critical input:

$$DER = \frac{\%\Delta DY^m - \%\Delta DY}{\%\Delta DY^m}$$

where

$\%\Delta DY^m$ is the maximum percent change in direct output
$\%\Delta DY$ is the estimated percent change in direct output

The major issue is what should be used as the maximum potential disruption. For ordinary disasters, a good starting point is a linear, or proportional, relationship between an input supply shortage and the direct disruption to the firm or industry (though see below for a discussion of nonlinearities associated with an extreme disaster, or catastrophe). This would be consistent with the context of an I-O model, which is inherently linear. The application of a simple version of this type of model implicitly omits the possibility of resilience.[6]

Note that the definition presented here (based on Rose, 2004b) is couched in deterministic terms. Though their definition of resilience (an off-shoot of the definition by Bruneau et al. 2003) differs from the one presented here, Chang and Shinozuka (2004) make a major contribution by providing a framework and illustrative example for evaluating economic resilience in probabilistic terms and in relation to performance objectives.

The measure of *total economic resilience (TER)* to input supply disruptions is the difference between a linear set of general equilibrium effects, which implicitly omits resilience and a nonlinear outcome, which incorporates the possibility of resilience. From an operational modeling standpoint this is the difference between linear I-O multiplier and CGE, or other comprehensive, nonlinear (e.g., econometric) model impacts as follows:

$$TRER = \frac{\%\Delta TY^m - \%\Delta TY}{\%\Delta TY^m} = \frac{M \cdot \%\Delta DYm - \%\Delta TY}{\%\Delta TY^m}$$

where

M is the economy-wide input-output multiplier
$\%\Delta TY^m$ is the maximum percent change in total output
$\%\Delta TY$ is the estimated percent change in total output

Our definitions of economic resilience have been stated in flow terms in relation to economic output. Is resilience applicable to stocks, i.e., property damage, as well? While property is important, paramount is the flow of goods and services it contributes to economic well-being. In relation to ecosystems, Holling (1973) defines resilience in terms of flow (productivity measures) as opposed to stocks. Resilience of more conventional capital assets (buildings, infrastructure) would pertain to the ability of the stock variable to absorb shocks (e.g., a building to withstand ground motion or the blast from a terrorist bomb). This would best be considered under the purview of engineering resilience. A more complex system, however, raises other issues. For example, an electricity system might be said to be less likely to fail if it has incorporated redundancy of power lines, or better communication between operators to avoid cascading failures. Again, this might be considered engineering resilience or perhaps economic resilience on the supply side (as opposed to the demand-side resilience that is the focus here).

Also, while the time-path of resilience is key to the concept for many analysts, it is important to remember that this time-path is composed of a sequence of steps. Even if "dynamics" are the focal point, it is important to understand the underlying process at each stage: why an activity level is achieved and why that level differs from one time period to another. As presented here, resilience helps explain the first aspect, and changes in resilience help explain the second.

MEASURING RESILIENCE

To date the only efforts to actually measure economic resilience in the face of disasters pertain to business interruption associated with utility lifeline disruptions. The initial question posed is: Will an X percent loss of electricity result in an X percent direct loss in economic activity for a given firm? The answer is definitely "no" if economic resilience is present. All of these analyses use as the measure of direct economic resilience, the deviation from the linear proportional relation between the percentage utility disruption and the percentage reduction in customer output. One of the most obvious resilience options for input supply interruptions in general is reliance on inventories. This has long made electricity outages especially problematic, since this product cannot typically be stored. However, the increasing severity of the problem has inspired ingenuity, such as the use of non-interruptible power supplies (capacitors) in computers. Other resilience measures include back-up generation, conservation, input substitution, and rescheduling of lost production. In many business enterprises, these measures are adequate to substantially cushion the firm against some losses of a rather short or moderate duration.

Next, the question is extended to: Will a Y percent loss in direct output yield much larger general equilibrium losses? Here both individual business and market-related adjustments suggest some muting of general equilibrium effects. As a starting point, it is appropriate to measure market, or net general equilibrium, resilience as the deviation from the linear outcome, e.g., the multiplier effect that would be generated from a simple I-O analysis of the outage. Adjustments for lost output of goods and services other than electricity include inventories, conservation, input substitution, import substitution and production rescheduling at the level of the individual firm, and the rationing feature of pricing and recontracting among suppliers and customers at the level of the market.

Table 14.1 summarizes loss estimates from utility service disruptions and the role of resilience.[7] The number of studies is rather sparse, because we have limited inclusion to those studies that used customer lost output as the unit of measure and that have also explicitly or implicitly included indirect (either ordinary multiplier or general equilibrium) effects. The first study in Table 14.1 is that of Tierney (1997), who collected responses to a survey questionnaire from more than a thousand firms following the Northridge Earthquake. Note that maximum electricity service disruption following this event was 8.3 percent and that nearly all electricity service was restored within 24 hours. Tierney's survey results indicated that direct output losses amounted to only 1.9 percent of a single day's output in Los Angeles County.

A study by Rose and Lim (2002) of the aftermath of the Northridge Earthquake used a simple simulation model of three resilience options to estimate adjusted direct losses at 0.42 percent and used an I-O model to estimate total region-wide losses of 0.55 percent. Although this study did not include the full range of resilience tactics as was inherent in the Tierney study, it is also likely that in the Tierney study the effects of production rescheduling would be underreported because not all businesses connect activities undertaken long after the

TABLE 14.1. SUMMARY OF LOSS ESTIMATES FROM UTILITY SERVICE DISRUPTIONS.

Study	Location/Event	Utility/Duration	Method or Model	Loss of Utility Services (%)	Direct Output Loss (%)	Total Output Loss from Adjusted Direct (%)	Direct Q Loss/Loss of Utility Services (%)	Individual Business Resilience (%)	Total Q Loss/Direct Q Loss (%)	Market Resilience (%)
Tierney (1995)	Los Angeles/Northridge EQ	Electricity/36 hrs	Survey	8.3	1.91	1.9b	22.9b	77.1	–	–
Rose-Lim (2002)	Los Angeles/Northridge EQ	Electricity/36	I-O	8.3	0.42c	0.55	5.0	95.0	131	79.3
Rose-Guha (2004)	Memphis/Hypothetical EQ	Electricity/First week	CGE	44.8	–	2.3d	5.1e	94.9	–	–
Rose-Liao (2005)	Portland/Hypothetical EQ	Water/First week	CGE	50.5	5.7f,g,h,i	7.0	11.3	88.7	122	75.6
Rose-Liao (2005)	Portland/Hypothetical EQ	Water/First week	CGE	31.0	3.5f,g,h,j	5.0	11.4	88.6	143	52.2
Rose et al. (2006)	Los Angeles/Hyp Terrorism	Electricity/Two weeks	CGE	100.0	9.4g	13.0	9.4	90.6	138	84.8
Rose et al. (2006)	Los Angeles/Hyp Terrorism	Water/Two weeks	CGE	100.0	10.2g	13.5	10.2	89.8	132	87.2

a. Survey response incorporates various undefined direct resilience practices
b. Explicitly includes only direct effects.
c. Resilience adjustments limited to time-of-day use, importance factor, and production rescheduling.
d. Model not able to incorporate very short-run elasticities; hence, flexibility of response is exaggerated.
e. Numerator is total output loss, since direct and indirect output losses could be distinguished in this model.
f. Does not include production rescheduling.
g. Production rescheduling (recapture) factors from Rose-Lim (2002) were applied to study results.
h. In addition to production rescheduling, the remaining resilience is attributed to conservation and input substitution for water, though other factors are implicitly present.
i. Prior to any mitigation.
j. After mitigation.

event with the affects of the disaster.

A CGE analysis by Rose and Guha (2004) of the impacts of a hypo-thetical New Madrid Earthquake on the Memphis, Tennessee econo-my indicated that a 44.8 percent loss Madrid Earthquake on the Memphis, Tennessee economy indicated that a 44.8 percent loss of utility services would result in only a 2.3 percent loss of regional out-put. However, this model did not explicitly include resilience meas-ures and was constrained from reducing major parameters, such as elasticities of substitution, to levels that truly reflected a very short-run crisis situation.

A study by Rose and Liao (2004) for a hypothetical earthquake in Portland, Oregon, and for water rather than electricity utilities, incor-porated engineering simulation estimates of direct output losses into a CGE model. The first simulation, which represented a business-as-usual scenario, indicated that a 50.5 percent loss of utility services would result in a 33.7 percent direct output loss, factoring in some resiliency measures. Further adjustment for production rescheduling reduces this to 5.7 percent. A second simulation, representing the case of $200 million capital expenditure initiative of replacing cast-iron pipes with modern materials, indicated that a 31percent loss of utility services would result in a 3.5 percent loss of direct output in the region. Direct resilience declined following mitigation (direct output losses as a proportion of utility outage levels increased), because miti-gation reduces initial loss of service and hence ironically narrows the range of resilience options that can be brought into play.

More recently, Rose et al. (2006a; 2006b) performed simulations for hypothetical terrorist attacks on the power and water systems of Los Angeles. They simulated total supply disruptions for the entirety of Los Angeles County for a two-week period. Their analysis incorporat-ed an extensive set of resilience options and found direct resilience to be over 90 percent for the case of the power outage and slightly less than 90 percent for the water outage. Market resilience was found to be almost as high. As noted in the following section, the resilience to these targeted attacks is likely to be relatively higher than that for nat-ural hazards. The former are focused on a key aspect of a communi-ty's infrastructure in the absence of any other devastation. On the other hand, for natural disasters and more widespread terrorist attacks (e.g., a "dirty bomb"), other aspects of a regional economy are affect-ed. This will reduce the ability to substitute inputs, bring in additional imports, or to rely on an effectively working market.

Individual business, or direct, resilience is presented in column 9 of Table 14.1. This measure is simply the complement of the figure in column 8 (the column 8 figure subtracted from 100 percent). The results of the several studies, using several alternative methods, indicate that individual business resilience is quite high and that results of analyses that included this factor would be between 77 percent and 95 percent lower than for analyses that neglected it (e.g., a purely linear model).

General equilibrium effects are presented in column 10 and indicate a moderate increase over direct (partial equilibrium) effects, ranging from 122 percent to 143 percent. The I-O model of the Rose-Lim (2002) study did not allow for ordinary multiplier effects, because of the assumed adequacy of inventories for goods other than electricity for the 36-hour outage period, and thus considered only "bottleneck effects" (see also Cochrane, 1997). Interestingly, the first simulation by Rose and Liao (2005) yielded general equilibrium effects on the order of 22 percent of direct effects, and the second simulation yielded general equilibrium effects 43 percent as great as direct effects. This means that mitigation not only lowered direct business resilience but also made the regional economy as a whole less resilient, thus offsetting some of this strategy's benefits.

Thus, in this group of studies direct resilience is a stronger force on the downside than are general equilibrium effects on the upside.[8] These two sets of effects do not cancel each other out, and a study that omitted both is still likely to significantly overestimate the effect that a terrorist attack on a utility lifeline has on the overall economy.

While I have assessed the implications of omitting general equilibrium effects, it is equally likely that they might be overestimated, especially if a linear model is used. The extent of this problem can better be appreciated by examining market resilience, or the percentage deviation between an analysis that takes the workings of the market into account and one that does not. Market resilience can, however, in part be taken into account in a linear model like I-O analysis, as in the work of Cochrane (1997), Rose et al. (1997), and Rose and Lim (2002). In the former case, the solution algorithm allows for market resilience by changing the pattern of imports and exports, while in the latter two it includes an assumption that customers without suppliers will find new suppliers without customers in a type of "recontracting" arrangement. Indirect effects in both of these approaches are thus limited to "bottleneck" effects, where one sector is so extensively disrupted that it limits the "smoothing" effects on supply and demand throughout the economy. Otherwise, if the standard I-O formulation is used, multiplier effects (as a proxy for general equilibrium effects) can be quite large. In the studies listed in Table 14.1, the L.A. County multiplier is about 2.5 and the Portland Metropolitan area multiplier is 1.9. Column one represents a measure of market (net general equilibrium) resilience as a percentage deviation from the purely linear result. However, even with the overestimation resulting from a standard I-O model, direct resilience appears to be the more dominant of the two effects.[9]

Note that the above analysis is generalizable and operational beyond the case of a utility service disruption. It can be applied to business interruption from property damage in general through the use of capital-output ratios (or related "functionality" factors in engineering).

CONCLUSION

The objectives of this paper have been severalfold. One is to clarify the major features of economic resilience and how it compares with closely-related dimensions in ecology, engineering, and organizational theory. Another is to offer an operational definition of the concept. It also summarizes studies that have attempted to measure resilience in accordance with this definition implicitly or explicitly. Finally, it offers insights into how resilience differs in various temporal contexts.

Several major conclusions can be drawn from the paper. First, that the definition of economic resilience can learn from, inform, and nicely complement definitions from other dimensions of the concept. Second, that in both static and dynamic terms, resilience is best conceived as reducing the consequences of disaster, so as to contrast it from mitigation, which reduces the probability that a disaster will occur. This bifurcation helps more clearly delineate the tradeoffs between pre- and post-disaster strategies. Third, an operational definition can be formulated. Fourth, resilience has been found to be a powerful way of reducing losses from disasters. Fifth, resilience is likely to be seriously challenged by catastrophes making it less effective in these contexts.

Klein et al. (2003; p.41) concluded that decades of research have not been able "to transform the concept [of resilience] into an operational tool for policy and management purposes." This chapter is intended to make significant progress toward this goal in the economic realm.

ENDNOTES

1. I-O models are linear and lack behavioral content. Econometric models are typically based on time series, which means they are an extrapolation of the past. Although non-linear and including behavioral considerations, the parameters of CGE models are typically based on normal operating experience and long-term adjustment, and would therefore overstate the flexibility, and hence the resilience of a system.

2. Bruneau et al. include "restoration of the system to its 'normal' level of performance" to their definition. This definition subsumes whether a system can "snap back" at all, i.e., the concept of *stability* as typically used in dynamics. My use of the term *desired state* is a generalization of possible responses, which would include return to pre-disaster status as a special case, but would at the same time allow for growth and change over time and implementation of mitigation practices, as well as considering obstacles to achieving the desired state.

3. In a similar vein, Chang and Shinozuka (2004; p. 741) state that: "It is useful to view robustness and rapidity as the desired ends of resilience-enhancing measures. Redundancy and resourcefulness are some of the *means* to these ends." Again, robustness and rapidity correspond to our static and dynamic definitions of resilience, respectively. The major difference between *ends* and *means* is an important reason not to extend the definition of resilience beyond the *ends* theme. Note also that subsequently in their paper, Chang and Shinozuka define robustness in economic terms as the reduction in Gross Regional Product, rather than its deviation from a maximum possible level given the characteristics of the hazard stimulus, as in this paper. Rapidity is defined by them, independently, in the same manner as in this paper, however.

4. Shaw and Harrald (2004) stress that for this to be successful organizational relationships and authorities must first be defined. In a situation analogous to issues emphasized in this paper, they point to the need to reconcile basic disagreements over the definitions of key concepts such as "crisis management' and "business continuity management." Their solution of combining the two terms into a single umbrella concept, however, would not be prudent in the case of resilience and various related terms such as sustainability, adaptation, vulnerability, or mitigation.

5. Broader dimensions of resilience in terms of the social fabric or community are not discussed here because they are beyond the scope of this paper (see, e.g., Tobin, 1999; Paton and Johnston, 2001). These dimensions focus on aspects of

resilience, such as psychology, sociology, and community planning, that are important to a holistic view of the topic of resilience and are discussed elsewhere in this volume.

6. Resilience can, however, be incorporated into I-O models in the manner of Rose, et al. (1997) and Rose and Lim (2002). See the analysis below for the results of the latter study.

7. Nearly all studies of power outages exclude resilience (see, e.g., Caves et al., 1992), except for those that use a resilience response as a proxy value of service continuity, as in the case of back-up generators (see, e.g., Bental and Ravid, 1986).

8. It should be noted that the various studies listed in Table 14.1 are not entirely independent. For example, Rose and Liao used some of the Tierney survey findings on resilience to recalibrate their production function parameters. In addition, the same production rescheduling (recapture) factors used in the Rose and Lim study were applied to all of the other study results by Rose and associates. It should be kept in mind, however, that these are only a few of several considerations that influence the numerical value of the results.

9. This is reinforced mathematically by the fact that business resilience is applied to the direct effect, which serves as the base for the market effect. For example, a 90 percent decrease in direct economic impacts due to resilience also reduces the general equilibrium impacts in absolute (though not in percentage) terms. However, a reduction in general equilibrium effects does not reduce individual business resilience.

REFERENCES

Adger, W. (2000). Social and ecological resilience: Are they related? *Progress in Human Geography, 24,* 247–364.

Applied Technology Council (ATC) (1991). *Sesimic Vulnerability and Impacts of Disruptions of Utility Lifelines in the Cotermininous United States,* report ATC-25. Redwood, CA: Applied Technology Council.

Bental, B., & Ravid, S.A. (1986). Simple method for evaluating the marginal cost of unsupplied electricity. *Bell Journal of Economics, 13,* 249–53.

Blaikie, P., Cannon, T., Davis, I., & Wisner, B. (1994). *At risk: Natural hazards, people's vulnerability and disasters.* London, UK: Routledge.

Bram, J., Orr, J., & Rappaport, C. (2002). *The impact of the World Trade Center Attack on New York City: Where do We Stand?* Federal Reserve Bank of New York, New York City, NY.

Bruneau, M., Chang, S., Eguchi, R., Lee, G., O'Rourke, T., Reinhorn, A., Shinozuka, M., Tierney, K., Wallace, W., & von Winterfeldt, D. (2003). A framework to quantitatively assess and enhance seismic resilience of communities. *Earthquake Spectra, 19,* 733–752.

Business Continuity Institute (2002). Good practice in business continuity management. *Continuity, 6,* 2.

Caves, D., Harriges, J., & Windle, R. (1992). The cost of electric power interruptions in the industrial sector: Estimates derived from interruptible service programs. *Land Economics, 68,* 49–61.

Chang, S., & Shinozuka, M. (2004). Measuring and improving the disaster Resilience of communities. *Earthquake Spectra, 20,* 739–55.

Chao, H. P., &. Wilson, R. (1987). Priority service: Pricing, investment and market organization. *American Economic Review, 77,* 899–916.

Cochrane, H. (1997). Forecasting the economic impact of a Mid-West earthquake," in B. Jones (ed.), *Economic Consequences of Earthquakes: Preparing for the Unexpected* (pp. 223–47). Buffalo, NY: NCEER.

Cochrane H. et al. (1997). Indirect economic losses. In *Development of standardized earthquake loss estimation methodology Vol. II.* Menlo Park, CA: RMS, Inc.

Corcoran, P. (2003). IBM Business Continuity Services. *Disaster Recovery, 16,* 26 & 28.

Comfort, L. (1994). Risk and Resilience: Inter-organizational Learning Following the Northridge Earthquake of 17 January 1994, *Journal of Contingencies and Crisis Management, 2,* 157–170.

Comfort, L. (1999). *Shared risk: Complex seismic response.* New York: Pergamon.

Common, M. (1995). *Sustainability and policy limits to economics.* Cambridge, UK: Cambridge University Press.

Dickinson, G. (2001). Enterprise Risk Management: Its Origins and Conceptual Foundation. *The Geneva Papers of Risk and Insurance 26,* 360–366.

Dovers, R., & Handmer, J. (1992). Uncertainty, Sustainability and Change. *Global Environmental Change, 2,* 262–276.

Eckles, J. (2003). SunGard Availabiltiy Services. *Disaster Recovery 16,* 28.

Federal Emergency Management Agency (FEMA) (2004) *Earthquake loss estimation methodology (HAZUS).* Washington, DC: National Institute of Building Sciences.

Gigerenzer, G., & Selten, J. (Eds.). (2002). *Bounded rationality: The adaptive toolbox.* Cambridge: MIT Press.

Handmer, J., & Dovers, S. (1996). A Typology of Resilience: Rethinking Institutions for Sustainable Development. *Industrial and Environmental Crisis Quarterly 9,* 482–511.

Holling, C. (1973). Resilience and Stability of Ecological Systems. *Annual Review of Ecology and Systematics, 4,* 1–23.

Klein, R., Nicholls, R., & Thomalla, F. (2003). Resilience to natural hazards: How useful is this concept? *Environmental Hazards, 5,* 35–45.

Mileti, D. (1999). *Disasters by design: A reassessment of natural hazards in the United States.* Washington, DC: Joseph Henry Press.

Paton, D., & Johnston, D. (2001). *Disasters and communities: Vulnerability, resilience and preparedness.* Disaster Prevention and Management, 10, 270–277.

Pelling, M. (2003). *The vulnerability of cities: Natural disasters and social resilience.* London, UK: Earthscan.

Perrings, C. (2001). Resilience and Sustainability. In H. Folmer, H. L. Gabel, S. Gerking, and A. Rose (eds.), *Frontiers of Environmental Economics* (pp. 319–41). Cheltenham, UK: Edward Elgar.

Petak, W. (2002). Earthquake Resilience through Mitigation: A System Approach.

Paper presented at the International Institute for Applied Systems Analysis, Laxenburg, Austria, July, 2002.

Rose, A. (2004a). Economic principles, issues, and research priorities of natural hazard loss estimation. In Y. Okuyama and S. Chang (Eds.), *Modeling of spatial economic impacts of natural hazards* (pp. 13–36), Heidelberg: Springer.

Rose, A. (2004b). Defining and measuring economic resilience to disasters. *Disaster Prevention and Management, 13*, 307–314.

Rose, A. (2005). Analyzing terrorist threats to the economy: A computable general equilibrium approach. In P. Gordon, J. Moore, and H. Richardson (Eds.), *Economic impacts of a terrorist attack.* Cheltenham, UK: Edward Elgar.

Rose, A., & Guha, G. (2004). Computable general equilibrium modeling of electric utility lifeline losses from earthquakes. In Y. Okuyama and S. Chang (Eds.), *Modeling the spatial economic impacts of natural hazards* (pp. 118–41), Heidelberg: Springer.

Rose, A., & Lim, D. (2002). Business interruption losses from natural hazards: conceptual and methodology issues in the case of the Northridge Earthquake. *Environmental Hazards: Human and Social Dimensions, 4*, 1–14.

Rose, A., & Liao, S. (2005). Modeling resilience to disasters: Computable general equilibrium analysis of a water service disruption. *Journal of Regional Science 45*, 75–112.

Rose, A., Oladosu, G., & Liao, S. (2006a). Business interruption impacts of a terrorist attack on the electric power system of Los Angeles: Customer resilience to a total blackout. In P. Gordon, J. Moore, and H. Richardson (Eds.), *Economic costs and consequences of a terrorist attack.* Cheltenham, UK: Edward Elgar (in press).

Rose, A., Oladosu, G., & Liao, S. (2006b). Regional economic impacts of a terrorist attack on the water system of Los Angeles: A computable general disequilibrium analysis. *Risk Analysis* (forthcoming).

Rose, A., Benavides, J., Chang, S. Szczesniak, P., & Lim, D. (1997). The regional economic impact of an earthquake: Direct and indirect effects of electricity lifeline disruptions. *Journal of Regional Science, 37*, 437–58.

Salerno, C. (2003). Powered up when the lights go out. *Continuity Insights: Strategies to Assure Integrity, Availaility and Secutity, 1*, 23–28.

Schuler, R. E. (2005). Two-sided electricity markets: Self-healing systems. Paper presented at the Second Annual CREATE Symposium on the Economic of Terrorism, USC, Los Angeles, CA, August, 2005.

Shaw, G., & Harrald, J. (2004). Identification of the core competencies required of executive level business crisis and continuity management. *Journal of Homeland Security and Emergency Management 1*, 1–13.

Tierney, K. (1997). Impacts of recent disasters on businesses: The 1993 Midwest Floods and the 1994 Northridge Earthquake. In B. Jones (ed.), *Economic consequences of earthquakes: Preparing for the unexpected* (pp. 189–222). Buffalo, NY: National Center for Earthquake Engineering Research.

Timmerman, P. (1981). *Vulnerability, resilience and the collapse of society: A review of models and possible climatic applications.* Institute for Environmental Studies, University of Toronto, Canada.

Tobin, G. (1999). Sustainability and community resilience: The Holy Grail of hazards planning? *Environmental Hazards, 1,* 13–25.

UN/ISDR. (2002). *Living with risk: A global review of disaster reduction initiatives* by the ISDR, Geneva, Switzerland.

Chapter 15

MANAGING COMPANY RISK AND RESILIENCE THROUGH BUSINESS CONTINUITY MANAGEMENT

DOUGLAS PATON AND ROSEMARY HILL

INTRODUCTION

Fundamental to societal resilience is the capacity of companies to sustain key business processes and functions despite adverse impacts upon their activities. In this context, any disturbance, whether from a failure of a key supplier or a natural disaster, becomes a crisis when it reveals an unambiguous failure of management actions and policy (Folke, Colding & Berkes, 2003; Levene, 2004). Levene, in an address to the World Affairs Council, argued, in the context of the fact that a lack of business preparedness accounted for about 25 percent of the $40 billion lost as a result of the September 11, 2001 terrorist attacks, for greater emphasis to be paid to developing company capacity to adapt to interruption to business activity from disasters. He also cited evidence to the effect that an estimated 90 percent of medium to large companies that can't resume near-normal operations within five days of an emergency will go out of business, and that 40 percent of companies hit by a disaster go under within five years. The fact that less than half of U.S. corporations have crisis-management plans in place illustrates both the scale of this problem and the urgent need for businesses to take action to remedy this problem. Doing so involves business continuity management.

How businesses manage risks and develop resilience is crucial for their survival (Elliott, Swartz & Herbane, 2002; Rose & Lim, 2002). Business continuity management (BCM) is a management process by which businesses can assess risk and develop plans and strategies to mitigate these risks (Hill, 1996; Paton, 1999; Shaw & Harrald, 2004). It influences societal resilience by contributing to sustaining the economic vitality of an area and continuity of employment. BCM also contributes to the effectiveness of recovery activities (e.g., ensuring the availability of building material suppliers, building contractors, welfare agencies). Business continuity planning and management thus has significant implications, not just for individual firms, but also for the wider society.

It is, therefore, important that businesses develop strategies to manage risk through improving their resilience. This chapter discusses those practices that comprise an effective business continuity plan and the procedures and competencies required to sustain organizational activity in the event of large-scale natural hazard activity.

BUSINESS CONTINUITY AND DISASTER

Shaw and Harald (2004) define business crisis and continuity management as comprising those practices that focus and guide the decisions and actions required to prevent, mitigate, prepare for, respond to, resume, recover, restore, and transition from a crisis event. Furthermore, they argue that such activities should be consistent with its strategic objectives and comprise activities that enhance resilience to disruption.

Business Resilience and Continuity

Resilience describes the capacity of the people and systems that facilitate organizational performance, to maintain functional relationships in the presence of significant disturbances as a result of a capability to draw upon their resources and competencies to manage the demands, challenges and changes encountered. Comfort (1994), in her study of risk and resilience in relation to the Northridge earthquake in the United States in 1994, describes resilience as a capacity to reorganize resources and action to respond to actual danger after it occurs.

A capability to reorganize resources will not just happen. Nor will it be possible to conduct such a reorganization during, or even immediately prior to, a crisis. Rather, it requires the systematic appraisal of the conditions that could necessitate change, and the development of the systems and staff competencies capable of facilitating continuity under atypical crisis conditions. While it is impossible to influence the likelihood of natural hazard activity, it is possible to manage risk by altering its consequences through better planning and preparedness. It is the latter activities that confer upon an organization and its employees a resilient capability to maintain levels of functioning during and following a disaster.

To create a resilient organization, business continuity planning requires three core elements. First, it requires that management and information systems are available (by safeguarding existing systems and/or arranging for substitutes) to facilitate continuity of core business operations (Davies & Walters, 1998; Duitch & Oppelt, 1997; Lister, 1996). Second, it requires crisis management systems and mechanisms for managing the transition between routine and crisis operations (Paton, 1997a; Shaw & Harrald, 2004). Competencies and systems must be designed to ensure continuity of functioning under the atypical crisis operating conditions necessitated by a large-scale natural disaster.

Disaster associated with natural hazard activity, such as that likely to accompany seismic, volcanic or flooding events, will occur at the upper end of the events that need to be considered within the continuity planning process (Reiss, 2004). Under these circumstances, for example, businesses must plan to deal with prolonged and/or intermittent loss of utilities (e.g., power, water, gas), conduct core operations away from their HQ, deal with casualties and deaths amongst staff, reconcile work with the family needs and concerns of staff, and ensure that staff fulfilling disaster continuity roles can deal with the high demands over prolonged periods of time (possibly several months).

The last point illustrates how continuity planning involves ensuring the availability of staff capable of operating these systems under challenging circumstances (Paton, 1999; Shaw & Harrald, 2004). They must thus be specifically selected and trained for these roles. Attention will also have to be directed to ensure that appropriate crisis management systems and procedures are in place. Transnational organizations would also have to accommodate the cultural dimension within this process.

This chapter examines how BCM strategy contributes to sustaining business activity following significant natural hazard activity and, thereby, to the social and economic resilience of a community. It commences with an overview of business continuity management. It then discusses the processes and competencies required to realize its benefits and the issues that must be considered to mobilize plans should disaster strike.

BUSINESS CONTINUITY PLANNING

BCM is a proactive and holistic management process that aims to ensure the continued achievement of critical business objectives (Standards Australia, 2003). It provides an iterative, structured process that incorporates planning, risk identification and management, training and the development of disaster recovery plans and procedures. BCM is built around understanding what the organization must achieve (its critical objectives), identifying the barriers or interruptions that may prevent their achievement, and determining how the organization will continue to achieve these objectives should interruptions occur. In order to achieve these objectives the following processes are recommended (Elliott et al. 2002; Business Continuity Institute, 2002):

- Understand the critical processes required to ensure the supply of goods and/or services to customers, provide income for the business, and maintain employment.
- Identify potential risks to the business in the context of its business, its geographical position (e.g., susceptibility to natural hazards), or its position in the marketplace.
- Assess the impact on the business of potential crises. Often referred to as "Business Impact Analysis," this involves assessing risk in terms of financial loss.
- Consider strategies and options available to mitigate identified risks to the business. These could include, for example, increasing the amount of insurance to transfer the risk; improving the structure of the building to withstand severe weather; installing an efficient back-up system for the computers so that data can easily be

retrieved.

- Draw up a business continuity plan that defines the action/s the business will take in the event of a disaster.
- Train staff and embed a culture of BCM within the business. Staff participation is an essential component of BCM. It helps inculcate continuity planning into the culture of the organization (i.e., BCM is "the way we do things round here"). It contributes to staff morale by heightening awareness that the business is concerned with their welfare. It also facilitates good communication within the business. The latter plays an important role in risk assessment and identifying realistic mitigation strategies.
- To accommodate changes in personnel, business practices or the external environment, the plan should be tested, maintained and revised.

Business Continuity Planning: What it Means in Practice

The underlying precepts of BCM contribute significantly to organizational resilience. The first is that BCM is a very individual process; there is no "one size fits all" complete solution. Each business must decide what its key processes are, what particular risks it faces, what the impact of particular interruptions would be on its business, and what resources are available to it to assist in developing contingency and disaster recovery plans. The individual business should ensure that these plans accommodate the interests of its stakeholders and its social responsibilities. This means that the business can focus its resources, both human and financial, in more cost-effective ways and ensure that plans and recovery measures are adapted to suit its particular circumstances. For example, Morgan Stanley, the investment bank, was the largest tenant in the World Trade Center in New York and they realized after the previous attack on the Center in 1993 that they were very vulnerable to future terrorist attacks. Accordingly they established contingency and continuity plans which were tested rigorously and regularly. As a result, the company began evacuating its employees to its three recovery sites one minute after the first plane flew into the World Trade Center and they lost only seven employees (Coutu, 2002).

The second precept is that BCM is about getting the business "up and running again." It is not intended as a method for returning the business to exactly the same state as it was before the disaster. One of the constituents of organizational resilience is the ability to deal with change and a disaster presents a major change for an organization. BCM facilitates managing change because it focuses on maintaining the key processes of the business, with the continuity plan providing a structure for the physical recovery of the business. It thus provides a basis for the business to move forward after a disaster. Depending on the extent of the disaster, the business has an opportunity to learn from the experience and to change its practices if necessary (see below). A survey of small businesses affected by disaster in the United States concluded that the extent to which the owner recognizes and adapts to the post-event situation is a significant predictor of survival. Those who continue to do business under the old paradigm, assuming that the community will return to pre-existing conditions, have all the cards stacked against their long-term survival (Alesch, Holly, Mittler & Nagy, 2002).

One of the main features of BCM is the inclusion of an operations management stage in the business continuity plan. This is a checklist of "who does what" in the event of an incident and includes details about cooperating with the emergency services, the utility companies, local authorities, the insurance companies and perhaps other businesses in the area (see the discussion on managerial competencies below). The procedures that are outlined in the continuity plan equip the business to deal with a power failure, a flood, a fire or any other kind of business interruption. The adoption of an all-hazards approach greatly increases the overall resilience of the organization.

To be carried out effectively, BCM requires an adequate allocation of resources, both financial and human. While many large businesses, particularly financial organizations, have risk-management policies in place which can be expanded into full BCM processes, for smaller businesses the allocation of resources for BCM is very much a discretionary expenditure. Consequently, managerial acceptance of risk and their commitment to BCM is essential to planning being initiated and developed to an appropriate state of readiness. There are, however, many factors that can conspire against their developing continuity plans.

The personal attitudes and background of the owner/manager are important (Ewing-Jarvie, 2002). Many small business owners believe that having an insurance policy is sufficient to protect them from the effects of a disaster (Hill, 1996). Insurance, however, will only provide monetary compensation, and not necessarily immediately after the disaster. It will not provide alternative premises, specialized equipment, or competent staff. Furthermore, claims on insurance are not always successful (Hill, 1996). Other influences include the attitude that disasters always happen to someone else, that some government or other external agency will come forward to help, or that disasters should be accepted as a normal part of life and one for which there is no point in preparing.

Organizational commitment to disaster business continuity planning can also be constrained by managers overestimating existing capabilities and ambiguity of responsibility (Gunderson, Holling, & Light, 1995; Paton, 1999; Shaw & Harrald, 2004). The last point is particularly important. Because continuity planning crosses several organizational role boundaries, responsibility for its performance may not fall within the purview of any one established organizational role. Consequently, a precursor to effective BCM is having responsibility vested in a key figure who can direct and sustain the planning process (Paton, 1999; Shaw & Harrald, 2004). Preparing plans and developing organizational capability is one important part of the process. The other is ensuring the availability of staff capable of implementing plans under atypical crisis conditions.

ESTABLISHING BUSINESS CONTINUITY CAPABILITY

The establishment and maintenance of BCM capability requires an immense commitment from management to ensure that it is effective in the event of a disaster. The problem remains regarding how to motivate managers to commit the necessary resources. "It *(BCM)* has all the ingredients of a nonstarter in corporate terms—it costs money but gives no direct return; it requires detailed planning yet has no clear endpoint; it does not offer the high flier a route to the Board and (worst of all) it forces managers to consider problems they would prefer to ignore" (Bird 1994, p 22). As with other organizational changes, BCM often requires a "champion" within the organization: someone who is committed to the concept of BCM and is in a position to "sell" the benefits to management and to those required to implement them.

For organizations that are subject to legislation, in particular legislation regarding corporate governance, obtaining management commitment is less of a problem. It is also less of a problem for organizations which already have effective risk management policies because these can provide a springboard for BCM. However, for other organizations, particularly small businesses, obtaining management commitment is more difficult. Increasingly, though, pressure for this to happen is coming from stakeholders who want to know that the organization is prepared to deal with crises so that their investments are protected. Larger organizations which have implemented BCM themselves are putting pressure on suppliers to protect themselves from any breakdown in the supply chain. For smaller businesses the pressure to adopt BCM may need to come from other agencies within the community so that they can work together to improve the overall resilience of the community. Encouragement for such planning may be forthcoming when the community understands the role of small business for employment and for the economic vitality of the community. They may, however, need assistance (financial and expertise) to put plans and competencies in place. In regard to the latter, a potential role for Chambers of Commerce of other groups (e.g., Rotary) can be identified. Making the decision to implement BCM is one thing, organizations then need to implement the necessary changes to culture, attitudes and practices.

BCM for disaster resilience is different to other organizational processes. For example, it involves developing a capability to manage disruption from events that have not occurred and that could present in a context of widespread societal disruption and devastation (such as occurred in New Orleans in 2005) that is difficult to anticipate and comprehend. Yet, managers must confront this task armed primarily with experiences derived from their own business history and the performance of routine activities.

A Capability for Change: Planning
for Success and Planning for Failure

Promoting effective change requires understanding the factors that predispose managers to think about this eventuality. An important issue here concerns the fact that, over time, the "mental maps" that inform managers' thinking and action become entrenched in the routine and insulated from environmental input. Under such circumstances, managers become cognitively complacent and render new, complex and ambiguous environmental data understandable by making it "fit in" with previous experience (Paton & Wilson, 2001). This makes it difficult for managers to consider, far less confront, nonroutine BCM contingencies. Consequently, those undertaking BCM planning must engage in a level of environmental monitoring, discussion with others (e.g., scientific and emergency management agencies), and develop a capacity for creative decision making that is unique to this activity. By understanding the cognitive processes that guide strategic thinking and the data upon which these processes operate managers can develop planning process and activities that challenge assumptions, facilitate change, and ensure that cognitive industry models most appropriate for identifying risk and developing BCM plans. The next issue concerns organizational willingness and/or ability to change.

There are various defense mechanisms which organizations adopt to deny their vulnerability to potential disasters. These include thinking that crises only happen to other organizations, that the organization is too big and powerful to be affected by a disaster and that a disaster will only affect a small part of the organization and therefore the organization can easily recover (Mitroff & Anagnos, 2001). Some organizations also choose to ignore signals within the organization that things are going wrong and therefore make no plans to mitigate or control a potential disaster (Paton, 1999; Paton & Wilson, 2001). These internal processes can mitigate against change, or render its implementation a more challenging endeavor.

Implementing change can be particularly problematic for organizations where power and authority are highly centralized (Gunderson et al., 1995; Harrison & Shirom, 1999). But if the organization has sufficient structural flexibility, it will be in a better position to develop its capability to manage significant disruptions (Alesch et al., 2001; Folke et al., 2003; Paton, 1997a). However, the structural capability to respond effectively need not always exist, and different categories of response can be anticipated.

At one end of the spectrum lies the "nonresponse." This occurs when bureaucratic inertia and vested political interests conspire to block change and, indeed, sow the seeds of future and more complex crises (Gunderson et al., 1995). A second type of response is where the organization responds, but lacks appropriate experience to do so effectively. This can occur as a consequence of a failure to consider risk from nonroutine events or because the organization has failed to learn lessons from previous disturbances. The consequent implementation of untried actions, even while recognizing a need for change, can increase resilience or it can increase vulnerability and exacerbate the loss of adaptive capacity (Folke et al., 2003). That is, the outcome, greater resilience or heightened vulnerability, is determined more by chance than by sound planning and good judgment.

Folke et al. (2003) emphasize the fact that, to increase resilience, experience of failure is required. The idea that a business should plan for failure as well as success is a difficult concept to accept. The majority of books and other literature written for businesses, particularly small businesses, are focused solely on strategies for success. However, "failing to plan to fail" is as important as "failing to plan to succeed."

Not only must the organization learn to live with risk and uncertainty, it must develop strategies to learn from the unexpected disturbances and failures that arise over time. Recognition of the importance of institutional learning leads to a third strategy, one capable of contributing to resilience. According to Folke et al. (2003), this involves several activities. Firstly, it requires the memory of prior crises, with personal experience of a disaster or knowledge of a disaster in a neighboring or similar business being potent motivational factors (Dahlhamer & D'Souza, 1995; Hill, 1996), and the lessons learnt being incorporated into institutional memory. Secondly, it requires a commitment to learn from these experiences and to develop future capability. Finally, these activities lead to the development of new rules and procedures. The effectiveness of this institutional learning approach can be enhanced by creating small-scale, controlled disturbances to facilitate the learning process and challenge complacency (Folke et al., 2003; Paton & Wilson, 2001). One of the outcomes of this process is the identification of the competencies and capabilities required of the staff who will be responsible for implementing the plan during a disaster.

BUSINESS CONTINUITY: SELECTION AND TRAINING

The atypical and complex environment within which business continuity plans are implemented will differ substantially from routine circumstances. Realizing the benefits of the BCM plan requires the availability of staff capable of applying them in a context defined by a need to confront challenging circumstances. This can be accomplished by selecting and training staff for their BCM roles.

Staff Selection

In addition to selecting for specific competencies (e.g., crisis decision making), staff selection decisions can be informed by knowledge of the demographic, dispositional and experiential factors that affect stress vulnerability and resilience. For example, older staff, ethnic minority staff, single parents and staff with young children may face levels of competing demands from nonwork sources that would reduce their capacity to respond effectively to crisis events (Paton, 1997a), making them less suitable for filling key response roles. Vulnerability is also affected by biological (e.g., heightened autonomic reactivity), historical (e.g., pre-existing psychopathology), and psychological (e.g., learned avoidance of threat situations, social skills deficits, and inadequate problem-solving behavior) elements (Scotti et al., 1995). Knowledge of these factors can be used to screen out staff. With regard to factors that can inform the selection of continuity staff, dispositional resilience factors such as, for example, hardiness, emotional stability, decisiveness, controlled risk taking, self-awareness, tolerance for ambiguity, and self-efficacy (Dunning, 2004; Flin, 1996; Lyons, 1991; MacLeod & Paton, 1999; Paton, 1989, Paton, 2003; Paton & Jackson, 2002) could be used.

Organizations may not, however, have the luxury of selecting staff in this manner. There may be insufficient flexibility to afford an opportunity to implement this option or staff may be cast into crisis roles by the unexpected timing of the crisis event. Under these circumstances, knowledge of predictors of stress vulnerability and resilience can be used for the post-event assessment of staff to identify those at risk and to prioritize them for support and monitoring during and after the disaster (Lyons, 1991; Paton, 1989; Tehrani, 1995). This strategy can facilitate staff recovery, hasten their return to work, and minimize recov-

ery costs (e.g., from compensation, absenteeism, illness, hiring temporary staff). Once selected, staff need to be trained.

Training for BCM Roles

Realizing the benefits of BCM also requires developing the competencies required to effectively action the plan (Grant, 1996; Paton,
1997a). The first step is a training needs analysis conducted explicitly
to identify the consequences likely to be encountered and the competencies required to manage them. Given the rarity of large scale disasters, practicing and evaluating the effectiveness of BCM procedures
and competencies is problematic. This limitation can be remedied
using exercises and simulations.

Simulations afford opportunities for BCM staff to develop technical
and managerial skills, practice their use under adverse circumstances,
receive feedback on their performance, increase awareness of stress
reactions, and rehearse strategies to minimize negative reactions (Flin,
1996; Paton & Jackson, 2002; Rosenthal & Sheiniuk, 1993). Detailed
process and content evaluation, conducted by someone with sufficient
authority and independence to be critical of the exercise/response and
make recommendations for future system and staff development,
should follow training exercises and actual crisis events. The results
should be incorporated into future planning and training agenda
designed to promote future response capability. These activities can
also contribute to the development of a supportive organizational climate (Folke et al., 2003; Paton, 1997a).

Significant differences between routine and post-disaster environments create novel and highly challenging demands for managers.
Training is thus required to enhance their response capability (Paton,
1997a). Training should cover, for example:

- hazard analysis and its implications for staff risk status and for
  operational continuity;
- developing a managerial style suited to identifying and planning
  to meet staff and business needs;
- adapting decision style under conditions of uncertainty (see
  below);
- familiarization with response plans and procedures and the use of
  problem-solving skills to adapt them to manage diverse (and

changing) circumstances;
- operating under devolved authority and planning for management succession (into crisis roles and from crisis back into routine operations);
- communicating and working with people with differing backgrounds and abilities;
- reconciling staff and business recovery needs (overtime), and
- staff monitoring and managing the return to work process.

A key area for training is information and decision management. While some communication problems result from hazard effects (e.g., loss of communication from seismic activity), lack of crisis information management expertise can generate additional problems. During the planning process, organizations need to consider what information will be required to maintain functions, how it should be collated, and how it should be interpreted and used to make decisions (Paton, Johnston & Houghton, 1998). During planning, dialogue should be entered into with information providers to discuss these issues. Staff should be trained to specify information needs, to interpret it appropriately on receipt, and, if required, to adapt information for different functions and end users. Organizations not only require information from diverse sources to manage response and recovery activities, they may also be called upon to distribute information to their staff, shareholders, suppliers and distributors, the community, the media, and board members.

In addition to considering information needs, decision-making procedures must be reviewed. Not only will decision procedures differ from those used in routine contexts, a capacity to adapt the style to suit the changing circumstances of the disaster response is also required (Flin, 1996; Paton et al., 1998). For example, long-term recovery planning requires an analytical approach to evaluate and compare options. During the disaster and its immediate aftermath rapid decisions are frequently required, making an intuitive or naturalistic style (Klein, 1997) more appropriate.

Given that a disaster can have community-wide consequences, all staff will be affected to some extent. Consequently, managers responsible for BCM will need to train to develop their capacity to facilitate both staff recovery and their return to normal functioning and productivity. Fulfilling the former involves their acting as good role models (e.g., acknowledging their own feelings) and providing feedback and information to staff (Paton, 1997b). This behavior demonstrates how to reconcile the personal impact of the event with continuing to work through a crisis or with returning to work. The latter is an important contributor to personal, business and societal recovery. Because it helps staff put their experience into perspective, allows access to support networks, and facilitates their regaining a sense of perceived control, returning to work is therapeutic and should be encouraged. However, managing the gradual return and reintegration into work requires careful planning and judgment. Managers should ensure that staff do not take on too much too soon and, because cognitive capacities may be temporarily diminished, remind them to take care when, for example, operating machinery, driving, or making complex decisions. Managers are also well-placed to help staff resolve their experiences in a beneficial manner. This can be facilitated by, for example, helping staff to identify strengths that helped them deal with this event and using the experience to focus on developing future capability.

Developing resilient staff is one part of this process. To fully realize its benefits, the attitudes, beliefs and values that constitute the organizational "culture" must sustain BCM activities. Recognition of the importance of organizational culture emphasizes the fact that developing people who are resilient does not guarantee the resilience of the organization as a whole (Coutu, 2002). Organizational resilience depends on the culture, structure and business practices of the organization as a whole. BCM provides a framework for building this resilience into an organization.

Business continuity plans should be developed in a consultative manner to ensure they are familiar to, and accepted by, those required to act on them and driven by the goal of developing the capability to respond effectively to any event (Lister, 1996; Paton, 1997a; Paton, 1999; Shaw & Harrald, 2004). Plans should be linked to training programs, resource allocation, and disaster simulation exercises. If not, plan effectiveness will be diminished when put into practice (Paton, 1997a).These collaborative activities provide staff with tangible evidence of organizational concern for their welfare, a shared responsibility for recovery (Powell, 1991) and help sustain staff loyalty (Bent, 1995), and ensure that planning and action occur within a supportive culture (Paton, 1997b). Organizational culture has another contribution to make. It provides the impetus to recognize a need for specialist crisis management systems and procedures.

Crisis Management Systems and Procedures

Key predictors of effective BCM are organizational characteristics (e.g., management style and attitudes, reporting and decision procedures) and bureaucratic flexibility (Doepal, 1991; Paton, 1997b; Powell, 1991; Turner, 1994). Rigid bureaucracies can, by persistent use of established procedures (even when responding to different and more urgent crisis demands), internal conflicts regarding responsibility, and a desire to protect the organization from criticism or blame complicate the response process. Effective response involves relaxing normal administrative procedures and replacing them with procedures designed specifically to manage response and recovery (both for staff and productivity) and, most importantly, accepting organizational ownership of the crisis and its implications (Elliot et al., 2002). Training programs for senior management and considerable organizational development may be required to plan and implement systems designed to support staff rather than (pre-existing) bureaucratic imperatives.

Crisis management systems will be required to cover, for example, delegation of authority; allocation of crisis response tasks, roles and responsibilities and the development of appropriate management procedures; identifying and allocating resources necessary to deal with the crisis, information management, communication and decision management, and liaison mechanisms. Flexibility in these systems is important. They will be required to deal not only with the uncharacteristic demands of the crisis, but also atypical demands emanating from dealing with unexpected emergent tasks; dealing with unfamiliar people and roles, and frequent staff reassignment (Paton, 1997a). Communication systems, designed to meet the needs of diverse stakeholders and response groups, are required for information access and analysis, defining priority problems, guiding emergency resource needs and allocation, coordinating activities, providing information to managers, staff and the media, and for monitoring staff and business needs (Bent, 1995; Doepal, 1991; Paton, 1997a). Information management and decision-making procedures are required (Bent, 1995; Paton, et al., 1998, Shaw & Harrald, 2004). Moreover, these activities may be required over a period of several months.

CONCLUSION

BCM provides a framework for developing the administrative and technical resources and staff competencies required to facilitate a capacity for business to adapt to adverse consequences. The organizational analyses that comprise BCM facilitate plan development, define the training and support needs of staff, and to identify the culture, systems and procedures that promote organizational resilience. Returning to productive capacity also requires that business continuity planning is a managed process which integrates staff and management systems via appropriately designed recovery resources. These integrated systems should be capable of adapting, over the course of the response and recovery period, to accommodate changing staff and business needs.

REFERENCES

Alesch, D. J., Holly, J. N., Mittler, E., & Nagy, R. (2002). *Organizations at risk: What happens when small businesses and not-for-profits encounter natural disasters.* [http://www.riskinstitute.org/ptr_item.asp?cat_id=1&item_id=1028] accessed 14th February 2003.

Bent, D. (1995). Minimizing business interruption: The case for business continuance planning. In A.G. Hull and R. Coory (Eds.), *Proceedings of the Natural Hazards Management Workshop 1995.* Institute of Geological and Nuclear Sciences, Lower Hutt, New Zealand.

Bird, L. (1994). What happens if peace breaks out?, *Survive! The Business Continuity Magazine, 1994,* Issue 2, p 22.

Business Continuity Institute (2002). Good practice in business continuity management. *Continuity, 6,* 2.

Comfort, L. K. (1994). Risk and resilience: Interorganizational learning following the Northridge earthquake of 17 January 1994. *Journal of Contingencies and Crisis Management, 2* (3), 157–170.

Coutu, D. L. (2002). How resilience works. *Harvard Business Review,* May, 46-55.

Dahlhamer, J. M., & D'Souza, M. J. (1995). *Determinants of business disaster preparedness in two U.S. metropolitan areas,* Preliminary Paper #24. Disaster Research Center, University of Delaware, U.S.

Davies, H., & Walters, M. (1998). Do all crises have to become disasters? Risk and risk mitigation. *Disaster Prevention and Management, 7,* 396–400.

Doepal, D. (1991). Crisis management: the psychological dimension. *Industrial Crisis Quarterly, 5,* 177–188.

Duitch, D., & Oppelt, T. (1997). Disaster and contingency planning: A practical approach. *Law Practice Management, 23,* 36–39.

Dunning, C. (2004). Reducing protective service worker trauma through pre-employment screening. In D. Paton, J. Violanti, C. Dunning, & L.M. Smith (Eds.), *Managing traumatic stress risk: A proactive approach.* Springfield, IL: Charles C Thomas.

Elliot, D., Swartz, E., & Herbane, B. (2002). *Business continuity management.* Routledge: New York.

Ewing-Jarvie, S. (2002). *Organizational Disruption in New Zealand.* Awesome Kiwi NZ Ltd., New Zealand.

Folke, C., Colding, J., & Berkes, F. (2003). Synthesis: Building resileince and adaptive capacity in social-ecological systems. In F. Berkes., J. Colding, & C. Folke (Eds.), *Navigating social-ecological systems: Building resilience for complexity an change.* Cambridge: Cambridge University Press.

Flin, R. (1996). *Sitting in the hot seat: Leaders and teams for critical incident management.* John Wiley & Sons Ltd, Chichester.

Grant, N. K. (1996). Emergency management training and education for public administration. In R.T. Styles and W.L. Waugh (Eds.), *Disaster Management in the US and Canada: The politics, policymaking, administration and analysis of emergency management* (2nd ed). Springfield, IL: Charles C Thomas.

Gunderson, L.H., Holling, C.S., & Light, S.S. (1995). *Barriers and bridges to the renewal of ecosystems and organizations.* New York: Columbia University Press.

Harrison, M. I., & Shirom, A. (1999). *Organizational diagnosis and assessment.* SAGE publications, US.

Hill, R. (1996). *An Investigation into Business Continuity Planning in the Melbourne Metropolitan Area,* unpublished thesis, Victoria University, Melbourne.

Holistic Disaster Recovery: Ideas for building local sustainability after a natural disaster, 2001. Natural Hazards Research and Applications Information Center, University of Colorado, US [http:www.Colorado.edu/hazards]

Klein, G. (1997). Recognition-primed decision making. In C. Zsambok & G. Klein (Eds.), N*aturalistic decision making.* LEA, Mahwah, N.J.

Knight, R. F., & Pretty, D. J. (1998). *Value at risk: The effects of catastrophes on share price. Risk Management, 45* (5), 39–41.

Levene, Lord (2004). *Taming the beast–managing business risk.* Lloyd's of London, 21 April.

Lister, K. (1996). Disaster continuity planning. *Chartered Accountants Journal of New Zealand, 75,* 72–73.

Lyons, J.A. (1991). Strategies for assessing the potential for positive adjustment following trauma. *Journal of Traumatic Stress, 4,* 93–111.

MacLeod, M.D., & Paton, D. (1999). Police Officers and Violent Crime: Social psychological perspectives on impact and recovery. In J.M. Violanti, and D. Paton (Eds.), *Police trauma: Psychological aftermath of civilian combat.* Springfield, IL, Charles C Thomas.

Mitroff, I. I., & Anagnos, G. (2001). *Managing Crises Before They Happen.* AMACOM, New York.

Paton, D. (1989). Disasters and Helpers: Psychological Dynamics and Implications for Counselling. *Counselling Psychology Quarterly, 2,* 303-321.

Paton, D. (1997a). D*ealing with traumatic incidents in the workplace* (3rd ed.). Queensland, Gull Publishing.

Paton, D. (1997b). Managing work-related psychological trauma: An organisational psychology of response and recovery. *Australian Psychologist, 32,* 46–55.

Paton, D. (1999). Disaster business continuity: Promoting staff capability. *Disaster Prevention and Management, 8,* 127–133.

Paton, D. (2003). Stress in disaster response: A risk management approach. *Disaster Prevention and Management, 12,* 203–209.

Paton, D., & Jackson, D. (2002). Developing disaster management capability: An assessment center approach. *Disaster Prevention and Management, 11,* 115–122.

Paton, D., Johnston, D., & Houghton, B. (1998). Organizational responses to a volcanic eruption. *Disaster Prevention and Management, 7,* 5–13.

Paton, D., & Wilson, F. (2001). Managerial perceptions of competition in knitwear producers. *Journal of Managerial Psychology, 16,* 289–300.

Powell, T.C. (1991). Shaken, but alive: Organizational behaviour in the wake of catastrophic events. *Industrial Crisis Quarterly, 5,* 271–291.

Reiss, C.L. (2004). *Risk management for small business.* Fairfax, VA: Public Entity Risk Institute.

Rose, A., & Lim, D. (2002). Business interruption losses from natural hazards: conceptual and methodological issues in the case of the Northridge earthquake. *Environmental Hazards, 4,* 1–14.

Rosenthal, P.H., & Sheiniuk, G. (1993). Business resumption planning: Exercising the disaster management team. *Journal of Systems Management, 44,* 12–16.

Scotti, J.R., Beach, B.K., Northrop, L.M.E. Rode, C.A., & Forsyth, J.P. (1995). The psychological impact of accidental injury. In J.R. Freedy & S.E. Hobfoll (Eds.), *Traumatic stress: From theory to practice.* Plenum Press, New York.

Shaw, G.L., & Harrald, J.R. (2004). Identification of the Core Competencies Required of Executive Level Business Crisis and Continuity Managers. *Journal of Homeland Security and Emergency Management, 1,* (Article 1), The Berkeley Electronic Press (bepress) http://www.bepress.com/jhsem

Standards Australia (2003). Business Continuity Management, HB 221:2003.

Tehrani, N. (1995). An integrated response to trauma in three Post Office businesses. *Work & Stress, 9,* 380–393.

Turner, B. (1994). Causes of disaster: Sloppy management. *British Journal of Management, 5,* 215–219.

Chapter 16

RESILIENCE IN EMERGENCY MANAGEMENT: MANAGING THE FLOOD

DOUGLAS PATON AND TREVOR AULD

INTRODUCTION

When disaster strikes, responsibility for the management of the consequences falls to emergency management agencies and the professional and volunteer personnel that staff them. Their performance in this capacity takes place against a backdrop of challenging and dynamic consequences whose nature exceeds the capacity of the resources available to manage them. Resilience, under these circumstances depends on their capacity to make choices regarding the allocation of resources to ameliorate anticipated and emergent demands, while working with others to determine how best to action these decisions. Furthermore, they have to perform these tasks under highly stressful circumstances. Because stress affects the ability to attend to information, render it meaningful, and make decisions with it (i.e., it influences adaptive capacity), stress risk management is fundamental to ensuring effective response (Paton, 2003).

This chapter focuses on emergency managers operating at the tactical or coordinating level in an emergency operations center (EOC) (Flin & Arbuthnot, 2002). The response management, team and interagency issues that characterize this level of response management are illustrated by drawing upon the emergency response to a major flood event in Manawatu, New Zealand in February 2004 (the Manawatu flood). The second author (TA) fulfilled an emergency management

267

role during this event, and his experience informs the identification of issues selected to illustrate adaptive capacity in emergency managers. Discussion also accommodates the fact that the contexts in which managers operate change over time. While, during a disaster, the warning, response and reintegration phases are seamless and run together, they are discussed separately here to articulate how adaptive capacity can be managed over the course of the disaster experience.

WARNING, ALARM AND MOBILIZATION

Emergency managers' involvement in a disaster is often viewed as commencing at the point when hazard activity occurs. Seismic hazards, for example, can occur with no warning, resulting in emergency managers being immediately thrust into response mode. However, under other circumstances, involvement begins earlier when a warning is triggered, or when conditions (e.g., weather) signal the possible onset of significant hazard activity. For example, volcanic, storm and floods hazards can present warning periods measured in hours, days, or months. With slow onset events, emergency manager involvement should start well before the onset of hazard activity.

Events such as the Manawatu storm/flood fall into the latter category. Under these circumstances, the Emergency Management Officer (EMO) will be checking on the area well before any event takes place. From personal experience (TA), stress during this period, which precedes warning being issued, reflects a realization that everything that you have trained for is about to happen.

Adaptive capacity at this point is a function of the quality of managers' situational awareness (Endsley & Garland, 2000) and its application to environmental monitoring or assessment. Under these circumstances, that component of situational awareness concerned with anticipating likely future conditions is particularly relevant. This capacity can be developed through contingency planning that integrates assessment procedures with local knowledge (Paton & Jackson, 2002). Where imminent hazard activity is indicated, the disaster experiences moves to the next phase.

Several hazards can create prolonged warning periods. For example, volcanic crises can have warning periods that extend over several months. Under these circumstances, the EMO faces demands in the form of maintaining motivation, vigilance and readiness over long periods of time. This uncertainty also increases demands on the EMOs from the public. For example, it can involve, first, dealing with public anxiety and then possibly public apathy if the hazard signalled by a warning fails to eventuate. This is not an easy issue to deal with. Good public engagement processes (see below) may go some way to ameliorating demands from this quarter. If hazard activity does materialize, warning gives way to mobilization.

During mobilization, EMOs must acquire information, differentiating fact from inference, making sense of information, adapting plans to accommodate emergent disaster demands, and identifying and deploying the resources required for effective response. Contingency planning and good situational awareness, developed in realistic simulation exercises (see below), represent strategies capable of mitigating stress risk and enhancing decision-making effectiveness under these circumstances.

At this juncture, the quality of the organizational procedures used to manage the transition from routine to disaster roles also influence the capacity of personnel to adapt to the reality of disaster response. Consequently, planning should cover issues such as role allocation, the delegation of authority and responsibility, emergency resource procurement and deployment and multiagency and multijurisdictional liaison (e.g., with other response agencies, scientific agencies). Procedures for developing effective multiagency collaboration are discussed later in this chapter. The mobilization process is also influenced by when activity commences.

The Manawatu flood event started on a Sunday night. About 1930 hrs, staff mobilized themselves. There were, however, problems with mobilizing the controller. Given that hazard consequences such as loss of infrastructure can prevent EOC personnel from getting through, ensuring that someone takes a leadership role is vital. Mobilization procedures should accommodate this contingency and training for the controller role should extend to cover a wider range of personnel.

In the case of the Manawatu flood, the establishment of an Emergency Management Committee (EMC) that had met regularly prior to the February event facilitated the transition from routine to disaster conditions. Notwithstanding, its effectiveness was still compromised by "turf protection" issues. This reflects the atypical nature of the response, the pre-existing mechanistic structure of many emergency organizations, and the lack of specific disaster operating procedures (Paton, 1997). The management of these issues is discussed below.

Mobilization stress risk can be affected by factors unrelated to the event. It is greater if personnel are responding at the end of a shift, by transient (e.g., illness, occupational stress) and family factors. The personal and transient nature of these factors renders them difficult to manage. However, risk management programs that enhance EMOs knowledge of these limiting factors, their performance implications, and the need to adopt appropriate reduction strategies (e.g., increased teamwork) can reduce their deleterious influence on performance effectiveness and well-being as managers turn their attention to managing the consequences of the disaster.

RESPONSE MANAGEMENT AND WELL-BEING

During the response phase, adaptive demands emanate not just from the characteristics of the disaster. They can also emerge from role stress, organizational and management practices, and media and public scrutiny. In this section, media and public issues are briefly discussed before considering risk factors and adaptive mechanisms relating to the disaster per se.

Media coverage of the response makes significant demands on managers. Sensationalizing or misreporting the response and its management are prominent stressors. For example, during the Manawatu flood one radio station issued unsubstantiated reports of bridges collapsing, causing chaos in the wider community. To manage such problems, the Manawatu District Council allowed the media to remain in the EOC. This strategy reduced the incidence of sensationalist publication and assisted the transfer of information. Ensuring that there is only one dedicated media liaison role for media releases, with the release issued on letterhead and signed by the chief executive was another beneficial element of the media strategy.

In the Manawatu flood, unrealistic public expectation of the response effort contributed to stress risk. This problem is growing as people increasingly transfer responsibility for their safety to emergency management agencies (Gregg et al., 2004; Paton et al., 2000). This example illustrates how assumptions inherent within emergency plans regarding community readiness may not be accurate (Lasker, 2004). A discrepancy between plan assumptions and actual public response represents an additional source of uncertainty for emergency managers. Response planning should be based on realistic estimates of what people will actually do (Lasker, 2004), with knowledge of the latter being derived from a process of community engagement.

Syme, Bishop and Milich (1992) demonstrated that engaging community members about hazards increased their commitment to take responsibility for their own safety. It also reduced the likelihood of community members wanting to scapegoat those responsible for emergency planning. This appeared to be due to greater community knowledge of the trade-offs involved in creating safer environments.

The demands on emergency managers can also be traced to the event itself. Managers must contend with uncertainty about, for example, the duration of a disaster, the period of their involvement, and recurrence or additional threats (e.g., earthquake aftershocks, secondary hazards such as building collapse or lifeline disruption (flood waters washing infrastructure and lifelines away or rendering them unusable). The fact that hazard consequences typically exceed the resources available to deal with them (Flin & Arbuthnot, 2002) creates a high and unrelenting level of demand on managers to make decisions regarding the distribution of available resources. Before proceeding to discuss decision making, it is worth noting how these circumstances can have secondary consequences for adaptive capacity and well-being.

During the Manawatu flood, it proved difficult to get staff to take breaks and to leave the EOC at the end of a shift. A culture of "I'm too important to leave" emerged quickly amongst those on duty. This describes what Raphael (1986) called *counterdisaster syndrome.* In complex events, role expectations interact with intense physical and psychological demands to create a situation where emergency manager's perceive their involvement as essential for the successful management of hazard consequences. The net effect of this overinvolvement is fatigue and a decline in operational effectiveness and well-being. Time spent actively managing incidents should, therefore, be limited and adequate rest breaks taken (Paton, 1994). In the Manawatu flood, explaining the importance of rest breaks and time-out remedied this problem.

Information and Decision Management

Sarna (2002) characterizes disaster as an event in which "There's a 1,000 things happening, you're aware of 100, and you can do something about 10" (p. 40). Central to the tactical EOC role is making choices about how to deploy limited resources to manage consequences that exceed a capacity for comprehensive response. Adaptive capacity under these circumstances reflects the quality of the information management and decision-making systems and competences, and the capacity to exercise these competencies within an interagency environment.

As the initial incident controller (TA), the management response was complicated by difficulties obtaining information from other emergency services. This proved to be a significant issue for all the Emergency Management Officers from the greater Manawatu area responding to this event. Future training with the EMC groups will hopefully alleviate the problem. However, a great deal of breaking down of old cultures will need to occur to facilitate better integrated emergency management in the future. Strategies for developing interagency collaboration are discussed below. We start this section with a discussion of decision making.

Emergency managers make decisions under conditions of incomplete or inaccurate information, using data from several nonroutine agencies, in a context of complex evolving hazard consequences and response objectives, under considerable time pressure. Managers need to acquire information and render it meaningful in relation to the hazard consequences to be managed. While this task can be affected by hazard activity (e.g., damage to communication infrastructure), adaptive capacity is primarily a function of managers' situational awareness (Endsley & Garland, 2000).

Situational awareness reflects a capability to operate on limited cues to impose coherence on complex hazard consequences (Paton & Hannan, 2004). By imposing coherence, it is possible to identify the subset of consequences that can be managed. That is, situational awareness facilitates a capacity to utilize limited resources in the most effective way. This process is complemented by effective information management procedures (Paton & Flin, 1999). Information needs must be anticipated and defined. Once information needs are identified, networks with information providers and recipients can be organized.

To use these resources, EMOs must be able to access, collate, interpret and disseminate information compatible with decision needs and systems under disaster conditions (Paton et al., 1999). Differences between disaster and routine circumstances mean these competencies must be developed.

For trained personnel, the heightened alertness, faster reactions and thinking skills associated with emergency response can enhance their ability to take decisions under pressure (Flin, 1996). However, counterdisaster syndrome (see above) can, as a consequence of managers experiencing tunnel vision, failure to prioritize, freezing, and loss of concentration, significantly reduce decision making effectiveness (Flin, 1996) and increase stress risk. Countering this possibility requires taking rest periods, rotating personnel, and ensuring that EMOs are trained in crisis decision making and have the capacity to adapt the decision process to the circumstances developed.

One process describes analytical decision making, where the individual or team consider alternative courses of action and selects the best option. This contrasts with intuitive or naturalistic decision making. Naturalistic decision making, where a person recognizes the type of situation encountered and, from previous experience, selects an appropriate course of action, is highly adaptive in high risk disaster environments (Flin et al., 1997). Naturalistic decision making affords greater stress resilience than the more intellectually demanding analytical approach (Klein, 1996). Given that responding to disaster can present rapidly changing demands, skill in naturalistic decision making is an essential competence for emergency managers. Because success in naturalistic decision making is a function of the ability to match current and prior situations, decision effectiveness is enhanced by having more options to match. This ability can be developed through experience or simulation.

These circumstances also call for a level of creative decision making that exceeds that required for routine emergencies (Jackson et al., 2003; Kendra & Wachtendorf, 2003; Paton et al., 1999). While some decisions will be made by EMOs themselves, other decisions will be made in collaboration with other EOC team members and sometimes with representatives of external agencies (e.g., scientific, technical, police).

Team Performance

In effective teams, the provision of unprompted (implicit) information between members facilitates better tactical decision making and resource allocation (Pollock et al., 2003). For this to occur effectively, team members must share a *team mental model* specifically relating to the goal-related information required by decision makers at critical periods. As the level of team work and planning activity increases, emergency managers develop a capacity to think in the same way as their team members and to understand how their role interacts with those of others. That is, they develop more similar schema or mental models of response environments and the roles and tasks to be performed within them. This, in turn, increases implicit information sharing during high workload periods, enhancing team performance (Paton & Jackson, 2002; Pollock et al., 2003), increasing the adaptive capacity of the EOC team and mitigating stress. The benefits of controllers working as a team for stress management was endorsed by the Manawatu District Council controllers after the Manawatu flood; working together lowered the stress impact considerably.

Large-scale disaster also results in the team expanding to include multiagency and multijurisdictional input. The complex nature of disasters brings together agencies that rarely interact or collaborate with one another under routine circumstances. Prior to a disaster, they are unlikely to have had the opportunity to work with other agencies in ways that would allow shared understanding of their respective roles to develop. However, simply bringing together representatives of agencies who have little contact with one another under normal circumstances will not guarantee a coordinated response. Rather, such ad hoc arrangements are more likely to increase interagency conflict, result in a blurring of roles and responsibilities, and fuel frustration and feelings of inadequacy and helplessness (Carafano, 2003; FEMA, 2004; Jackson et al., 2003; Kendra & Wachtendorf, 2003; Paton, 1994; Paton et al., 1999). However, training in multidisciplinary team skills, and extensive joint planning and team development activity involving agency representatives can enhance this aspect of response management. It does so by building a capacity to arrive at consensus about tasks, goals and priorities, and developing a culture of cooperation and teamwork that focuses the team on managing hazard consequences rather than interteam and political issues (Flin & Arbuthnott, 2002; Pollock et al., 2003).

To facilitate effective interagency collaboration, several factors need to be taken into account (Paton et al., 1999; Paton et al., 2003). One concerns how each agency defines interagency collaboration. For example, *turf protection* increases interagency competition and, consequently, stress risk. The constraining presence of this factor during the Manawatu flood was described above. Organizations must accept the value of collaboration (e.g., the need for diverse perspectives) if complex problems are to be understood and managed effectively. A second factor concerns the patterns of interaction between group members in relation to institutional policies, structures and culture, and the language and terminology used. Managing these issues requires that agencies are integrated into a super-ordinate group whose membership is prescribed by their collective role in managing complex events and that exists solely for the purpose of managing a disaster. This involves their accepting this role for the duration of the disaster and separating their disaster role from their routine role. Some strategies for achieving this are described later in the section on simulation. A third factor concerns agencies understanding of integrated emergency management policies and practices, and the status and power accorded to different members. Operating practices (e.g., information and decision management) must be developed specifically for disaster response. It is also important that members suspend normal status relationships and accept the need for authority to be vested in those with the expertise to manage the disaster. A fourth issue concerns the level of trust between partners.

At one level, these issues reflect the need for structural integration between agencies to be matched by corresponding procedural or operational capacity to act in concert during a crisis (Paton et al., 1999). However, it also encompasses participants' understanding of their respective contributions to the same plan and their shared understanding of each member's role in the response (Paton & Flin, 1999). This contributes to their capacity to share a common understanding of evolving events, to work towards common goals over time and, importantly, to anticipate the needs of those with whom they are collaborating (Flin, 1996; Pollock et al., 2003). This anticipation plays an important role in facilitating adaptation to rapidly evolving events. While performance of these tasks will often occur when all parties are in one location, large scale events can necessitate performing this role when key decision makers are distributed throughout several locations.

The concept of distributed decision making recognizes the need for contributions from people who differ with respect to their profession, functions, roles, and expertise, and who may be in different locations (FEMA, 2004; Paton & Flin, 1999). The quality of shared understanding thus determine the capability of the multiagency team to utilize its collective expertise, even if dispersed or contributing different perspectives, to manage the response. It also increases the likelihood of their operating with a shared mental model of the situation that facilitates the effective and efficient allocation and use of limited resources. Consequently, high levels of interagency planning and training will play a prominent role in the development of emergency management resilience. The question is then one of how this can be accomplished.

Several factors, including pragmatic issues associated with bringing agency representatives together to exercise and the diversity of collaborative relationships (e.g., agencies can be differentiated with regard to those with whom they will collaborate) that will comprise the overall response makes developing this capacity a complex task. In an attempt to circumvent these problems, Paton (2001) proposed a method based on defining decision making and information needs.

Using realistic disaster scenarios that require input from several agencies to define and resolve problems, this approach involves, firstly, defining the decisions required to manage anticipated demands. The second stage involves each agency identifying the information they require to make decisions. Agency identification of the data and information needed to make nonroutine decisions provides a foundation for conceptualizing their interagency networks and how they will relate to other agencies during a crisis. A similar approach for managing distributed operations (in which decision makers must coordinate their actions from geographically dispersed locations) when dealing with nonroutine, multiagency response was proposed by van der Lee and van Vugt (2004). Other models have also been proposed.

Burghardt (2004) proposed the COMBINED Systems model. According to this model, effective response to complex crises can be facilitated by, firstly, delegating well-structured tasks to artificial systems which leaves more time for human decision makers to deal with emergent demands. Secondly, control is delegated to self-organizing subsystems (e.g., search and rescue role, evacuation) supported by decision support systems that accommodate the complex psychological, cultural and political interactions that characterize multiagency response environments. Irrespective of the model adopted, emergency managers need opportunities for practice and to review and progressively develop plans and skills. Simulations are increasingly being used for this purpose (Crego & Spinks, 1997; Paton & Jackson, 2002).

Exercises and simulations afford opportunities for emergency managers to develop, practice and review technical, management and team skills under realistic circumstances and to construct realistic performance expectations. They also provide opportunities to practice dealing with high pressure situations in a safe and supportive environment, increase awareness of stress reactions, and to rehearse strategies to minimize negative reactions.

Many exercises fail to mirror the complexity of disaster response environments. This can occur because of time and resource constraints. However, it can also reflect cultural attitudes. Civil Defense exercises are designed to succeed. If an exercise fails then the exercise writer has failed. This belief does not recognize that failure in an exercise plays an important role in identifying future training and management needs. It is only by identifying problems that future capability can be developed. It is, therefore, necessary to change the meaning of success. Exercises should be designed in ways that allow individuals and teams to progressively push their boundaries and develop progressively more sophisticated competencies (Paton & Jackson, 2002).

Only through exposure to exercises that challenge assumptions and allow personnel to confront novel events can preparation for disasters, whose complexity will exceed even the most extreme simulation, enhance response effectiveness. What is required is an attitude change to accommodate the fact that exercise allow both the maintenance of strengths and identify areas for skill and procedural change. The identification of weaknesses also makes an important contribution to the analysis of residual risk and to making more accurate assessment of response effectiveness. This process will allow more realistic estimates of recovery and rebuilding needs to be developed.

To be effective, simulations should integrate emergency roles, tasks, responsibilities, skills and knowledge required for effective all-hazards management with the disaster characteristics and response demands (e.g., scale of damage, multiagency operations, rapid role change) likely to be encountered (Paton, 1994; Paton & Jackson, 2002). They should be designed to facilitate competence in, for example, identifying risk factors and their consequences for disaster stress; the transla-

tion of plans into action and their adaptation to cater for events differing in type, scale or complexity. They should also cover team processes and management; delegation of authority and responsibility; information management and communication, creative problem solving,
multiagency response management, and decision making under conditions of uncertainty; (Paton, 1997). Given that EMOs will be called
upon to function under highly challenging and dynamic circumstances, it is pertinent to ask what contributes to their stress resilience.

Adaptive Capacity: The Characteristics of Emergency Managers

Several dispositional and cognitive appraisal characteristics influence EMOs capacity to function. Coping strategies (e.g., emotional
support and expression and positive reframing) and dispositional factors (e.g., extraversion, openness to experience, agreeableness, consci-
entiousness, self-efficacy, optimism and hope) have been implicated as
predictors of resilience and adaptive outcomes in emergency populations (Linley & Joseph, 2004). The significance of personality data for
emergency organizations relies on its predictive validity and the extent
to which it can be used by organizations to make choices about staff
resilience using selection procedures. In a prospective study, Smith
and Paton (2002) found that Extraversion was the only personality
characteristic to predict posttraumatic growth outcomes in police officers. This finding is consistent with Thompson and Solomon's (1991)
conclusion that well-being in members of body recovery teams
reflected levels of extraversion elevated relative to population norms.

A pertinent issue here is the fact that emergency managers, many of
whom are volunteers, elect to enter a profession that increases the likelihood of their exposure to disaster. This can reflect an underlying
motivation to help people under trying circumstances (Miller, 1995).
While self-selection may predispose emergency managers to find benefit in the challenging aspects of emergency work, it does not, however, prepare them for all the eventualities they may encounter.
Sustaining these motivational benefits during disaster work reflects the
capacity of their cognitive appraisal to render highly challenging experiences meaningful.

In emergency professions, finding meaning in work increases satisfaction and contributes to a capacity to find benefit from traumatic

experiences (Britt, Adler, & Bartone, 2001). Paton, Cox and Andrew (1989) found that disaster volunteers reported significant benefits from their disaster experience. Beneficial consequences derived from their struggle with traumatic recollections, usually over a period of several months, and were manifest as a stronger sense of individual and professional competence, a greater sense of the importance of family and work relationships, increased empathy, and a stronger sense of life appreciation. These benefits persisted over time, and were reflected in a continued commitment for volunteer disaster work. The question then becomes what influences *how* this is accomplished?

The retrospective nature of the above study precluded identifying specific predictors of beneficial outcomes. However, a subsequent prospective study revealed how the derivation of benefit was linked to training designed specifically to develop schema that helped render the challenging aspects of disaster experience meaningful. This study compared the experiences of a group who had received this training with a control group of firefighters who had not (both of whom responded to the same disaster). Analysis revealed that training that enhanced a capacity to impose meaning on the disaster experience and personal reactions to it resulted in more salutary outcomes and a sense of personal and professional growth (Paton, 1994). According to Paton, this training developed more flexible and sophisticated mental models. These enhanced officers' capacity to make sense of their experience and to learn from it in ways that facilitated their personal and professional growth. The outcome was a capability for challenge appraisal that reduced the likelihood that hazard demands would exceed the person's perception of the resources available to them to cope with the ensuing demands (Tugade & Frederickson, 2004).

These findings are consistent with others that endorse a role for positive reframing and benefit finding as predictors of posttraumatic growth (Linley & Joseph, 2004). The finding of a similar relationship between positive cognitive appraisal of threat and beneficial outcomes in civilian populations (Tugade & Frederickson, 2004) adds weight to the argument that this process represents a natural resilience mechanism. Importantly, from the perspective of organizational choice, a capacity for challenge appraisal or positive reframing can be developed through training (Paton, 1994).

Training to develop challenge appraisal should address three areas (Inzana, Driskell, Salas, & Johnston, 1996; Dunning, 2003; Paton,

1994). Firstly, it should include procedural issues such as ensuring that managers have realistic outcome and performance expectations and learn to differentiate personal from situational constraints on effective response. Secondly, training should address sensory and experiential elements. This would include providing systematic exposure to the sights, sounds, smells or disaster (e.g., using morgue visits, reviewing accounts of experienced personnel and specially prepared training videos) and understanding what constitutes normal emotional reactions and feelings under atypical circumstances. These issues were built into the training that preceded the Manawatu flood. They helped mitigate adverse stress reactions during the flood. Notwithstanding, some personnel developed serious stress reactions. Consequently, it is important to ensure that a residual stress risk assessment is included in the risk management process. Stress levels in staff need to be monitored constantly, and personal exhibiting signs of stress during an event must be treated immediately. Thirdly, training should develop officers' interpretive processes. This can include, for example, developing procedures (individual and group) to review experiences as learning opportunities that enhance future competence.

The incorporation of these elements in realistic simulations increases the effectiveness of training and contributes to the development of competencies, such as self-efficacy, that have been implicated as predictors of posttraumatic growth (Linley & Joseph, 2004; Paton & Jackson, 2002). Developing these more sophisticated psychological structures requires that simulations are constructed to reconcile event characteristics (e.g., exposure to biohazards, personal danger, dealing with human remains and cross-cultural aspects of death and loss) with the competencies required to manage them (e.g., hazard identification and interpretation; adapting plans; team and multiagency operations; information and decision management) in ways that promotes adaptive capacity (Paton, 1994; Paton et al., 1999; Pollock et al., 2003). Training for Manawatu District Council staff revolved around "challenging" scenarios in training exercises, such as the town of Feilding losing water supply, roads being washed out and large areas of the town being flooded. On February 15th all of these scenarios came to pass. Training needs analysis derived from these exercises identified the need for training to address both technical and psychological issues, and specialist training from a psychologist had been included to training.

Because response, and the training that precedes it, are performed under organizational aegis, organizations are thus well-placed to make choices regarding the development of a capacity for challenge appraisal through their selection and training systems. Training is also a component of the process of organizational socialization. It not only develops pertinent skills and competencies, it also inculcates EMOs into the fabric of the organizational culture. Training is also put into practice in a context defined by organizational membership. Because organizational membership influences how personnel make sense of organizational experiences (Weick, 1995), its potential to influence challenge appraisal must be considered. Thus, the organization has the potential to make a significant contribution to facilitating adaptive capacity.

Organizational Factors

When responding to disasters, EOC personnel do so within a context defined by their membership of an organization whose structures and procedures reflect the performance of routine roles. In the study of disaster workers discussed above (Paton, 1994), a switch from the autocratic management style normally prevailing within emergency organizations to one in which responsibility was devolved to those actively dealing with hazard consequences was strongly implicated as a determinant of their adaptive capacity. Similar findings by Alexander and Wells (1991) reinforce the fact that organizational factors influence resilience. In this regard, the organizational culture has a prominent role to play. Positive aspects of organizational culture (e.g., having responsibility, empowerment, recognition of good work) enhance adaptive capacity, while organizational hassles (e.g., lack of consultation, poor communication, red tape) inhibit effective response and undermine well-being.

A culture that empowers personnel, delegates authority, support a flexible, consultative leadership style and practices that ensure that role and task assignments reflect incident demands facilitate adaptive capacity (Paton et al., 2003). Adaptive capacity can be reduced if organizations assume that response practices (e.g., command structure, level of autocracy, degree of devolved authority, level of training) derived from routine contexts, are appropriate for managing disaster consequences (Carafano, 2003; Kendra & Wachtendorf, 2003; Paton & Hannan, 2004). Persistent use of routine decision and reporting procedures, inadequate delegation of authority and responsibility, and senior management interference designed to protect the organization from criticism or blame rather than assisting response management increase stress risk. Systems must be designed specifically to support disaster response. Autonomous emergency management systems, a flexible, consultative leadership style, and role and task assignment based on empowerment principles can ameliorate disaster stress and enhance response effectiveness (Alexander & Wells, 1991; Gist &Woodall, 2000; Johnston & Paton, 2003; Paton, 1996).

Recognition of the organizational role is important. Emergency organizations can use knowledge of the relationship between personality, cognitive appraisal and organizational factors and disaster resilience to proactively prepare EMOs for future disaster work. These activities also contribute to the development of the personal and cultural competencies conducive to developing adaptive capacity, managing emergent demands and safeguarding well-being.

When developing this strategy, it must be acknowledged that fully realizing its potential can take weeks to months (Linley & Jospeph, 2004). Because the period within which growth occurs will transcend the period of involvement in a specific disaster, the capacity of the post-event environment to sustain this process must be considered. This issue is addressed in the next section.

RECOVERY AND REINTEGRATION

Termination of involvement in disaster response and returning to normal life poses its own challenges. For emergency managers, reintegration risk factors include dealing with reporting pressures within routine bureaucratic systems, catching up with any backlog of work, dealing with sociolegal issues, and reintegration back into normal family life. While significant in themselves, stress risk is compounded by the interaction between these demands and prevailing organizational climate and practices (Paton et al., 2004). The importance of considering this reflects the fact that the organizational culture provides the context within which future adaptive capacity is nurtured or inhibited. Strategies for facilitating adaptive capacity are discussed here with reference to support and management practices. Just as teamwork enhances adaptive capacity during response, social support can act in a similar capacity during reintegration. It must, however, be structured in ways that facilitate learning.

Membership of a cohesive team may sustain posttraumatic growth (Lyons, Mickelson, Sullivan, & Coyne, 1998; Park, 1998; Paton & Stephens, 1996). Lyons et al. (1998) used the term "communal coping" to describe how team activities can contribute to growth through, for example, shared acceptance of psychologically challenging events and cooperative action to resolve problems and sustain positive emotions. Acknowledging and building on effective collaboration during a disaster, and working together after it to develop better preparedness for future crises, they argue, contributes to the development of personal and team resilience.

While identifying a context in which growth outcomes are facilitated, it is important to consider the mechanism that mediates the effectiveness of resources such as communal coping. One candidate for the latter is Frederickson's Broaden and Build model (Frederickson, 2001; 2003). It represents a mechanism for explaining how positive emotions (sustained by communal coping) can result in new ways of thinking. Positive emotions broaden peoples' attention and thinking in ways that encourages more creative, integrative and flexible thinking. This facilitates the development of social (e.g., sense of cohesion), intellectual (e.g., problem solving), and psychological (e.g., sense of identify, optimism) resources that contribute to a capacity to experience growth following crises events (Frederickson, Tugade, Waugh, & Larkin, 2003). This process can also be implicated in the development of positive threat appraisal (Tugade & Frederickson, 2004) and contributes to the further development of mental models capable of imposing a sense of coherence on nonroutine, complex and threatening disasters (Paton, 1994). In emergency professions, however, this process, and the content of the schema developed, will also be influenced by the context in which EMOs work.

A significant issue for emergency professions concerns how organizational culture determines how people make sense of experiences (Weick, 1995). An important component of this concerns the transmission of cultural characteristics through managerial behavior and attitudes. For example, during reintegration, managerial attitudes to allocating blame and supporting emotional expression exercise a significant influence on the expression of positive emotion (Paton, Violanti & Smith, 2003). If the benefits of the Broaden and Build theory are to be fully realized, the role of organizational climate as a determinant of its effectiveness must be considered.

Berkes, Colding and Folke (2003) argue that, to develop new conceptual frameworks and enhance the organizational contribution to resilience, experience of events that challenge assumptions is essential. This can be achieved by critically reviewing crises and using simulations to challenge complacency. This provides the foundation for the collaborative learning, creative decision making, and sense of coherence that characterize an organizational culture that facilitates growth (Berkes et al., 2003; Paton, 1994; Paton & Jackson, 2002; Paton, Violanti & Smith, 2003).

Acknowledging the fact that support practices are offered within an organizational culture, Dunning (2003) adapted Lissack and Roos (1999) model of coherences to identify a set of principles to guide the integration of support resources and organizational practices in ways designed to increase the likelihood of personnel deriving benefit from their experience. These principles include, for example, recombining information to rehearse potential new situations, recognizing the multiple roles and cohesive team ethos of emergency responders, allowing procedural flexibility, and ensuring managers have field experiences that enhance their empathy. Senior managers can increase the likelihood of beneficial outcomes by helping personnel appreciate that they performed to the best of their ability, accept the impact of uncontrollable situational constraints on performance, learn about their reactions and support positive expression of emotion.

Adaptive outcomes are more likely if managers work with EOC personnel to understand their experiences within an organizational climate of care that acknowledges and legitimizes emotional expression and that promote self-help (Dunning, 2003; Gist & Woodall, 2000; Lissak & Roos, 1999; Paton et al., 2000). This includes assisting EOC staff to identify the strengths that helped them deal with the emergency, and building on this to plan how future events can be dealt with more effectively. That is, by encouraging the interpretation of experience as learning opportunities that contribute to personal and professional growth. These actions also contribute to the development of an organizational culture that nurtures strengths, provides a context conducive to increasing social support, builds and sustains EMOs capacity for challenge appraisal. By incorporating these activities into risk management planning, estimates of emergency managers' capability to manage disaster will increase substantially, as will confidence in the planning that precedes their deployment to deal with disasters.

REFERENCES

Alexander, D.A., & Wells, A. (1991). Reactions of police officers to body handling after a major disaster: a before and after comparison. *British Journal of Psychiatry, 159,* 517–555.

Berkes, F., Colding, J., & Folke, C. (2003). *Navigating social-ecological systems: Building resilience for complexity and change.* Cambridge: Cambridge University Press.

Britt, T.W., Adler, A.B., & Bartone, P.T. (2001). Deriving benefits from stressful events: The role of engagement in meaningful work and hardiness. *Journal of Occupational Health Psychology, 6,* 53–63.

Burghardt, P. (2004). *Combined Systems.* Proceedings of ISCRAM 2004. Brussels: ISCRAM.

Carafano, J.J. (2003). *Preparing responders to respond: The challenges to emergency preparedness in the 21st Century.* Heritage Lectures #812. Washington, DC.: The Heritage Foundation.

Crego, J., & Spinks, T. (1997). Critical incident management simulation. In R. Flin, E. Salas, M. Strub & L. Martin (Eds.), *Decision making under stress.* Ashgate, Aldershot.

Driskell, J., & Salas, E. (1996). *Stress and human performance.* Hillsdale, NJ: Lawrence Erlbaum.

Dunning, C. (1999). Post-intervention strategies to reduce police trauma: A paradigm shift. In J.M. Violanti, J.M., and D. Paton (Eds.), *Police trauma: Psychological aftermath of civilian combat.* Springfield, IL: Charles C Thomas.

Dunning, C. (2003). Sense of coherence in managing trauma workers. In D. Paton, J.M. Violanti, & L.M. Smith (Eds.), *Promoting capabilities to manage posttraumatic stress: Perspectives on resilience.* Springfield, IL: Charles C Thomas.

Endsley, M., & Garland, D. (2000). *Situation awareness. Analysis and measurement.* Mahwah, NJ: Lawrence Erlbaum.

FEMA (2004). *Responding to Incidents of National Consequence.* Washington, DC.: FEMA.

Flin, R. (1996). *Sitting in the Hot Seat. Leaders and Teams for Critical Incident Management.* Chichester: Wiley.

Flin, R., & Arbuthnot, K. (Eds.) (2002). *Incident Command: Tales from the hot seat.* Ashgate, Aldershot.

Flin, R., Salas, E., Strub, M., & Martin, L. (Eds.) (1997). *Decision making under stress.* Ashgate, Aldershot.

Fredrickson, B. L. (2001). The role of positive emotions in positive psychology: The broaden-and-build theory of positive emotions. *American Psychologist, 56,* 218–226.

Frederickson, B.L. (2003). The value of positive emotions. *American Scientist, 91,* 330–335.

Frederickson, B. L., Tugade, M.M., Waugh, C.E., & Larkin, G. (2003). What good are positive emotions in crises?: A prospective study of resilience and emotions following the terrorist attacks on the United States on September 11th, 2001. *Journal of Personality and Social Psychology 84*:365–376.

Gist, R., & Woodall, J. (2000). There Are No Simple Solutions to Complex Problems. In J.M. Violanti, D. Paton, & C. Dunning (Eds.), *Posttraumatic stress intervention: Challenges, issues and perspectives.* Springfield, IL: Charles C Thomas.

Gregg, C., Houghton, B., Paton, D., Swanson, D.A., & Johnston, D. (2004). Community preparedness for lava flows from Mauna Loa and Huallai volcanoes, Kona, Hawaii. *Bulletin of Volcanology, 66,* 531–540.

Inzana, C.M., Driskell, J.E., Salas, E., & Johnston, J.H. (1996). Effects of preparatory information on enhancing performance under stress. *Journal of Applied Psychology, 81,* 429–435.

Jackson, B.A., Baker, J.C., Ridgely, M.S., Bartis, J.T., & Linn, H.I. (2003). *Protecting emergency responders Volume 3: Safety management in disasters and terrorism response.* Cincinatti, OH: National Institute for Occupational Safety and Health.

Johnston, P., & Paton, D. (2003). Environmental resilience: Psychological empowerment in high-risk professions. In D.Paton, J. Violanti, & L. Smith (Eds.), *Promoting capabilities to manage posttraumatic stress: Perspectives on resilience.* Springfield, IL: Charles C Thomas.

Kendra, J., & Wachtendorf, T. (2003). Creativity in emergency response to the World Trade Center disaster. In Monday, J.L. (Ed.) (2003), *Beyond September 11: An account of post disaster research.* Special Publication #39. Boulder: Institute of Behavioral Science, University of Colorado.

Klein, G. (1996). The effect of acute stressors on decision making. In J. Driskell & E. Salas (Eds.). *Stress and human performance.* Hillsdale, N.J: Lawrence Erlbaum.

Lasker, R.D. (2004). *Redefining readiness: Terrorism planning through the eyes of the public.* New York, NY: The New York Academy of Medicine.

Linley, P.A., & Joseph, S. (2004). Positive change following trauma and adversity: A review. *Journal of Traumatic Stress, 17,* 11–21.

Lissack, M., & Roos, J. (1999). *The next common sense: Mastering corporate complexity through coherence.* Naperville, IL: Nicholas Brealey Publishing.

Lyons, R.F., Mickelson, K.D., Sullivan, M.J.L., & Coyne, J.C. (1998). Coping as a communal process. *Journal of Social and Personal Relationships, 15,* 579–605.

Miller, L. (1995). Tough guys: Psychotherapeutic strategies for law enforcement and emergency services personnel. *Psychotherapy, 32,* 592–600.

Park, C.L. (1998). Stress-related growth and thriving through coping: The roles of personality and cognitive processes. *Journal of Social Issues, 54,* 267–277.

Paton, D. (1994). Disaster relief work: An assessment of training effectiveness. *Journal of Traumatic Stress, 7,* 275–288.

Paton, D. (1997). *Dealing with traumatic incidents in the workplace* (Third Edition) Gull Publishing, Queensland, Australia.

Paton, D. (2001). *Information and decision management in an emergency operations center.* Auckland: Auckland City Council.

Paton, D. (2003). Stress in disaster response: A risk management approach. *Disaster Prevention and Management, 12,* 203–209.

Paton, D. Cox, D., & Andrew, C. (1989). *A preliminary investigation into posttraumatic stress in rescue workers.* Robert Gordon University Social Science Research Reports #1. Aberdeen, Scotland: Robert Gordon University.

Paton, D., & Flin, R. (1999). Disaster stress: An emergency management perspective. Disaster Prevention and Management, 8, *261–267.*

Paton, D., & Hannan, G. (2004). Risk factors in emergency responders. In D. Paton, J. Violanti, C. Dunning & L. Smith (Eds.), *Managing traumatic stress risk: A proactive approach.* Springfield, IL: Charles C Thomas.

Paton, D., & Jackson, D. (2002). Developing disaster management capability: An assessment center approach. *Disaster Prevention and Management, 11,* 115–122

Paton, D., Johnston, D., Houghton, B., Flin, R., Ronan, K., & Scott, B. (1999). Managing natural hazard consequences: Information management and decision making. *Journal of the American Society of Professional Emergency Managers, 6,* 37–48.

Paton, D., & Stephens, C. (1996). Training and support for emergency responders. In Paton, D. & Violanti, J. (Eds.), *Traumatic stress in critical occupations: Recognition, consequences and treatment.* Springfield, IL: Charles C Thomas.

Paton, D., Violanti, J., & Dunning, C. (2000). *Posttraumatic stress intervention: Challenges, issues and perspectives.* Springfield, IL: Charles C Thomas.

Paton, D., Violanti, J., Dunning, C., & Smith, L.M. (2004). *Managing traumatic stress risk: A proactive approach.* Springfield, IL: Charles C Thomas.

Paton, D., Violanti, J.M., & Smith, L.M. (2003). *Promoting capabilities to manage posttraumatic stress: Perspectives on resilience.* Springfield, IL: Charles C Thomas.

Pollock, C. Paton, D.Smith, L., & Violanti, J. (2003). Team resilience. In D. Paton, J. Violanti, & L. Smith. (Eds.), *Promoting capabilities to manage posttraumatic stress: Perspectives on resilience.* Springfield, IL: Charles C Thomas.

Raphael, B. (1986). *When disaster strikes.* Hutchinson, London.

Sarna, P.V (2002). Managing the sSpike: The command perspective in critical incidents. In R. Flin, R. & K. Arbuthnot (Eds.), *Incident command: Tales from the hot seat.* Ashgate, Aldershot.

Smith, C., & Paton, D. (2002). *Personality predictors of occupational well-being in police officers.* Unpublished research data. Wellington, New Zealand Police.

Syme, G. J., Bishop, B. J., & Milich, D. (1992). Public involvement and dam safety criteria: Towards a definition of informed consent. *ANCOLD Bulletin, 92,* 12–5.

Thompson, J., & Solomon, M. (1991). Body recovery teams at disasters: Trauma or challenge? *Anxiety Research, 4,* 235–244.

Tugade, M.M., & Frederickson, B.L. (2004). Resilient individuals use positive emotions to bounce back from negative emotional experiences. *Journal of Personality and Social Psychology, 86,* 320–333.

van der Lee, M., & van Vugt, M (2004). *IMI–An information system for effective multidisciplinary incident management.* Proceedings of ISCRAM 2004. Brussels: ISCRAM.

Weick, K.E. (1995). *Sensemaking in organizations.* Thousand Oaks, CA.: Sage.

Chapter 17

PLANNING FOR HAZARD RESILIENT COMMUNITIES

DAVID KING

INTRODUCTION

The United Nations designated the 1990s as the International Decade for Natural Disaster Reduction (IDNDR). This drove a shift towards an emphasis on mitigation—awareness and preparedness. The aim was to identify vulnerability and to reduce it. During the International decade this shifted to a preference to identify and enhance strengths, specifically resilience. The outcome was the strategy of building hazard resilient communities. Despite IDNDR, loss of life and economic costs from natural hazards have continued to increase. Mitigation has been pushed by both political and economic necessities.

A response in Australia was to identify and quantify economic costs (BRS, 2001), followed by the Council of Australian Governments (COAG, 2002) review, a high-level review to establish mitigation priorities. The COAG review requires mitigation at all levels of government, and puts responsibility on planners as well as requiring an enhancement of resilience through civil responsibility, education and warnings. "Take action to ensure more effective statutory State, Territory and local government land use planning, development and building control regimes that systematically identify natural hazards and include measures to reduce the risk of damage from these natural hazards." "Reduce the problem of public infrastructure repeatedly

288

damaged by natural disasters through cost-effective mitigation measures to make infrastructure more resilient. . . ." "Develop jointly improved national practices in community awareness, education and warnings. . . ." The review goes on to identify specific actions. (COAG 2002 p. 4). The emphasis is on strengthening communities through awareness, education and warnings in order to enhance mitigation, and placing responsibility on Local Government Councils and land use planners.

PLANNING AND COMMUNITY: CONCEPTS AND MEANINGS

Thus, we have an enhanced relationship between strengthening communities, making them more resilient and an increased responsibility of planners to avoid hazards or protect new developments in hazard-prone locations. The terminology of mitigation has been driven by international and national agencies. There are, of course, many other areas of increased mitigation but this chapter will concentrate on the role of planners in relation to the enhancement of hazard resilient communities. These are ideas and needs that are easily stated by high-level government groups but which are much more complex down at community level.

The chapter title summarizes these aspects of mitigation to five short words that are in no way a simple relationship. Each of these terms is complex, and clearly a desired outcome is the hazard resilient community. Thus, to deal with each in turn the chapter begins with planning and planners.

Plan, planning and planners are used extensively in a number of settings and concepts. The basic plan in emergency management is the state disaster plan, which is supported by legislation. There are all sorts of plans that may plan for risk; rolling, strategic, sectoral etc. at all levels of government and private enterprise. However, planning as a component of mitigation is used in its narrower context–land use planning, or the profession of planning as it is defined by professional organizations in many countries. The Planning Institute of Australia (2005) defines it as follows:

Planning deals with many different issues. Planners guide and manage the way suburbs, cities and regions develop, making sure that they are good places in which to live, work and play. Planners are involved in making decisions about land use proposals and other types of developments whilst balancing the needs of communities and the environment. Planners are responsible for a range of tasks including:
- Shaping the form of neighborhoods and cities
- Controlling the spread of urban regions
- Ensuring sustainable natural environments
- Working towards economic and cultural development
- Ensuring vibrant and liveable communities
- Providing advice on planning matters to the public and stakeholders

The role of planners is becoming more important, as society places greater emphasis on balancing environmental and development issues, promoting liveable communities and securing high-quality urban design. As cities and towns continue to grow in terms of size and population, planners are in increasing demand to manage these changes. They frequently work alongside and often coordinate the work of other specialists and professionals such as engineers, architects, building surveyors, economists, developers, politicians, scientists, and environmental scientists (website).

There is no reason why this definition should not include emergency management and hazard mitigation. In the United States many more emergency managers are from a planning background than in Australia.

However, emergency management and hazard mitigation are not core activities of planners or planning. In Australia in particular this is a relatively new direction in the increasing complexity of the planning profession. Hazard mitigation is generally accepted as a challenge rather than an imposition, but it is still far from the highest priority. This is illustrated by the subject content of professional journals. For example, in Australia two similar kinds of journals exist for the professions of planning and emergency management; the *Australian Planner* and the *Australian Journal of Emergency Management*. A content scan of each of these journals over the last seven years of issues revealed hardly any papers concerned with hazards in the *Australian Planner,* but more than 20 in the *Australian Journal of Emergency Management,* for example, community mapping (McRae, 2001), duty of care (Proctor, 1998), emergency management and local government councils (Gabriel, 2003; Kanarev, 2001), guidelines and land use (Gillespie, Grech, & Bewsher, 2002; Pardy & Daly, 2001), New Zealand planning (Becker & Johnston, 2002), legislation and education (Barnes, 1999), and flood liability (Yeo, 2003). Clearly planners are less interested in hazards than emergency managers are in planning. There is a different situation in the United States where similar issues of mapping, mitigation, flood control and resilience were strongly represented in the *Journal of Planning* (El-Marsi & Tipple, 2002; Henderson, 1999; Lee, 2004; Milheizler & Schneider, 1997; Srinivasan, 2003; Stalberg, 1995; Steinberg & Burby, 2002; Tibbetts, 1994). However, while emergency management may be better integrated with planning in the United States, new developments dominate planning worldwide and hazard mitigation is one of many considerations in development assessments.

Thus, it cannot be argued that hazard resilient communities are planned by planning professionals. Formerly such communities have emerged by chance, although legislation is steadily pushing planners to take greater cognizance of hazard mitigation. A chapter title of planning hazard resilient communities would not have reflected the current roles of planners. The word "for" has been used to indicate the gap that exists—that planning is an entity in itself and hazard resilient communities are a desired outcome, in which the act of planning has to be harnessed to enhance mitigation. The use of planning is a noun rather than as a verb which is an important distinction. Planners cannot plan resilience. They may make plans that reduce vulnerability and enhance mitigation, and they may contribute to the future resilience of the community through good design, creation of a sense of place, and the provision of appropriate services and facilities. But the fact remains that planning is a process, a profession that creates plans, and natural hazard risks have not formally concerned them to any great extent.

It is no simpler when defining the hazards that are to be mitigated. Emergency management has targeted all hazards for mitigation, such that multihazard assessments have been carried out in several Australian locations (Granger, Jones, & Scott, 1999). For the local government councils who were the recipients of these assessments, priorities were necessary to operationalize the information. Predictable, gradual onset hazards such as flood, cyclone/surge, associated landslides and bushfire could be targeted and formally prepared for. In accepting such a planning responsibility the Queensland government developed a state planning policy on hazards that required mapping and development controls in specified hazard zones for flood, fire and landslide, while surge was covered by the coastal zone management legislation and wind damage by building codes. Low probability events like earthquake and tsunamis are not addressed by legislation, while extremely common droughts are not considered in Australia to be a natural hazard (although government support is given to drought declared regions). The United Nations International Secretariat for Disaster Reduction does consider drought to be a hazard. Also at odds with the rest of the world (like Kyoto) Australia and the United States at the World Conference On Disaster Reduction in Kobe January, 2005 refused to acknowledge climate change as a disaster or natural hazard. Consequently, legislation and planning are restricted to mitigation of a relatively narrow range of natural hazards.

Generally, communities mitigate and build resilience against the predictable local hazards, paying scant attention to low probability hazards. This is further accentuated by local government councils and local communities preparing for the highest probability of their local hazards, i.e., preparation for categories one to three of cyclones, 100-year floods and so on. When the extreme event occurs the community is devastated, although realistically most places and households simply cannot afford to mitigate against the worst scenario. While planning has been pushed towards hazard mitigation in land use and development, the hazards are selective and the probabilities legislated for are at the high frequency lower end of impacts.

Planning can actively enhance resilience through the core goal of planners to create liveable communities, a sense of place and a sense of community. Indirectly best practice planning is an activity that strengthens resilience. However, documents and legislation like a planning policy do what most legislation does–they specify minimum standards–what must be avoided or what must be done as a minimal act of legislation. The Integrated Planning Act in Queensland attempted, like similar planning acts elsewhere in Australia and other parts of the world, to facilitate best practice. Consequently, it is extremely complex and expensive to administer. Generally, legislation is fixed to minimum standards rather than best practice. Reducing vulnerability to hazards requires the setting of minimum standards. Enhancing resilience is best practice; a desirable outcome but extremely difficult to measure, let alone legislate.

Analysis of the social impact of hazards was initially dominated by vulnerability, especially in the early part of the IDNDR. Identifying vulnerability proved extremely difficult because of the diversity of factors and human characteristics that make up vulnerability (Granger, 1995; Keys, 1991). On the other hand, if it could have been defined precisely it could have provided a clear minimum standard to improve on, as is the case with a similar kind of vulnerability—poverty eradication. Reducing vulnerability in the broadest sense is a role of many government departments and international agencies. As poverty was identified as one of many contributors to hazard vulnerability, then poverty eradication programs contribute to a part of hazard vulnerability mitigation.

Planning again is an indirect reducer of vulnerability through its role in developing services, facilities, infrastructure and access. These things do not necessarily enhance resilience. Vulnerability is not the opposite of resilience. These characteristics of an individual or a community are best seen as separate scales that may intersect on specific characteristics, but it is quite possible for a community to be both vulnerable and resilient simultaneously, i.e., a low income or indigenous closely-knit community that has endured many floods or cyclones and has learned to minimize loss. Vulnerability reduction can be legislated by specific minimum standards, but in a sense it represents a weakness of "at risk" areas, or individuals or groups. Many vulnerability characteristics are immutable; the very young, the very old so that a vulnerability analysis is only of use to emergency managers in determining where to concentrate resources.

Resilience on the other hand consists of strengths and capacities. By identifying these elements, the community may be assisted in mitigating its own hazards. The assumption is that resilience will strengthen mitigation and enhance response and recovery. Hazard resilience is the ability to cope with a crisis and bounce back. Enhancing resilience takes place through activities like education, prevention, communication and unity of purpose, or shared beliefs and values. It is a characteristic that grows out of the people and their communities. It can be facilitated but not legislated.

The community that is the target of hazard mitigation is also a complex concept. Having gained ascendancy as a planning and mitigation cliche the word community often stands for "the public" or "people."

Communications like community hazard warnings or community preparedness or community education and many others are essentially
targeted towards individuals, or households, or families. There is no
expectation that a whole "community" will receive, accept and
respond homogenously to an education or preparedness campaign, or
a warning.

However, in land use planning and physical elements of hazard mitigation, the community is viewed as a group target with an assumption
of relative homogeneity and a geographical locale. Hazard impact
occurs differently from one geographical area to another; from coast
to inland, river floodplain to hill slopes, from valley to ridge. Thus,
hazard mapping, as used by planners and emergency managers, identifies hazard zones within which specific communities of people and
their houses are identified. Jane Jacobs' (1961) evocation of dynamic
urban communities has profoundly influenced New Urbanism
(Congress for New Urbanism, 2005), which advocates close-knit interactive communities. Yet, this is not a realistic model of the average
suburban community. People only spend a portion of time in their
houses. In particular, residential suburbs are dormitories that are emp-
tied for much of each working day, and even at weekends.
Furthermore, Jacobs' vision of the dynamic, partying neighborhood is
not the reality for most urban residents. Neighbors are not the basis of
community even if a whole street shares demographic and socioeconomic characteristics. Proximity does not make a community. But
urban communities are multiple networks, described by Alexander
(Alexander 1966) as a lattice of interconnections. Even the family or
household is not homogenous in its makeup or community membership. Individuals are simultaneously members of several communities
based on workplace, school, recreation, gender, values, use of facilities, friendships, extended families, organizational membership and so
on. The urban population is mobile, multilocational and interconnected.

Mitigation of hazards and the enhancement of hazard resilient communities is not achieved by simple targeting of a geographical collection of streets and houses, although that is one of the layers of communities. The rest of the mitigation effort must take place through all
of the other communities. For example, schoolchildren can be educat-
ed for hazard awareness and preparedness within the relatively
homogenous environment of the school classroom where it is possible

to inculcate hazard knowledge that will stay with individuals for life. Children take their lessons and homework into the home where they frequently influence parents, siblings and other friends and family. The school itself is a community centered on teachers and children, but it interacts directly as a broader community that includes parents and local residents. A ripple effect flows out from the community center, the school, through the broader geographical community. Enhancement of a hazard resilient community therefore develops from an educational activity at the core.

Another view of hazard resilience in communities is through what happens when a crisis or disaster occurs. At one level emergency organizations and response agencies are directly involved, but a plethora of community-based formal and informal organizations involve themselves both directly and indirectly alongside or independently of the emergency organizations.

Although natural disasters are extremely unequal in their impacts, with some places and individuals losing everything alongside neighbors or neighboring suburbs where little loss occurred, most disasters

TABLE 17.1. ORGANIZATIONS INVOLVED IN EMERGENCY MANAGEMENT.

Direct	Indirect	Residual & Spontaneous
International	Businesses	Culture
Government Organizations	Economic Organizations	Community Networks
Non-Government Organizations	Recreational organizations	Internet
Privatized Specialists	Religous organizations	Residual Leadership
Grass Roots Organizations	Cultural Groups	Volunteers
Community Organizations	Interest Groups	Fixers & Tradespersons
	Political Groups	Illegal Groups
	Media	Family & Household
		Individuals & Visitors

cause an impact over a wide area. Usually many communities, both in a geographical sense as well as the complex urban networks, are affected by a disaster. Where individuals are at the time of the hazard event, may determine their roles in response and recovery. The response will vary enormously according to the day of the week, the time of day and even season. The hazard-resilient community may be a neighborhood block, a workplace, school or shopping mall. Recovery of the workplace may be far more important in the short-term than recovery of the home. This was powerfully visible in Phuket (Thailand) during the days after the Boxing Day, 2004 Indian Ocean tsunami. Tourist businesses and facilities are the core of the economy and security. Employees and business owners explained how crucial it was to clear up, reopen and attract tourists back as quickly as possible, as the tsunami had struck at the peak of the tourist season. Other losses existed, but without a functioning economy any other kind of recovery would not have been feasible.

The response to a disaster is often far from orchestrated, whatever the pre-crisis disaster plan may have anticipated. Everyone is affected and most will become involved in response and recovery. Table 17.1 illustrates the formal and informal organizations and communities that have a stake in responding to a disaster. The formal organizations have a plan and a procedure, while the other groups and networks have priorities and agendas. In many situations these groups may work together, but that is not necessarily the case. It is just as likely that formal organizations and community groups will work in parallel. The more empowered and resilient a community is, the less dependent it will be upon the formal organizations, and the more likely it will be to pursue its own priorities.

MITIGATION, RESPONSE, AND RECOVERY

A community that is hazard resilient is empowered to prepare for and cope with an actual disaster, along with appropriate support. People will want to be involved at all stages, regardless of the actions of emergency managers and response agencies, because they have a stake in their own communities. They also possess local knowledge, although not necessarily the big picture. The community may be resilient in recovery or mitigation or in response but is not necessarily good at all of these things.

The conventional emergency management model (Crondstedt, 2002) expresses a circular process from mitigation (encompassing both hazard prevention and preparation), through response to a crisis followed by recovery. It is seldom that linear in a disaster, as both communities and emergency management agencies respond at different rates. Some communities may begin recovery while others have not yet experienced a crisis response. Mitigation also continues throughout an event (even though it may not be the highest priority), as decisions about future prevention and preparation will be made in relation to the reality of the actual disaster. At the emergency management preparation stage it is rational to separate the different stages of mitigation, response and recovery, but once a crisis occurs all these things will happen at the same time according to community and response agency resources, agendas, priorities and the needs.

Therefore, it is useful to examine community resilience in relation to each of the conventional emergency management stages. Three brief case studies are used to illustrate how hazard resilience may function alongside existing planning shortcomings.

Mitigation

During the late 1990s, Cairns in Far North Queensland was the focus of the multihazard assessment of Geoscience Australia's (GA, then AGSO) Cities Project. The Centre for Disaster Studies played a role in vulnerability assessment, especially in relation to cyclone and storm surge. Anderson-Berry (Berry 1996) carried out a series of longitudinal household surveys in the northern beaches suburbs of Cairns. These surveys contained some measures of vulnerability and some of resilience. As the 1996 census figures became available during the first of these studies, vulnerability indicators (identified initially by Granger, 1995; Keys, 1991) were compiled from census data to construct a ranking of vulnerable communities (census collection districts) in the northern beaches suburbs. The household surveys included some census-type questions (which were used to test for significance in the survey), but most were qualitative questions concerned with cyclone knowledge and preparation. The results of this research did not provide a neat assessment of vulnerability and resilience. Firstly, the census vulnerability indicators did not correlate with the survey hazard vulnerability indicators, and secondly vulnerability indicators did not correlate with resilience indicators (King & Melick, 1996).

These results were expected, as the range of indicators was very diverse. Socioeconomic characteristics may indicate vulnerability, but do not necessarily have anything to do with lack of cyclone knowledge or preparation. Similarly, resilience indicators were a different set of measures to those of vulnerability. They are not opposite ends of the same scale, but are two separate, occasionally interconnecting scales from low to high vulnerability and from low to high resilience (Buckle, 1999). Thus, a community could be both highly vulnerable and highly resilient. One particular suburb of Cairns stood out very strongly as both extremely vulnerable while demonstrating strong resilience characteristics. This was Machans Beach, immediately adjacent to Cairns International airport. It is a beachside suburb on very low land that is an island in the delta of the Barron River which drains from the tableland ranges that flank Cairns. In order to gain a better understanding of resilience in a hazard vulnerable location postgraduate planning students carried out quantitative appraisals in both Machans Beach and in the similarly vulnerable inner-city suburb of Portsmith, which is situated next to the port of Cairns (Guy & Wellington, 1997, cited in King, 1997).

Portsmith is a zone in transition with very little sense of community. It has a large number of low rental dwellings, is low-lying and vulnerable to flood and storm surge. The attitude of residents towards flood or surge warnings was to evacuate immediately. Machans Beach had a very strong sense of community, although many dwellings were still low-cost rental. There were several local organizations and associations and local community events. If devastated by a disaster they would probably exhibit strong resilience in recovery. However, their resilience extended to community members making their own decision as to when it was necessary to evacuate. They expressed an intention to use open dinghies to ferry residents across the Barron River in the middle of a cyclone. We concluded an impression of a community whose resilience was unrealistic in the face of a catastrophic event and extreme hazard vulnerability. Having a sense of community does not necessarily make a community hazard safe.

Both of these low-lying suburbs are located in vulnerable places because of planning decisions made over 100 and 50 years ago respectively. While planners are now responsible for mitigating hazard vulnerability in new developments, most of the existing vulnerable locations are the result of historical decisions about which modern planners can do very little until a redevelopment application is made.

Response

The multi hazard assessment of Cairns also recorded every building, against which it was possible to assign individual elevations above sea level. Analysis of this GIS to examine potential storm surge impact showed an overwhelming concentration of critical infrastructure in low-lying areas adjacent to the coast (King, 1997). In fact, the residential housing in Machans Beach and Portsmith was an exception. Most housing in Cairns is outside storm surge zones. Emergency services, community buildings, infrastructure, services and commercial buildings on the other hand are all especially concentrated in vulnerable locations. This experience of Cairns is repeated in most other Queensland cities and other places in northern Australia. These are relatively new urban centers that were established around a port access which became the subsequent city center. There are of course numerous other cities in the world that are vulnerable for the same reason (Queste, 2005).

Because of this concentration of critical infrastructure in hazard vulnerable urban centres, such cities as Cairns will be severely constrained in responding to a disaster. This was exactly what happened to Townsville in 1998 when over 700mm of rain was dumped on the city in 24 hours. Over 50 percent of all emergency facilities, services, government and community infrastructure were inaccessible or flooded.

The incapacitation of response agencies during a crisis puts greater emphasis on community resilience, and its ability to organize its own response in recovery. Phuket City in Thailand is an example of an administrative and commercial center that is well outside the coastal hazard zone. The 2004 Indian Ocean tsunami struck the western beaches of Phuket Island as well as islands and the mainland of Krabi to the southeast and Khao Lak to the north. The immediate response to the tsunami came from its victims. The first priority of dealing with the dead and injured involved local residents, visitors, and emergency response teams.

The priority then shifted to the reestablishment of the tourist industry and businesses as rapidly as possible in order to rescue the remainder of the tourist season. Because critical infrastructure was not concentrated in the wave impact zone, the response was rapid, organized and intensive. Within a week after the tsunami, the beach areas of Phuket had been cleaned up and returned to as much functionality as possible.

It is unrealistic to argue that it was good planning that gave government and private enterprise in Phuket a locational advantage in relation to a rapid response. In this instance it was more good luck, combining with competition from tourist operations for beachfront locations. However, the response was rapid and efficient because a focused community with strong economic motivation was backed up and led by capable government, with subcontracted private enterprise builders and all of their heavy equipment and machinery.

Recovery

Resilience aids disaster recovery—the speed and extent to which a community bounces back from disaster is a measure of resilience. This will most clearly be observed during the recovery phase. Recovery is the most complex of the three emergency management stages: there are realms of the personal and household, the economy, the State infrastructure, and both personal and community trauma. Recovery may advance in one of these realms but not in others.

Economic and infrastructural recovery are especially difficult where the community is less developed. In Papua, New Guinea the town of Rabaul was devastated by volcanic eruptions in 1994. Despite a highly successful evacuation without loss of life, the consequence of poor governance and the lack of development funds resulted in Rabaul remaining a ghost town 10 years later with most of its population, economy and government functions lost. Its population of around 30,000 had reestablished in less hazardous locations away from Rabaul, rebuilding some of the former functions but little of the economy. If the investment and relief funds had been available and wisely administered, a new town could have been built within a few years. The community did not lack resilience; the problems lay in the political and economic system.

The same experience is likely in areas impacted by the 2004 Indian

Ocean tsunami. Aceh will probably take many decades to recover its functionality, but Thailand will probably achieve its pre-tsunami economic level within five years. In Thailand there was inequality of impact. Recovery on Phuket is rapid; it may be fully functional by the following tourist season. The large tourist resorts to the north were severely damaged. Recovery will require rebuilding structures, landscapes and tourist confidence, probably taking several years.

Three observations during fieldwork on Phuket in the week immediately following the tsunami, illustrate important elements of the recovery process and the role of resilience in that process. These concerned mitigation, hazard attitudes and community linkages. The Thai government identified mitigation through land-use controls to restrict the development of small cottages and tourist accommodation on the beachfront, stipulating a 100m development free zone. While it is possible that this may not be achieved in reality, the mitigation idea developed directly from the hazard recovery. Mitigation and response and recovery were simultaneous processes. Secondly, the attitude that was expressed towards the tsunami was that it was less awful than having to deal with a human generated disaster, like the Bali bombing. Thirdly, community linkages were strong in some of the smaller beach communities where tourist small businesses were linked by family involvement. In a situation where most did not carry insurance, reliance on extended family support is an important aspect of resilience in recovery.

After a major disaster people have to make their own arrangements, getting on with picking up the pieces with little outside support, at least in the short-term. In the complex humanitarian disaster of post-Civil War recovery in Sierra Leone in 2002 (a small country in West Africa with a population of 5 million), resilience was expressed through independent community-led rebuilding and reconstruction. In a situation where governance, physical infrastructure, economy and residential dwellings had been systematically destroyed over a 10-year period, the government that regained authority after UN intervention had very little structure with which to initiate recovery. Sierra Leone facilitated a National Government Organization (NGO) policy, to encourage international and national NGOs and relief agencies to lead post-war recovery. In the face of enormous displacement and destruction, most NGOs concentrated on their traditional skills in such areas as health, displaced persons, food relief and capacity building. Inevitably their impact was random and neglected communications infrastructure and residential dwellings. The priority for civil society was to rebuild their houses and reestablish the economic base, which needed a transport system. Thus, the community pursued a parallel route to recovery, which interconnected with the efforts of the NGOs, but which was in no way led by them. During 2002 people were returning to their war-ravaged towns and villages to rebuild the civil society that had existed before the war. They worked within traditional structures that gave them the organizational resilience to begin rebuilding a country from thousands of small communities.

CONCLUSION

This chapter has structured planning and hazard resilient communities within the emergency management processes of mitigation, response and recovery. Planning is primarily concerned with new developments and land-use changes. Hazards and hazard zones are a complication and a nuisance that get in the way of new developments and settlement growth. Planners and developers will only confront hazard mitigation when structured by legislation. At a broader level, planning for communities is the responsibility of all agencies and organizations. Community resilience is enhanced indirectly through the provision of many services, safeguards and structures. The corollary is that the resilience of civil society and communities is undermined by inappropriate siting of supporting infrastructure.

Communities are diverse, multilayered and interconnecting with each pursuing its own response and recovery according to local priorities. Formal agencies and communities follow parallel routes in response and recovery with neither necessarily providing primary leadership. Community strength and resilience may be positive in some situations or hazard levels, but may endanger its citizens in other situations. Resilience is hazard, community and temporally specific. These are realms of resilience that do not exist as absolute characteristics which can be reached as an ultimate goal. Resilience needs constant enhancement and capacity building, both from within the community and from outside agencies. Planners will develop passive positive community characteristics. Hazard resilience will otherwise remain a responsibility of emergency managers working with communities to build mitigation capacity.

REFERENCES

Alexander, C. (1966). A city is not a tree. Architectural Forum, April 1966; reprinted in Design, No. 6 February 1966. Revised (1986) for Zone 1/2, New York; revised version reprinted in Thakara, J. (1988) *Design After Modernism.* London: Thames and Hudson.

Barnes, J. (1999). The role of legislation in the advancement of community education Part 1: Is the law enforceable in the courts? *Australian Journal of Emergency Management, 14,* 51–59.

Becker, J., & Johnston, D. (2002). Planning for earthquake hazards in New Zealand: A study of four regions. *Australian Journal of Emergency Management, 17,* 2–8.

Berry, L. (1996). *Community vulnerability to tropical coastal cyclones and associated storm surges: Case study of the Cairns northern beaches townships.* Townville, Australia: James Cook University, Centre for Disaster Studies and Centre for Tropical Urban and Regional Planning.

BRS (2001). *The economic costs of natural disasters in Australia.* Canberra: Bureau of Transport Economics.

Buckle, P. (1999). Redefining community and vulnerability in the context of emergency management. *Australian Journal of Emergency Management, 13,* 21–26.

Council of Australian Governments. (2002). *Natural disasters in Australia* (DoTARS Report. Canberra: Department of Transport and Regional Services, Retrieved 19/10/05 from http://www.dotars.gov.au/localgovt/naturaldisasters/COAG report.aspx

Congress for the New Urbanism. (2005). About New Urbanism. Retrieved 17/10/05, from http://www.cnu.org/about/index.cfm?CFID=11870021&CFTOKEN=7764 2732

Crondstedt, M. (2002). Prevention, preparedness, response, recovery - an outdated concept. *Australian Journal of Emergency Management, 17,* 10–13.

El-Marsi, S., & Tipple, G. (2002). Natural disaster, mitigation and sustainability: The case of developing countries. *International Planning Studies, 7,* 157.

Gabriel, P. (2003). The development of municipal emergency management planning in Victoria, Australia. *Australian Journal of Emergency Management, 18,* 74–80

Gillespie, C., Grech, P., & Bewsher, D. (2002). Reconciling development with floods risks - the Hawkesbury-Nepean dilemma. *The Australian Journal of Emergency Management, 17,* 27–32

Granger, K. (1995). *Community vulnerability: The human dimensions of disaster.* Paper presented at AURISA/SIRC 95–The 7th Colloquium of the Spatial Information Research Centre.

Granger, K., Jones, T., & Scott, G. (Eds.). (1999). *Community risk in Cairns: A multi-hazard risk assessment* (Cities Project). Canberra: AGSO.

Henderson, H. (1999). An ounce of prevention. *Planning, 65,* 25.

Jacobs, J. (1961). *The death and life of great American cities.* New York, NY: Random

House.

Kanarev, N. (2001). Assessing the legal liabilities of emergencies. *The Australian Journal of Emergency Management, 16*(1), pp. 18–22.

Keys, C. (1991). Community analysis: Some considerations for disaster preparedness and response. *The Macedon Digest, 6,* 13–16.

King, D. (Ed.). (1997). *Cyclone and storm surge impact in Cairns. 1996/97 Research Reports.* with reports by King "An Atlas of Cyclone and Storm Surge Impact on Cairns", Berry, Goudie, Guy and Wellington. Townsville: James Cook University, Centre for Disaster Studies, Tropical Cyclone Coastal Impacts Program.

King, D., & Melick, R. (1996). Community vulnerability to cyclone storm surge in Cairns, far North Queensland. In R. Heathcote, C. Cuttler, & J. Koetz (Eds), *NDR96.* Proceedings of the National Disaster Reduction 96 Conference, Gold Coast: Institution of Engineers, Canberra. (pp. 363–364).

Lee, A. (2004). Early planning for hazards brings benefits to Biloxi. *Planning, 70,* 51.

McRae, R. (2001). Community Mapping–An aid to emergency management. *Australian Journal of Emergency Management. 16,* 22–27.

Milheizler J., & Schneider, P. (1997, July). FEMA on the job. *Planning, 63,* 8–9.

Pardy, S., & Daly, M. (2001). Hazard and risk management: Guidelines for local authorities. *The Australian Journal of Emergency Management, 16,* 62–64.

Planning Institute of Australia. (2005). *What is Planning?* Retrieved 17/10/05, from http://www.planning.org.au/index.php?option=com_content&task=view&id=10 2&Itemid=103

Proctor, H. (1998). Issues for local government. *Australian Journal of Emergency Management, 13,* 2–4

Queste, A. (2005). *Vulnerability of modern societies towards natural disasters–The impact on critical infrastructures.* Retrieved 17/10/05, from http://www.unisdr.org/wcdr/thematic-sessions/cluster4.htm#c4-8

Srinivasan, D. (2003). Battling hazards with a brand new tool. *Planning, 69,* 10.

Stalberg, C. E. (1995). Disaster patrol. *Planning, 61,* 18–21.

Steinberg, M., & Burby, R. J. (2002). Growing safe. *Planning, 68,* 22.

Tibbetts, J. (1994). Waterproofing the Midwest. *Planning, 60,* 8–13.

Yeo, S. (2003). Effects of disclosure of flood-liability on residential property values. *The Australian Journal of Emergency Management, 18,* 35–44.

Chapter 18

DISASTER RESILIENCE: INTEGRATING INDIVIDUAL, COMMUNITY, INSTITUTIONAL, AND ENVIRONMENTAL PERSPECTIVES

DOUGLAS PATON

It is the decisions that you are able to make, not the situation in which you find yourself in that will define your destiny.
Anonymous

INTRODUCTION

The contents of this text testify to the fact that a capacity to adapt to, and even experience benefit from, the experience of disaster is a reality for many communities. To some extent, this should not come as a surprise. Humankind has a long history of confronting and adapting to the devastation caused by war, pestilence, disaster and other catastrophic events. That such experience can have beneficial consequences has, however, often been overlooked by research that has focused primarily on physical losses and the anguish of survivors during the immediate aftermath of disaster. However, when the time frame within which analyses are conducted and the range of outcomes assessed is extended, evidence for positive outcomes has been readily forthcoming (Bolin & Stanford, 1998; Joseph, Williams & Yule, 1993; Linley & Joseph, 2004; Pe'rez-Sales et al., 2005; Sarason, 1974; Taylor, Wood & Lichtman, 1983; Tobin & Whiteford, 2002; Va'zquez et al.,

2005). The salutogenic paradigm (e.g., Antonovsky, 1990) clearly has much to offer emergency planning.

That a capacity for adaptation and growth exists should not be taken to imply that communities can just be left to fend for themselves. A corollary of identifying adaptive capacities has been recognition that many places and sectors of society lack this capacity. This was graphically illustrated by the 2004 Indian Ocean tsunami and hurricane Katrina in New Orleans in 2005. These events illustrated how disaster can create a need for affected populations to draw upon their own resources and be self-reliant. They also demonstrated how risk was influenced by relationships between people/communities and their ecological, economic and societal contexts. If, however, the predictors of adaptive and growth outcomes at ecological, social, and community levels are understood, proactive steps can be taken to include their development and maintenance in emergency planning and community development agenda (see Chapters 5 and 17).

What is clear is that deficit and loss outcomes should not be assumed to be a fait accompli of exposure to disaster. Rather, deficit and loss outcomes co-exist with a capacity to confront challenging circumstances in ways characterized by adaptation and growth. A corollary of this has been recognition of a need to reconsider how risk is conceptualized, assessed and managed.

Contemporary use of the risk concept tends to portray risk and loss as synonymous. This reflects a conceptualization of hazard consequences derived from a predominant focus on vulnerability. This does not represent the risk paradigm in a way that renders it readily capable of encapsulating evidence of adaptive and growth outcomes. The emphasis on deficit or loss outcomes is, however, of relatively recent origin. A return to the original conceptualization of the risk concept, as the probability of an event occurring combined with an accounting for the *gains and the losses* that the event could represent if it occurred (Dake, 1992), can remedy this problem.

In this context, it is not risk per se that is managed. Rather, this is achieved by making choices regarding the losses (vulnerability) and gains (resilience) that could prevail within a given community. That is, risk reflects how hazard characteristics interact with those individual, community and societal elements that facilitate a capacity to adapt (i.e., increase resilience) and those that increase susceptibility to experiencing loss (i.e., increase vulnerability) (Figure 18.1). Conceptualiz-

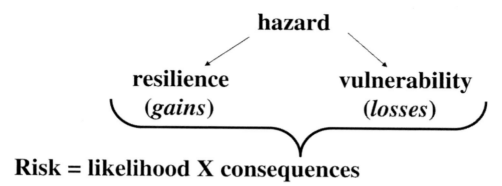

Figure 18.1. The relationship between risk, resilience & vulnerability.

ing the consequences of hazard exposure as comprising gains and losses represents a more appropriate framework within which to capture the essence of a contemporary emergency management that seeks to promote sustainable practices, resilience and growth as well as mitigating loss. It is important that vulnerability and resilience are conceptualized as discrete, co-existing elements within the risk management process (Figure 18.2).

VULNERABILITY

As with their resilience counterparts, vulnerability factors exist at several levels. Factors such as personality (e.g., neuroticism), denial-based coping, learned helplessness and developmental immaturity influence vulnerability at the level of the individual (Violanti & Paton, 2006). Vulnerability has also been described with respect to demographic (e.g., age, ethnic minority status, educational level) and environmental (e.g., marginalized political and economic status, family dynamics, community fragmentation) characteristics (Bolin & Stanford, 1998; Bravo et al., 1990; Fothergill, Darlington & Maestos, 1999; Kaniasty & Norris, 1995; Lindell & Whitney, 2000; Schwarzer et al., 1994).

The well-documented potential of these factors to increase susceptibility to loss means they have a key role to play in estimating risk. It would, however, be incorrect to automatically equate their presence in a community with increased risk. Rather, vulnerability factors can co-exist with factors that facilitate a capacity to adapt to adverse circumstances (Buckle, 2001; Cadell et al., 2003; Handmer, 2003; Kaniasty & Norris, 1999; Linley & Joseph, 2004; Paton et al., 2001; Saegert, 1989; Schwarzer et al., 1994; Tobin & Whiteford, 2002). These complementary factors do not reduce vulnerability per se; they have an action that is independent of vulnerability and act specifically to enhance adaptive capacity (see Chapters 6 and 17). It is the relative balance of the vulnerability and resilience factors available or mobilized when confronting hazard effects that determine risk (Figure 18.2). Resilience resources and processes are developed within readiness/mitigation programs and mobilized during response, recovery and rebuilding.

This volume focused on identifying factors that influence resilience. Identifying adaptive resources and processes provides emergency planners and communities with the capacity to influence their risk status (i.e., the kind of outcome they desire). They can do so by making choices about the characteristics of their communities, the relationships that exist between their members, and about their relationship with the wider society. Understanding how interdependencies between people, their communities, and societal institutions influence adaptation thus becomes important. In this context, risk management

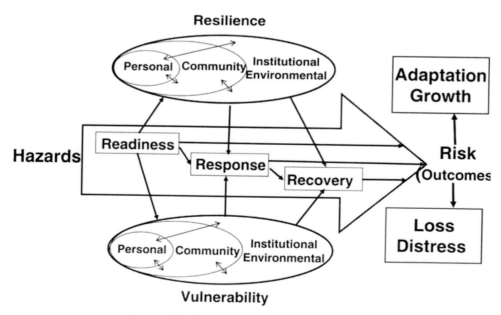

Figure 18.2. The hazard and risk relationship.

is an iterative process that contributes to societal resilience by facilitating a capacity to make decisions about personal, community and societal characteristics and providing the resources required to implement them.

RESILIENCE

The contents of the preceding chapters illustrated the many and varied resources that societies and their members can draw upon to develop the adaptive capacity required to sustain societal functions in the event of disaster. Some of these are intrinsic aspects of culture. Others reflect personal dispositions and the formal and informal ways in which people organize themselves, and in societal and institutional characteristics and the ways in which they decide to perform their functions. While cultural attributes are not amenable to change through a planning process, they must be accommodated when estimating risk and crafting risk reduction and recovery plans. Cultural knowledge can also play a valuable role in identifying adaptive capacities that could be developed through community development initiatives.

Modeling Comprehensive Adaptive Capacity

To summarize the contents of this volume, a tentative model of adaptive capacity is outlined. The model includes: a) the individual (e.g., self-efficacy, sense of community, sense of place), community (e.g., reciprocal social support, collective efficacy) and societal/institutional (e.g., business continuity planning) resources required to support adaptation, and b) the mechanisms that facilitate interaction within and between levels (e.g., social justice, community competence, trust, empowerment) in ways that promote cohesive action to enhance adaptive capacity, minimize disruption, and facilitate growth.

People bring key resources to the community. This includes their specific knowledge and expertise, as well as dispositional factors such as commitment (e.g., sense of community) and self-efficacy that influences the range of plans developed and levels of persistence in their application (Paton, 2003). However, through cooperative effort, the depth and breadth of collective expertise that can be brought to bear on problems can far exceed the sum of its parts (e.g., collective efficacy). Cooperation cannot, however, be taken for granted. In increasingly pluralistic societies, people and groups differ with regard to their needs, perceptions, goals and expectations. In this context, the sustained availability of a collective capacity will require an ability to resolve conflicts and reconcile needs, costs and benefits in ways that are fair and just. The fact that the costs and benefits of hazard mitigation may not be equally distributed, either physically or socially, makes this particularly important. Risk management strategies based on social justice principles and community involvement in decision making about acceptable levels of risk and the strategies used to mitigate this risk positively influence risk acceptance and increase both collective commitment to confront hazard consequences and community acceptance of responsibility for its own safety (Lasker, 2004; Paton, 2005; Paton, et al., 2001; Paton & Bishop, 1996).

Community competence (e.g, Eng & Parker, 1994, see also Chapter 10) is a construct well-suited to the role of conceptualizing and assessing the community dynamics that will influence levels of collective capacity. It describes a community with regard to, for example, the extent to which it encourages participation in making decisions about salient community issues, the existence of mechanisms to articulate collective views, and the existence of procedures for managing relations with the wider society. A community with high levels of community competence will have the capacity to formulate ideas, transmit them to institutions, and to mobilize and sustain action to implement initiatives within the community. However, fully realizing the potential of this capability requires a corresponding level of civic reciprocity.

The ability of a community to realize its goals will be a function of the degree to which societal institutions (e.g., civic agencies, emergency planners) possess an organizational culture that embraces the value of empowering communities and that translates this into decisions and actions that support bottom-up, community-led initiatives. That is, the degree to which civic agencies sustain community capacity by distributing power, resources and expertise in ways that empower community members (Dalton et al., 2001; Rich et al., 1995) to achieve the outcomes the community thinks are important. Some of these relationships are summarized in figure 18.3 to illustrate how the process may operate as a comprehensive resource capable of facilitat-

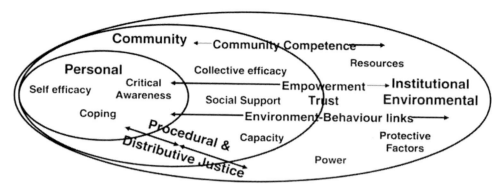

Figure 18.3. Multilevel resilience model showing selected resources at each level and selected transactional resources.

ing societal capacity to adapt to adverse circumstances.

It is also pertinent to consider the cross-cultural applicability of this framework. On the basis of the work presented in this text, there are grounds for assuming this to be the case. For example, certain parallels can be drawn between the elements of the Hakka Spirit described in Chapter 11 and the resilience factors identified in other chapters. For example, perseverance despite adversity (self-efficacy), focus on responsibilities and issues rather than emotions (problem-focused coping), optimism, and an underlying sense of self-reliance, social responsibility and commitment to family and neighbours (sense of community) can be discerned in Jang and LaMendola's discussion of culturally-derived resilience. The difference is that the Hakka Spirit is transmitted and sustained through cultural mechanisms. In Western populations, more active community development work is required to achieve the same capacity for adaptation and growth. The investigation of cross-cultural similarities remains an area for future research.

Changes in Adaptive Resource Availability

Breaking adaptive capacity down into its individual, collective (community), and societal levels offers other insights into resilience. One of these has particular relevance for response management. This arises from how it assists appreciation of how adaptive pressures are negotiated as the disaster evolves through its impact, response and recovery phases (Figure 18.2).

During the immediate impact phase survival is influenced by the level of protective measures that have been adopted. For example, failure to have ensured the structural integrity of a house and secured internal furnishings and fittings increases the householders' risk of injury and death. Such protective actions not only directly influence their survival, they also affect their availability to participate in subsequent response (e.g., assisting search and rescue) and recovery (e.g., getting back to work to minimize economic losses) efforts.

Adaptation during the period immediately following impact (the first three or so days and possibly considerably longer) is also a function of levels of readiness. During this time, people are isolated from external assistance and have limited, if any, access to normal societal resources and functions. Under these circumstances, the effectiveness of adaptive and coping efforts will be a function of prevailing levels of individual/household preparedness (e.g., household emergency plans, stored food and water, heating source) and their capacity for self-reliance (see Chapter 7). Given that disaster strikes with no or very little warning, the foundation upon which adaptive capacity rests involves ensuring that the requisite knowledge and resources are organized in advance and can be used to good effect when disaster strikes.

Preparedness research has focused, usually for pragmatic reasons, on households. Irrespective of levels of household preparedness, its utility must be qualified by acknowledging that some or all household members spend only limited periods of time at home (see Chapter 17). To accommodate this, community preparedness has been conceptualized in ways that include workplaces, schools, and places where people spend time (e.g., shopping malls) (Lasker, 2004). As Lasker points out, such activities can facilitate more general levels of preparedness. For example, work-based programs can help instill the importance of preparing into the community consciousness and increase the likelihood of preparation in a range of contexts.

As the impact phase subsides, people will have more opportunities to work with neighbors and other community members to confront local demands. At this stage, adaptive capacity will reflect the capacity of community members to work with others to plan and execute tasks. Fully realizing the benefits of this collective capacity to deal with local issues will be influenced by the degree to which emergency response agencies possess an organizational culture that espouses community empowerment (e.g., developing mechanisms for mobilizing and coordinating community volunteers to assist recovery efforts).

As the event progressively moves through the response phase, adaptive capacity will increasingly involve interaction between communities and societal-level institutions (e.g., businesses, emergency response). The quality of reciprocal relationships between communities and societal institutions will influence the quality of the community experience of recovery. It will also determine whether rebuilding (which may extend over several months or years) enhances the subsequent quality of community life and lays the foundations for future resilience (or vulnerability).

The introduction of a temporal component to the concept of adaptive capacity raises other issues. The inclusion of the term "capacity" in the definition makes it easier to appreciate that communities have only so many resources to draw upon; adaptive capacity is finite. Consequently, planning must consider how adaptive pressures may change over time as well as how long these demands will persist. That is, what is the time frame over which people, communities and societal institutions will have to continue to function and at what point might available resources become exhausted? The implications of this exhaustion must be considered. Consideration should also be directed to the period prior to impact. For example, volcanic crises can have precursory periods that may last for months. Under these circumstances, economic resilience may be an important means of dealing with threats to future investment and employment. The next question is how to translate this into practice. One approach involves integrating hazard planning with community development (Paton, 2000; see also Chapters 5 and 17).

RESILIENCE AND COMMUNITY DEVELOPMENT

Several studies (Bishop et al., 2000; Lasker, 2004; Paton & Bishop, 1996; Paton et al., 2001; Pearce, 2003; Rich et al., 1995) have identified prior involvement in community activities and functions (e.g., membership of clubs or social action groups) as a significant predictor of adaptation to hazard consequences. That is, adaptive capacity can be forged and sustained through community engagement in activities concerned with identifying and dealing with local issues even if they have little or nothing to do with hazard readiness per se. Participation in identifying shared problems and collaborating with others to develop and implement solutions to resolve them engenders the development of several resilience competencies (e.g., self-efficacy, action coping, community competence). The effectiveness of these activities can be increased when motivated and sustained by active community leadership (Dalton et al., 2001). Lasker (2004) revealed community members' preference for community-based hazard planning to be based around competent and credible individuals from within their community who are trained (e.g., to provide advice, assist them to make decisions that reconcile protective actions and their needs) specifically to assist their fellow community members. Nothwithstanding, emergency management planning may profit from being actively integrated with community development planning (Paton, 2000; see also Chapters 5 and 17).

To facilitate this integration, representatives of community groups (e.g., community boards or action groups, neighborhood watch, religious and ethnic groups) could be invited to review hazard scenarios with regard to the potential challenges, opportunities and threats they could pose for each group (Lasker, 2004; Paton, 2000). The outcome of this process would provide the information and resource requirements necessary for community-led mitigation strategies that are more consistent with the diverse beliefs, values, needs, expectation, goals and systems within the diverse groups that comprise contemporary communities. This point reiterates the need for emergency management planning to value community empowerment. That is, they focus on mobilizing community resources to facilitate adaptive capacity rather than imposing institutional decisions on a community.

One approach to achieving this would involve emergency planners assimilating and co-ordinating the needs and perspectives derived from community consultation, and providing the information and resources necessary to empower community groups and sustain self-reliance and resilience. Emergency management agencies would thus act as consultants to communities (e.g., facilitators, resource providers, change agents, coordinators) rather than directing the change process in a top-down manner (Paton, 2000). This approach can help embed the processes by which adaptive capacity is developed into the fabric of community life (see also Chapter 17).

CONCLUSION

Resilience is about nurturing and sustaining the capacity of people, communities and societal institutions to adapt to and experience benefit from disaster. The contents of this volume provide valuable insights into how this might be achieved. It advocates an approach to risk management based on the bottom-up development of community development initiatives that foster and sustain a capacity to adapt to the vicissitudes of life irrespective of their origin.

While knowledge of how to develop resilience is available, the realization of this community potential cannot, of course, be prescribed. Making information on the issues about which choices can be made available does not guarantee that the necessary decisions will be made by communities and societal institutions. In some cases choices will not be made on financial grounds (e.g., derived from risk assessment, cost-benefit ratios). In other cases, action may not be taken because the competencies required to do so are not present and must first be developed. What is important is that a commitment to develop this capacity is present. Indeed, the absence of this commitment will make a significant contribution to future community vulnerability. However, even if a decision is made not to implement specific resilience resources, knowledge of resilience resources can inform the assessment of residual risk, identify strategic community development goals, and provide a framework for the intervention to achieve these goals.

There remain many issues that have to be tackled if comprehensive models of resilience are to be developed. One such issue is the need for future work to accommodate the fact that communities may face significant challenges during the pre- and post-event periods, not just when actively confronting the disaster. For example, volcanic events may be preceded by long precursory periods which will pose challenges for economic resilience whether an eruption takes place or not. Suddenly occurring earthquakes would not pose similar demands. Different hazards also create different adaptive demands during rebuilding. For example, extensive lava flows will require the wholesale redevelopment of entire communities. In contrast, seismic activity could result in reconstruction of pre-existing infrastructure.

The nature and capacity of resources will change from place to place. Adaptive capacities will also change over time with changes in societal priorities (e.g., from natural hazards to terrorism), hazard-scapes (e.g., from global warning, environmental degradation), as well as community membership, goals, needs and expectations. The assessment and development of adaptive capacity is a dynamic and iterative process.

By ensuring that risk management strategies are developed and delivered within a salutogenic paradigm, the potential for adaptation can be optimized, and community development strategies more readily integrated with the engineering, lifeline, natural hazard planning and public policy initiatives that contribute to community resilience. When this happens, estimates of community capability to adapt to, deal with and develop from exposure to natural disaster will increase substantially, as will confidence in the planning and policies that define societal responsibility and the actions they stimulate to develop resilience in communities at risk.

REFERENCES

Antonovsky, A. (1990). Pathways leading to successful coping and health. In Rosenbaum M., (Ed.), *Learned resourcefulness: On coping skills, self-control, and adaptive behavior.* New York: Springer.

Bishop, B., Paton, D., Syme, G., & Nancarrow, B. (2000). Coping with environmental degradation: Salination as a community stressor. *Network, 12,* 1–15.

Bolin, R., & Stanford, L. (1998). The Northridge earthquake: Community-based approaches to unmet recovery needs. *Disasters, 22,* 21–38.

Buckle, P. (2001). Managing community resilience in a wide-area disaster. *Australian Journal of Emergency Management, 16,* 13–18.

Bravo, M,, Rubio-Stipec, M., Woodbury, M.A., & Ribera, J,C, (1990). The psychological sequelae of disaster stress prospectively and retrospectively evaluated. *American Journal of Community Psychology, 18,* 661–680.

Cadell, S., Regehr, C., & Hemsworth, D. (2003). Factors contributing to posttraumatic growth: A proposed structural equation model. *American Journal of Orthopsychiatry, 73*(3), 279-287.

Dake, K. (1992). Myths of nature and the public. *Journal of Social Issues, 48,* 21–38.

Dalton, J.H., Elias, M.J., & Wandersman, A. (2001). *Community psychology.* Wadsworth: Belmont, CA.

Eng, E., & Parker, E. (1994). Measuring community competence in the Mississippi Deltas: The interface between program evaluation and empowerment. *Health Education Quarterly, 21,* 199–220.

Fothergill, A., Darlington, J.D., & Maestos, E. (1999). Race, ethnicity and disasters in the United States: A review of the literature. *Disasters, 23,* 156–173.

Handmer, J. (2003). We are all vulnerable. *Australian Journal of Emergency Management, 18,* 55–60.

Joseph, S., Williams, R., & Yule, W. (1993). Changes in outlook following disaster: The preliminary development of a measure to assess positive and negative responses. *Journal of Traumatic Stress, 6,* 271–279.

Kaniasty, K., & Norris, F.H. (1995). In search of altruistic community: Patterns of social support mobilization following hurricane Hugo. *American Journal of Community Psychology, 23,* 447–478.

Kaniasty, K., & Norris, F.H. (1999). The experience of disaster: Individuals and communities sharing trauma. In R. Gist, R. and B. Lubin (Eds.), *Response to Disaster.* Taylor & Francis: Philadelphia, PA.

Lasker, R.D. (2004). *Redefining readiness: Terrorism planning through the eyes of the public.* The New York Academy of Medicine, New York: NY.

Lindell, M.K., & Whitney, D.J. (2000). Correlates of household seismic hazard adjustment adoption. *Risk Analysis, 20,* 13–25.

Linley, P.A., & Joseph, S. (2004). Positive change following trauma and adversity: A review. *Journal of Traumatic Stress, 17,* 11–21.

Paton, D. (2000). Emergency planning: Integrating community development, community resilience and hazard mitigation. *Journal of the American Society of Professional Emergency Managers, 7,* 109–118.

Paton, D. (2003). Disaster preparedness: A social-cognitive perspective. *Disaster Prevention and Management, 12,* 210–216.

Paton, D. (2005). Community resilience: Integrating hazard management and community engagement. *Proceedings of the International Conference on Engaging Communities.* Brisbane. Queensland Government/UNESCO.

Paton, D., & Bishop, B. (1996). Disasters and communities: Promoting psychosocial well-being. In D. Paton and N. Long (Eds.), *Psychological aspects of disaster: Impact, coping, and intervention.* Dunmore Press: Palmerston North.

Paton, D., Millar, M., & Johnston, D. (2001). Community resilience to volcanic hazard consequences. *Natural Hazards, 24,* 157–169.

Pe´rez-Sales, P., Cervello´n, P., Va´zquez, C., Vidales, D., & Gaborit, M. (2005). Post-traumatic factors and resilience: The role of shelter management and survivours' attitudes after the earthquakes in El Salvador (2001). *Journal of Community & Applied Social Psychology, 15,* 368–382.

Pearce, L. (2003). Disaster management and community planning, and public participation: How to achieve sustainable hazard mitigation. *Natural Hazards, 28,* 211–222.

Rich, R.C., Edelstein, M., Hallman, W.K. & Wandersman, A.H. (1995). Citizen participation and empowerment: the case of local environmental hazards. *American Journal of Community Psychology, 23,* 657–677.

Saegert, S. (1989). Unlikely leaders, extreme circumstances: Older black women building community households. *American Journal of Community Psychology, 17,* 295–316.

Sarason, S. B. (1974). *The psychological sense of community: Prospects for a community psychology.* San Francisco: Jossey-Bass.

Schwarzer, R., Hahn, A., & Schroder, H. (1994). Social integration and social support in a life crisis: Effects of macrosocial change in East Germany. *American*

Journal of Community Psychology, 22, 685–706.

Taylor, S.E., Wood, J.V., & Lichtman, R.R. (1983). It could be worse: Selective evaluation as a response to victimization. *Journal of Social Issues, 39,* 19–40.

Tobin, G.A., & Whiteford, L.M. (2002). Community resilience and volcanic hazards: The eruption of Tungurahua and evacuation of the Faldas in Ecuador. *Disasters, 26,* 28–48.

Va´zquez, C., Cervello´n, P., Pe´rez-Sales, P., Vidales, D., & Gaborit, M. (2005). Positive emotions in earthquake survivors in El Salvador (2001). *Anxiety Disorders, 19,* 313–328.

Violanti, J.M., & Paton, D. (2006). *Who gets PTSD? Issues of vulnerability to poasttraumatic stress.* Springfield, IL: Charles C Thomas.

INDEX

A

Adaptive capacity, 8, 12, 14, 191, 193, 202, 228, 234, 268, 281, 308, 311
Adversarial growth, 169
Altruism, 176
Attitudes, 113, 199, 200, 204, 254, 298, 301
Attribution theory, 116

B

Building codes, 32, 34, 63, 81
Business continuity planning, 252, 253
    staff selection, 259
    staff vulnerability, 259
    staff resilience, 259

C

Change, 99
Community
    aboriginal (Australian), 131
    attachment, 165
    capacity, 90, 99, 162, 163
    competence, 163, 165, 166, 169, 309, 310, 314
    conflict, 144, 198
    development, 12, 70, 76, 164, 313, 314
    diversity, 13
    engagement, 13, 206, 271, 313
    leadership, 76, 98, 112, 314
    participation, 164
    planning, 12, 76, 76
    sense of, 17, 149, 164, 167, 169, 204, 298, 309
    sustainability, 35, 40, 66, 79, 163

Consensus building, 80
Content minimalization error, 149
Coping, 90, 120, 166, 278, 283, 314
Counter disaster syndrome, 271
Critical awareness, 112,
Culture, 14, 15, 116, 129, 140, 147, 174, 177, 262, 281, 283, 309

D

Decision making, 13, 68, 71, 98, 149, 236, 261, 263, 269, 272, 273, 276, 280
Diversity, 233
Disaster, 6, 21, 144
    catalyst for development, 8
    continuity planning, 17, 229, 235, 249
    loss estimation, 227
    sociopolitical, 167

E

Electricity transmission, 42, 48, 53
Emergency management, 17, 72, 74, 79, 217, 295
    inter-agency, 267, 274
    simulations, 277, 280
    teams, 267, 274
    training, 77, 279
    planning, 269, 271, 314
Emergency Planning and Community Right to Know Act (1986), 73
Empowerment, 97, 98, 281, 309, 310
Environment, 79
    peri-urban, 5
Equity, 14, 121, 205, 301
Evacuation, 132, 155, 300

319

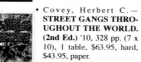
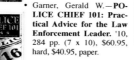
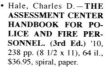

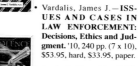
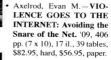
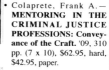
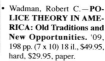
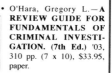